Astride a Fierce Wind

Astride a Fierce Wind

HUBERTA HELLENDOORN

to Matt
with love

Huberta H.

First published in 2017

Typesetting and book design by Paul Stewart
Edited by Mary McCallum

Cover image of Huberta in 1947, Hellendoorn family collection.
Author photo by Janice Rowley.
'Palm Sunday procession', 'Walking through the village to our
wedding, 1959' and 'Four years old, 1941' by Zeylemaker,
Zutphen, used with permission. 'Damage by V1' by JB Thate,
used with permission. Other photographs by Judith Birchall,
Pauline Clark, Raymond Hellendoorn, Lydia Ruiterkamp
and Wim Ruiterkamp.

Epigraph on p.11 is from *The Envoy from Mirror City*
by Janet Frame (Vintage 2000), used with permission.

© Huberta Hellendoorn 2017

Find out more about Huberta on http://otagowritersnetwork.co.nz/

ISBN 978-0-473-39521-6

This book is copyright apart from any fair dealing as
permitted under the Copyright Act, and no part may
be reproduced without permission from the publisher.

A catalogue record for this book is available from
the National Library of New Zealand

Printed by Your Books,
Wellington, New Zealand

submarine
an imprint of Mākaro Press
PO Box 41-032 Eastbourne 5047
makaropress.co.nz

Contents

PART ONE

Leaving	15
The cellar	19
Escape	24
The journey	25
The farm	30
Sounds of the night	34
Bombardments and fairies	35
Dreams	38
Going home	39
Freedom	43
Peace	45
Scarlet fever	48
Honeymoon decisions	50
School	54
Always that fear	58
Cabbage and cake	60
My beginnings	68
Palm Sunday	72
Oma's bonnets	78
Pretending princesses	85
Promises of heaven	88
The organist	96

Greta's friendly visit	105
The sea	110
Que sera, sera	113
The yellow bikini	114
The windmill camp	119
Au pair	123
Courting	129
Brother	130
Spring 1959	131
Official news	136
White bread and sheep waiting	137
The kitchen table	139

PART TWO

St Clair Pool	143
That April morning	145
Life on the ship	146
Melbourne	155
Welcome to New Zealand	169
Welcome to Dunedin	172
Reality	175
Always time for coffee	177
What's in a hat	182
Wonderful weekends	185

Sick for home	189
The birthday party	192
Employment	197
Integrating	200
New life	203
Unto us a child	204
Miriam	208
A family	213
New arrivals	216
Growing shoots	221
Visitors	232
Finding a balance	236
A working wife	239
A trip to Holland	241
Sounds and words	247
Back to Dunedin	252
Renovating (again)	255
Learning to fly	257
Another journey	261
Surprising ourselves	266
Singing	270
How to deal with grief from a distance?	273
The apple tree	276
Filling the house	282

PART THREE

Retirement	295
Where did she go?	299
Where did they go?	307
More changes	310
A defining speech	311
Fly me to the sun	313
A woman I am	315
Flying off again	319
I am coming home	328
A certain hill	329
The writing life	332
A journey without an itinerary	341
Life, eh!	348
Echoes from the cellar	349
Home	354
Acknowledgements	359

Dedicated to Bart

All writers are exiles wherever they live and their work is a lifelong journey towards the lost land.

JANET FRAME

PART ONE

I'VE TRIED TO BE A GOOD WIFE AND MOTHER. MY YEARS OF preparation for this were being a good daughter.

Honour your father and mother … This was drummed into me. I loved my mother and tried to honour my father, but at 22 I left my family and our small village in Holland to start a new life in the southern hemisphere. I left astride a fierce wind.

Leaving

Oh, yes. Bart and I were ready to leave Warnsveld – and Holland. Neighbours in winter coats pulled over pyjamas, slippers on their feet, came to say goodbye to us. They had known me since I was born in October 1937 and it is now April 1960.

I cried as I promised my mother, 'I'll be back.' I kissed my father on the cheek.

He turned his head away. He did not utter one word.

My mother's quiet, loyal voice: 'He is very sad you're going. He now has to do all the work on Sunday mornings.'

We climbed into the waiting car. The gears of the Mercedes crunched as it moved slowly forward in the dark.

I took Bart's arm, squeezed it tight against my breast.

We both turned to look through the back window. Cars with family members waited on the village square ready to follow us to the docks of Amsterdam. We drove in convoy through the flat landscape where bare trees stood like soldiers on both sides of the road, through villages with narrow streets and across newly built bridges spanning wide rivers. When we reached Amsterdam I stared at rows and rows of houses, the straight streets, the lights, people riding bikes to work.

At the end of the day those people would return to their homes while we would be on the ship heading for Southampton, our first port of call after leaving Amsterdam.

Inside the car it was warm, but the dampness of the streets seemed to filter into my body, the cold clinging to me. Yet there was excitement too, moving cautiously at first, slowly building and heating my marrow; already my fear of the journey ahead was dissolving.

Bart shouted, 'I can see the ship!'

My fingers touched the large gold clasp of my three-strand necklace of coral beads. My mother had fastened it around my neck when I turned 20, telling me, 'This necklace belonged to my grandmother. It will keep you strong and protect you from ill-health. You must wear it.'

Bart put an arm around my thin shoulders, tightened his grip. 'We'll make it.'

'Yes, we will.'

We stood close together for those last moments, Bart and I and our sisters and brothers, milling awkwardly together. None of us had ever done such a thing before – never said goodbye not knowing if or when we would see one another again.

There was the ship, the *Johan van Oldenbarnevelt*. I kept glancing towards it. Was it moving?

Soaring above us were the giant chimneys, yellow at the base with a black band at the top. The portholes were like many dark eyes, and I could smell the seawater. I clutched Bart's hand, 'Look at the lifeboats on the top deck. At least if the ship sinks we can get away.'

Bart squeezed my hand: 'You and your imagination.'

All those memories. Bombs. Droning aeroplanes. Hiding in a cellar. I'd learnt danger is always around.

A man stood at the gangplank and people began to move forward, giving him their tickets.

Lydia cried out, 'I'll miss you, Huub. I'll miss you and Bart so much.'

'One day you'll visit us?'

There were hugs, kisses and tears.

Leaving

Loura said, 'You must write. Every week – promise?'
Yes. Write soon.

High up on the top deck we looked down at the small figures below, waiting close to the railings. Waving, and calling, *'Goeie reis, tot ziens.'*

Bon voyage. Farewell. We'll meet again.

Bart had his arm around my shoulders. 'It's really happening. Our new life. I'll work hard. I'll make a go of this.'

'We'll do it together.'

Bart walked to the bow of the ship, his legs confidently swinging. Those long legs.

I REMEMBERED A FREEZING NIGHT, MINUS 15°C. I'D DECIDED to go to the skating rink and, circling the large, frozen area by myself, heard my name called out. 'You're back! How are you?'

A tall young man in a green anorak was skating towards me. Turning my feet inward, I braked.

He shook my hand. 'How was your holiday in Switzerland? You look different.'

We skated, talking, till the rink closed. Slowly we biked towards the village where I lived. As we reached my house Bart touched my arm. 'Come with me to the film tomorrow night?'

'Why not?' I said, already mentally composing a letter to my long-time best friend, Ans, now studying in Amsterdam. He's lovely. He's changed since we last saw him. He's no longer shy. So thoughtful.

Ooh la la. He even kissed me.

Ans. My best friend since the first day at school. I stood at the railing of the *Johan van Oldenbarnevelt* and knew she was now just a memory. Already home had become the

ASTRIDE A FIERCE WIND

place where things happened in the past.

Bart and I stayed at the railing while the ship headed out from the canal into the open sea, slowly picking up speed as the coastline retreated, the thick line of land in the distance turning into a dark sliver, then disappearing.

18

The cellar

5 April 1945

The wooden staircase below the cellar door is steep but there is no handrail. I sit on the fifth step up with my feet on the one below, elbows on my knees and head resting in my hands. Soon it'll be my seventh birthday. I watch and I listen.

There are mattresses on the cold stone floor. They're covered in green ticking, with buttons to keep the ticking in place. Each family has brought its own, and blankets. People sit or lie, talking to each other. About their families who are sheltering in other underground rooms. About the good times that will happen again – walks in the forest or biking around the local villages, feeling the warm sun and wind on their bodies, eating fresh white bread and crispy apples.

I look at the faces of the grown-ups, tired from sleepless nights while the roaring outside goes on and on.

Black cloth is spread over the small barred window. Light isn't allowed to escape to the outside so not much daylight can come inside. Around the walls of the cellar are shelves, deep shelves that before the war held jars of preserves. Small jars with apple sauce. Large jars filled with white pears, halved and left with a round gap where the core was. Creamy pears to eat with smooth, pale yellow custard. Now those shelves hold blankets and warm coats and things that mean a lot. A white handbag, a black handbag. A box with jewellery. Toys.

I don't like this half-darkness. I want the window open so I can breathe. I shiver in my cotton dress. It's springtime, but the sun cannot reach the cellar.

In one corner stands an earthenware pot, grey with blue stripes. One day my mother will put beans in the pot again, or sauerkraut, held down by a stone on the round wooden lid that covers the wide opening. She promised me last week that next winter we'll eat sauerkraut again. She said, 'The war is nearly over. I can't remember the taste of sauerkraut.'

The last few days we've been hiding in this cellar as the fighting continues. I want to play outside but we've been told to stay inside until there is no more shooting and until there are no more bombardments. Bombardments are scary.

Like the bomb last week. I was woken by a dark noise, then sirens, people screaming outside on the street, the light of a glowing fire flickering through jagged glass.

Moving my hands over my sheet, I felt the pieces of glass. Papa stood at the edge of the bed.

'Huub, come on. I must carry you downstairs – there are too many glass splinters on your bed and on the floor. A V1 has crashed into the houses a few streets away. All our windows are broken.'

'No, no. I can walk. I don't want to be carried – I want to walk on my own. *I* can do it.'

'Be quiet.' My father's voice sounded angry.

Carefully I got out of bed, my feet feeling for the glass fragments around me, but Papa lifted me up and carried me down the stairs. There were people in the doorway, a red light outside as if a giant candle had been lit, a constant movement of lanterns in the street, and people carrying stretchers. Some stretchers bore strange shapes covered with blankets.

The cellar

People I recognised from the village walked past, their hands and faces covered in blood. I saw Joke and Jannie. They were crying and holding tightly to their mother who had a red ribbon dripping from her hair. I was scared then, watched what the men were dragging away.

Now in our cellar I wonder what it will be like when there is peace. I hate the war.

Out on the street it is quiet. Not the quietness of the night when people are asleep and only the nightingale sings. We know this stillness cannot be trusted. Too many bombs have fallen around us and damaged houses. Even the house of my friends Jannie and Joke. That's why they are staying in our cellar. They sit next to their mother, Hans, who is feeding the new baby. Hansje is so tiny and sweet as she sucks her mother's milk. Their father, Jan, sits near them, moving restlessly.

My baby sister, Lydia, is asleep in a wooden cot. I remember the day she was born. I asked Papa, 'How long before the new baby arrives?' He said, 'Go and play with Heli and then you can watch our upstairs window from her house. If you wait long enough you'll see the stork carrying the baby in its beak and dropping it through the window of our bedroom.'

I knew all about storks, the huge white birds with their nests high up on the poles in the meadows outside our village.

Heli and I played in the garden – I remember rolling in the grass – then we went to her house across the road and played dolls in her bedroom. My eyes never left the window of my mother's bedroom as I waited for the special white bird who would bring the new baby to our house. I was really cross when Papa told me I had a baby sister. I asked him what happened to the stork, but he said he was busy.

I'm getting hungry. We don't have much food in the house.

ASTRIDE A FIERCE WIND

Joke and Jannie's family must be hungry too.

Jan gets up, fiddles with his hands, sits down, gets up again, walks to the tiny window. He removes the blackout cover from one corner and tries to look outside. 'I'll have to go over the road and see how my sisters are. I haven't seen them for days.'

'Oh, Jan, don't be so stupid, don't go. It's still too dangerous. Blanche and Ger will be fine, just like we are.' Hans starts to cry, tears falling past her nose and onto her white breast until they reach her bared nipple.

Jan looks at his wife and children. He shapes his mouth as if he is biting into an apple. He says, 'Look, I'll be gone for just a minute. Don't worry, it'll be safe. I'll be back before you can take another breath.'

'Stay with me. I want you to stay with me.' Her voice has a stronger plea now.

No sound comes through the thick red-brick walls. Jan fixes his eyes on Hansje, then turns to the other people with their thin, tight faces. He says, 'It should be all right to go now – it's been quiet for so long.'

Papa stands up. 'Jan, I don't think you should go yet. Wait a while until this has all settled down. Your sisters are fine. Your wife and children need you here.'

'It's no good. I can't stay here while maybe they need help. There they are, sitting in the dark. It's bad enough that there wasn't room for them in this cellar. You can say what you like – they're my sisters and I have to go and see if they need anything.'

I can tell he is angry. He takes a few steps, moves past me on the staircase. I hear Jannie's voice: 'Don't go, Papa. Stay here with us.'

As he opens the cellar door a thin ray of light fleetingly reaches the nearly dark, enclosed space with its prisoners. The menacing blackness enfolds us again and I hear the front door close with a bang.

The cellar

Only a few minutes have passed when I hear the shrill whistling of a grenade. An explosion. Then silence again.

Somebody tries to make a joke. Nobody laughs. People whisper to each other; some sit and stare. The baby is asleep in Hans' arms. She rocks her gently. I start to sing the words of a Sunday school song, 'Jesus bids us shine with a clear, pure light ...' In the gloomy dark we wait.

We wait for footsteps outside, for the sound of the front door closing. For the cellar door to open.

Hans looks at my father, 'Will you go and see? Jan should have been back by now.'

My father turns to my mother. Her eyes are moist and pleading, her glasses damp with the steam of her sweat. He says, 'Give it another 15 minutes. Then I'll go.'

He opens the old black Bible and reads slowly, 'They that dwell in the secret place of the most High shall abide under the shadow of the Almighty.'

My mother begins to cry, but sitting on the staircase I imagine that secret place as a scary dark cave hidden in a towering mountain with walls so thick I won't be able to hear the guns. There will be no windows through which I can see the dead bodies. There will be no doors that people can be lost through. This will be a hiding place where enemies cannot reach us, where the daylight won't expose us to danger.

Escape

Years later I learnt that on the afternoon of the cellar, our village of Warnsveld had been liberated. The third Canadian Infantry Division had gradually moved towards nearby Zutphen, setting free many of the small villages in the area, including Warnsveld. The liberation documents were signed by Canadian, German and local representatives and many of the villagers rushed outside thinking that freedom had arrived, only to be killed by German soldiers who were hiding in the neighbourhood, looting houses and shooting anybody who came near them. The Germans in Zutphen refused to surrender to the advancing Canadians, and couldn't accept that Warnsveld was no longer at war with them. They sent out a warning that they would try to take over our village again using a fresh load of grenades.

It was a few hours after this that Jan went into the house across the road to check on his sisters. He didn't come back. A stray grenade threw him to the ground, killing him instantly.

People felt betrayed by the refusal of the Germans to accept that the village had been liberated, and while this entrenched enemy and our liberators prepared to confront each other, my family and other groups of people from our neighbourhood decided to seek refuge in Vorden, a village nine kilometres away that had been successfully liberated by the Canadians.

The journey

Slowly the long line moves forward. If a pilot flew above us, watching from a low-flying aeroplane, he would see no end, no beginning. Only an endless snake coiling between the houses. The people are like its scales, their drab clothes reflecting the tough years. Coats and trousers in dull colours, torn at the cuffs, shiny in parts, thin where the solidly made material has given way.

Everybody has got used to the sounds of heavy fighting getting closer, to the air raids, to the random killings along the roads. Farmhouses being burnt. We've listened to a V1 rocket landing close to the old windmill at the end of our street. Watched dead bodies being carried away in the middle of the night.

Now we have abandoned our homes in the tree-lined streets, our gardens full of budding shrubs and spring flowers. Homes filled with treasures – books and precious rugs, silverware and photographs. A red plush cloth on the table, a clock with a softly ticking pendulum on the mantelpiece, still telling the time though there's no one there to appreciate it. Ticking away into emptiness.

The forces of the young countries – America, Canada, Australia, New Zealand – are ready to push back the invader. It's only a matter of weeks till freedom.

Low-hanging clouds touch the earth. They touch the people inching along, people whose faces mirror the greyness of the day. Families with older children are at the front of our convoy, those with young children next, and any older people who can still walk for a day to a temporary safe place. One elderly woman is transported on a carrier she shares with two grandchildren, pulled by two family members on bikes. At the rear is a group of older boys who are nearly adults.

The snake grinds forward. My family is in the middle. Around us children run ahead and to the side, talking and joking with other children. I walk between my parents, close and safe. *I've got to hold on to my mother. Hold on, and then I'll be safe.* My older sisters and brother march along at the front.

Papa carries a bag in each hand – nightwear, towels, woollen jerseys, nappies for the baby. There is no toothpaste, no soap. I wear a homespun, knitted cardigan underneath a dark blue coat that has been made from an old overcoat belonging to my father. I remember watching my mother unravelling a previously knitted jersey, winding the wool into tight balls, and later knitting the cardigan, her fingers moving in a steady rhythm, the white wool lumpy with knots.

Then she embroidered tiny pink flowers with green leaves on the front panels and added pink buttons from an old dress. A cardigan made especially for me. I'd hugged my mother, 'Moeke, I love it. I love it, it's beautiful.'

Hans is also in the queue, Joke and Jannie close to her. She pushes a pram that holds the baby and the few possessions she can take with her. She tells my mother again how she waits in the night for her husband to come back, long lonely nights when there's nobody to talk to, nobody to share her pain. How she waited for him to return to the cellar, waited for his reassurance that all would be well again soon. 'How could he do it? Why couldn't he have stayed

26

The journey

with us? He should've thought of me and the children, not of his sisters.'

I know that a grenade plunged through the roof as Jan walked through the house where his sisters were hiding safely in the cellar. Hans' loss and loneliness are marked on her face and in the dreamlike way she walks and speaks. I feel scared when I see her face. I hope she won't die.

I beg, 'Moeke, please let me push Lydia's pram. She likes it when I sing for her.' I want to hold on to the pram. That makes me feel safe. I must stay close to the baby, I know that, and if I push the pram we must stay together. We will not get separated.

But my mother frowns. 'Huub, I need to push the pram. It gives me something to hold on to. Besides, pushing her would be too heavy for you after a while. Run along with the other children. That will make you sleep well tonight.'

I think about the unknown room where I'll sleep. There is light around us now, but what will that new darkness be like? I want to stay close to the grown-ups so I can watch and hear everything.

The line of people plods through a forest with wide lanes, each branched with uneven paths that spread out like veins on an old face. Resembling soldiers on parade, the trees are planted in straight rows along the paths, the ground soft and spongy with the fallen pine needles of many generations.

The forest ends and the narrow road winds on through flat countryside, and now I can see a procession of machines moving towards another village of empty homes – soldiers on heavy trucks, or in armoured tanks, which show only the faces and helmets of their occupants. These are the liberators, ready to fight the enemy, to free the next village. Men who sing and shout in a language I can't understand. I see them laughing.

I think of the shattered places in our village and the

nearby town, buildings that have collapsed like carefully created structures in a sandpit. Dead bodies on stretchers.

I don't want to go back to the village yet because I'll die too. Our bodies will be crumpled up like the bodies of our neighbours. Blood. Screams in the night. I know the enemy soldiers hide inside the houses.

The trail of people reaches the liberated area. There's an old manor house. Soldiers stand in the front garden. They smile and use their hands to point us towards tables.

'We've got tea and bread for you. Come, help yourself.'

I look at the beautiful house. A path like a half-moon leads to the massive oak front door, and on either side of the door are tall dark-green cypresses that stand out against the white-painted brick. As I near the front door I catch a glimpse of a wide staircase. I want to walk up that staircase. What would I find there?

I taste the white bread. It is so whole, so soft that I don't want to swallow it. I imagine a country where people sit around long tables all day, eating nothing but white bread, chunky slices covered with golden butter and orange jam. I've heard my parents talking about the foreign soldiers who live in a golden country, where the hills are green and the mountains high and the lakes wide. A country where the Dutch princesses now live and where there is plenty of butter.

In that country there is sunlight and people wear dazzling clothes and laugh a lot. I wonder if there are words of love in their language especially meant for me.

I don't want to move on. The soldiers in khaki uniforms smile at me and I grin back. They pick me up and hold me high, as if they can make me fly away to the country they came from.

They use their hands to describe what they say in their strange language. Oh, how I would love to understand their

The journey

words. They give me tea in a big metal mug, steamy and so sweet as it swirls around the inside of my mouth.

I hear the laughter of my parents. A soldier gives my father a cigarette. He holds it in his hand, turns it and says, 'I'll enjoy that tonight.' Another soldier gives my mother chocolate and soap. I jump up and down. 'I want to smell the soap!' I close my eyes and inhale the beautiful scent.

But now we are told to move on. Will there be food at the end of our journey? I've heard that there'll be farms and houses where we can stay, that we'll find beds in houses that have been opened for us. The long, slow-moving queue is on its way again. There is lightness in the faces of the people and in their voices. A lightness that comes from hope.

The farm

Later that afternoon we arrive at a small farm where we'll be staying until it is safe to go back to Warnsveld. The farmer's wife says, 'You need a good wash and some clean clothes.' We look at each other, know that we are smelly and dirty, hungry and exhausted. Moeke uses a handkerchief to wipe her eyes. She looks so tired as she holds Lydia in her arms, eyes closed, rocking her gently.

Clean towels and buckets with warm water appear in the scullery and we take turns washing ourselves, using the new soap sparingly. Dressed in clean clothes, we sit around the long table and eat a warming meal of wheat porridge made with skim milk. Papa says, 'I'm sure we won't have to stay here too long. It's just a matter of days. The Germans must know by now that they are defeated.'

We smile. Soon we'll be home.

I hear Papa tell the farmer about the transport planes that, with their monotonous droning and humming, day and night, had become such close companions they were given names by the villagers. He says, 'We called one *The Droner* and a fast plane was called *The Bolter*. Now those planes have disappeared. And we don't want them back.'

I remember those planes. Scary sounds in the darkness of the night.

The farmer asks about the bridge over the IJssel. Papa lights the cigarette given to him by the Canadian soldier,

The farm

closes his eyes as he takes a puff, then opens them and hands the cigarette to the farmer, who repeats the procedure. Papa says, 'Pontoon bridges have had to be laid over the rivers so the liberators can reach the occupied areas.'

The next day Papa says it's not safe yet for us to return home. It is quiet in the farmhouse where we're staying. There are sandy roads around the farm buildings that go to the river and the village – roads that could offer escape to safety or lead to fear and destruction.

Words are sparse on that farm. The farmer, his wife and sons are tight-lipped; they let us know we aren't welcome. Hunched shoulders at meal times, grunts as answers to questions, yet there is comfort that we haven't known for a long time. In the kitchen it's warm, a blackened stove radiating heat on the cool spring days, and we gather around the rough wooden table for the midday meal and gaze with hungry eyes at small pieces of fried meat in brown gravy, fresh vegetables, milk. We bow our heads when the farmer lifts off his black cap, places it on the table next to his plate and blesses the meal. Lydia and I sleep in the same room as our parents – Lydia in a cot in the corner and my bed under a window. Eef, Jan and Jo sleep in another part of the farmhouse. Later at night in bed I wake when my parents come into the room, listen to them talking.

'I know he's been involved with the Germans.'

'Did you notice how the place is full of goods that don't seem right on this little farm? Have you seen the enormous grandfather clock in their bedroom? I wonder whose it was. The owners probably didn't even get a pound of meat for it.'

What are they talking about? I think we are lucky to be in a warm house. I turn over in the little bed, wanting to sleep.

During the day I play in the fields, watch the animals being fed and feel safe because Moeke is here. I like it when in the evening she comes to kiss me goodnight, *lekker*

31

slapen. Before I fall asleep I watch the trees moving in the breeze outside the bedroom window.

The days move fast as there's the cooking to be done, and the cleaning and other chores. Moeke helps with the washing, heating large kettles of water. She says, 'We have no soap but, oh, to spread the washing out on the fresh green grass. It feels as if the spring sun heats each bone in my body.' My mother talks a lot about her body; she must be so tired.

One morning after she's given Lydia her breakfast she says, 'It's safe for us to go home. Lots of other people have begun to move back. We'll start walking tomorrow.'

I dance around on the grass, jumping up high to grab a twig from the pear tree covered with blossom.

'Hooray, hooray, hooray. I can play with Joke and Jannie again. And with Heli. But what about the aeroplanes? Will there be more bombings? Do we have to hide in the cellar again?'

Moeke pulls me close to her. She smells like the air in the forest when we pick blueberries. 'Huub, it will be better for you to stay here for a while. You'll eat good food. Look at you – you're so skinny, and you know we haven't got the right food to feed us all well. Papa will come to take you home in a few days' time. It won't be long. The war is nearly over.'

I remember the food at home – the dry bread with a sprinkling of salt and fat, the grey barley-and-buttermilk porridge in the mornings. Strange-smelling oats. The soup kitchens in the village square offering onion slices and pieces of cabbage floating in water.

But I don't want to be left behind. 'Why is everybody else allowed to go home?'

'Lydia is a baby. She needs extra care so we can't leave her here.'

Maybe I've done something wrong. Would I be a danger

The farm

to the family? I remember the whispers and the sudden quietness at home when visitors arrived. Do my parents think I would say the wrong words? I already know about betrayal, but when we visited our neighbours – crawling along the hedge after the hour of curfew – I didn't talk. I didn't even whisper a word.

I stand near the gate as my family leaves. The green paddocks are no longer as green, the prunus blossom no longer as pink. In bed at night, before the dusk of the spring evening turns to darkness, I feel the loneliness of the cows in the meadows around the farmhouse, their dark brown eyes like the shadowy parts of the river in which I can see myself.

When will my family come back for me?

Sounds of the night

Lying in bed, I watch the plum tree outside the window with its deep-green branches. There's a new game I can play, pretending there are little fairies in those branches and I can tell them about my longing for home and safety, about Heli, my friend next door, and the fun we had together – hop-skipping and playing with her doll. Heli has the most beautiful doll with blonde hair and blue eyes that have black fringes around them. She wears a pink dress and shiny pink shoes. I'd love to have a doll like that.

Around me I hear the sounds of the family on the farm. The farmer and his wife in the bedroom next door, muttering to each other. The creaking of springs. I listen to the sons talking as they close the windows of the barn. I don't like them – their eyes are strange. And they make me do things, bad things. They pull my pants down and touch my bottom. 'If you tell your mother she'll sell you to the gypsies and they'll take you away to a faraway land where there are tigers and lions and other wild animals who eat naughty children.'

I say, 'I'm not naughty.' But what they do makes me feel naughty.

Bombardments
and fairies

I tell the fairies in the plum tree a story. It started with Moeke saying to me, 'Today we'll have lunch with my friend Gerda in the city and you can play with her daughter. Emma is seven years old, just like you.'

It was 28 September 1944 and the day had started out feeling so special. We were walking towards the city, Moeke pushing the pram, Lydia fast asleep. The lunch wasn't special – dry brown-grey bread – but after that, Emma and I were told we could play in the street close to the railway station. Taking the lunch dishes to the kitchen, Moeke said, 'You girls had better get some sunshine on your bodies before winter comes. Emma's mother and I will stay here with Lydia. We have to catch up on a lot of news.'

We'd been watching the trains – black monsters getting ready to steam away, loading up with ammunition for the enemy – when we heard and then saw the low-flying planes above us heading towards the station. The deafening noise … bombs falling. Somebody yelled at us to run to the next street. We ran. Pushed into a doorway and up stairs that took us over a small art gallery. An older man yelled over the noise, 'The English are bombing the German ammunition train at the station! Those wagons are filled with grenades.'

That's why it was noisy!

A young man said, 'At least they can't use those grenades any more.'

The stairway was dark, closed in and packed with other people. I wanted to breathe but I couldn't, my chest felt so tight. I remember crying, 'Where's my mother? I want my mother!' Emma was crying too, holding her hands over her head.

'Hush, children, hush – it'll soon be over.'

Even the older people around us were scared. The ferocity of this bombardment was unexpected. Lips muttered prayers, or swore, using whatever words they could think of.

Finally a quietness returned.

Slowly we made our way down the stairs and out into the street, the older people forming groups to talk about their experience.

Emma and I walked back to the house, the same way we'd come. At first our legs moved like lead. We didn't talk. Then I said, 'I was so scared. Were you?' Emma didn't answer. She kicked a stone on the footpath, then took off at great speed, racing ahead. I tried to catch up with her but I couldn't.

I remember my mother's outstretched arms. 'Oh, *kindje*, I was so worried about you, I thought you'd never come back. I thought we'd lost you.'

I TOLD THE FAIRIES ANOTHER STORY WHILE I WAITED FOR MY parents to take me home.

It was a Saturday afternoon. There have been no warnings of bombs, no sirens, so Papa has taken the older three children to visit his parents.

Bombardments and fairies

My mother sighs after they've left and makes a cup of tea. We are wearing our coats, sitting in the cold dining room, Lydia asleep in the pram. She'll soon have her first birthday.

The noise starts, no warning. The scary, wild noise that rattles and breaks windows and makes the house shake.

Moeke takes me on her knee. With her left hand she pushes the pram backwards and forwards while her right arm clamps around me. She chokingly begins singing and I join her, our two voices blending: 'Safe in the arms of Jesus ...'

My mother's voice, soft and gentle: 'Just hold on to me. Don't worry, soon we might go to the most beautiful country you can ever imagine. There is no pain, no war there, and we'll be truly happy. For ever and ever.'

I'm getting impatient. What's she talking about?

'What country? Will there be soldiers too?' I ask. 'What are we waiting for? Let's go now. Papa and the others can follow us as soon as they come home. You can leave a note to tell him where we've gone.'

I wonder why my mother cries and then laughs. Holds me so hard while bombs fall around us.

Dreams

As a child I wondered whether my mother dreamed about secret places where it would be safe to shelter. Perhaps her prayers were her dreams. Safe above the earth, in the deep blue heaven of her imagination, thinking that angels and archangels were waiting for us in silver-white robes.

Safe in the arms of Jesus.

In the dark night on the farm I try to go to sleep. Marbled colours and textures merge into pictures and feelings. I want my mother's arms around me again, taking me away from the people whose faces tell me I am an intruder. I think of the white bread, the rich feeling in my mouth, the safety of those soldiers in the right uniform – the khaki one. I remember my grandmother with a finely pleated bonnet on her head and a knitted black shawl around her shoulders. I will tell her stories about the farm animals, and the farm people with their unfriendly faces. I will tell them everything when I return – when I am safe on my mother's knee eating white bread with sweet orange jam.

Going home

The plum tree outside my bedroom window has become a familiar part of my life on the farm. I think of the fairies holding golden wands that glitter in the evening dusk. The tree has its own safe shadows and lots of blossoms.

But today is different. I'm going home. I'll see my mother again, and Lydia. I've missed her – the special smell of my little sister, her smiles and the softness of her tiny hands.

Before I fell asleep the night before I'd overheard the farmer's wife saying to the farmer, 'I'm glad the girl is going tomorrow.'

A grumpy answer: '*Ach,* Huub has been easy to look after – no trouble. But all those questions at meal times! When the food is on the table I want to eat.'

Now, beside the shabby, dull-green door of the farmhouse, they stand upright and silent, their faces expressionless. I run to greet Papa, arms outstretched. 'How is Moeke? How is Lydia? Will you take me home now, Papa?'

Hand-in-hand we walk back to Warnsveld, between trees full of leaves, passing green paddocks with yellow buttercups and white daisies, and along sandy paths in the forest with its mysterious darkness. We wave at people working in the fields, and when we cross a narrow wooden bridge we stop and look at the slow waters of the creek. Birds chirp in the trees and we sing about the little bird that sits on a green branch in the bright morning sun and sings too – till his heart bursts. We sing about standing up for Jesus, being soldiers of the cross. In my imagination I see myself lifting high the banners, marching on. We are the good soldiers who will save the world.

I want to cry when I hear Papa singing. His voice is as warm and velvety as the brown drapes in my grandparents' house. I don't know why I'm feeling sad in my heart.

This isn't a time for crying. It's daylight and the sun shines, and today I'm going home.

I want to ask more questions. I free myself from my father's hand, skip and dance ahead. 'Is it safe to return? Have the bombs gone? Are there no more aeroplanes in the night?'

Papa walks along steadily. He often says he needs to think.

There are the familiar buildings appearing now – a red-roofed barn, long tree-lined lanes, the big white mansion with a moat, and in the distance the church with its square tower. I need to ask more questions. It doesn't matter that Papa is quiet; at least I can think about home between my questions. Before we had to hide in the cellar, there were German soldiers living in our house. I am worried.

'Papa, will I sleep in my own bed tonight? Are the German soldiers still in my bedroom? You won't send me away again?'

My father laughs with a deep gurgle. 'Everything is back to normal. The German soldiers have left. A few houses in the neighbourhood were damaged during the last bombing but we were lucky – our house wasn't.'

And there is our house, close to the church. I run inside, look around, and luckily nothing has changed.

Moeke hugs me. 'I'm so pleased you're home. I've cooked a nice hot stew.'

'What's in it?'

Going home

Papa laughs. 'You'll enjoy it – it's frog stew.'

And yes, everything is nearly back to normal. We sit around the table – Papa, Moeke, my sister Jo, my brother, Jan, and me. Eef has hurt her leg and has gone to get better at Tante Sien's house, our favourite aunt in Deventer. Jo and Jan argue about things that happened in the village, the V1 that came down at the end of our street, close to the windmill. The damage it caused, how so many people died.

They can't understand when I don't want to eat. Why, there are those lovely pieces of meat drenched in rich gravy, and I must be hungry after having walked such a long way. But I can only hear the sound of the frogs at night in the pond close to the house, squawking. I remember how they sat on the waterlily leaves, waiting to jump off and chase each other through the murky water.

Moeke says, 'Huub, it's time to go to bed.'

Afterwards, in the stillness of the dark bedroom, I move the black cloth that covers the window and look out at the night, the moon fuller than I've ever seen it before. The clouds moving across the white expanse go so fast, I wonder if they would ever go as fast as a Spitfire. As I lie in the narrow bed under the window that looks out over the empty street I hear doors open and close, footsteps on the stairs.

Then there is the silence of the night. A silence so different from night at the farm.

Freedom

That first night of freedom.
At the end of the war
people danced in the streets.
In the stillness of my dark bedroom,
I moved the black cloth that covered the window.
The moon fuller than I'd ever seen before,
round and white with dancing shadows,
enchanting as magicians producing birds
from black jackets.

Clouds raced across the white expanse,
so fast, so fast, and in my childhood dreams
I wondered what bomber pilots had thought,
what dark dreams they had before they took off
for destructive missions,
flying under another moon
before we were free,
when we could not dance in the streets.

Freedom

The village is filled with people. Some are in uniform. Moeke says they are good soldiers, that they have liberated the village. Are they the same soldiers Papa and I sang about when we walked back, only a few days ago? Everyone's arms are around each other, holding on tight, and people are crying, 'We are free, free, free. We will never have a war again. We thought we were abandoned but our liberators came.'

Bells peal, and we gather in the church to sing about the solid foundation we have. I wonder what they mean but am happy that they no longer think the foundation has crumbled. I suppose it means that everyone can feel safe.

That night through the open window between the pulled-back drapes I watch the people dancing in the street. I see Jo with her shining black hair; she's dancing with a good soldier and they seem to laugh a lot. I'm glad the black window covers are finally gone.

When I hear the word liberation I imagine myself running through our wide open fields – my body floating in a beautiful white dress. Around me, yellow sheaves of rye and wheat ripple in the gentle breeze. Above me, endless pale-blue skies reach the heavens. There are no more dead bodies on stretchers, no soldiers in uniforms and nothing to prevent me from seeing Heli, my dear friend, again.

I don't think any more about the secret place in the cave of a high mountain. *Will I have white bread for breakfast from now on?*

Peace

At last there is peace in the country. It arrives slowly, creeping from village to village, city to city, river to river. That peace will require a great deal of understanding. Some people are living on the streets – former neighbours, their heads shaven as punishment for collaborating with the enemy. There is food again, though it is only available by handing over coupons, which buy sugar, oranges and soft mandarins.

The air is saturated with the sounds of the carillon ringing through narrow streets, across cobblestoned market squares, resounding above the wide rivers.

We are allowed to play in the fields surrounding the village. The golden field full of rye divided by narrow strips where my friends and I chase each other on our bikes, and where young couples walk arm-in-arm in the twilight.

The blueness of the skies is unmarred by grey bombers, yet the villagers no longer dance in the street, and the routines of each day are burdened once more with the frustrations that people didn't care about when their minds were laden with fear: petty annoyances like the weather, the irritating behaviour of politicians and the price of groceries.

On summer mornings housewives clean their homes. Cellars that provided safety during air raids will be used again to keep food cool and store summer fruits. Walls and floors and shelves have been washed with Lysol, and the black covers removed from windows. These women want to remove the smell and vermin of the dirty years.

As the women scrape the blue-and-grey stone pots and dry them in the sunshine they think of the harvest. White cabbages cut up for sauerkraut; green beans, fresh and ripe, thinly sliced and pickled – to eat with potatoes and smoked sausage in the middle of winter, when there will be displays of real meat in the shops again.

There's white bread, smooth and tasty. No butter to put on it – only rich people can afford butter – but thank God there's Blue Band margarine.

Outside the streets are full of rubble.

My bedroom is small, with painted walls and a little dormer window. The curtains have pink and yellow flowers, but the material is old and thin in places. Moeke has promised me some new curtains when the restrictions are over.

There is a toilet on the ground floor but no bath or shower. Each Saturday night I climb into a grey metal tub in the kitchen. Moeke scrubs my back, sighing and groaning as she bends down. Thin, brown hairs escape her tight bun and with a wet hand she pushes them away, back into the fold of her warm head, her face flushed and her body exhausted. For her there is still the renewed sensation of feeling the luxury of soap again, rubbing lather into the facecloth that is shaped like a glove without fingers. I like the touch of my mother's steady, soft hands.

This is the best time of the week. After the bath there will be steaming chocolate on the table, in a white cup with blue flowers from which Moeke's mother drank when she was a young girl.

'Come, *kindje*, drink up – it's past your bedtime.'

I glance at my mother, notice the tears. 'Where is Papa?'

She doesn't answer, but puts her arms around me and holds me tight. And then up the stairs we go, hand in hand.

Peace

A clean body, thick blankets to hide in. A stomach that doesn't feel empty.

I lie in bed, remembering the heavy tanks, the soldiers in blue uniforms. What will happen if they return? They will blow up the bridge again and how will I escape then? I can't swim, and even if I could I'd never be able to cross the wide river. I wake from nightmares to find my bed is wet.

There is a black-and-white photo on my bedroom wall of my parents and me. My parents are in wicker chairs in the garden and I'm on my mother's lap – a baby dressed in a knitted suit, my tiny hands in gloves. My mother told me it was a pink suit, such a pretty pink. 'Mevrouw Bauduin gave it to me when you were born.' I look at the faces of my parents in the photo and create a story where they talk to me as they stare out of the picture, their frozen smiles turning into laughter.

I like the way my photograph mother gazes at me through her spectacles. I remember my father's velvet voice, the singing, the talking. Him joking with his friends, his deep gurgling laugh.

In my story my parents take me on a holiday to a beach. But even there they are always in a hurry.

Scarlet fever

A Sunday night at home. 1942. The war is still in the streets of Warnsveld. I'm in a single bed under the dormer window in my parents' bedroom that also has their lits-jumeaux: twin mattresses side-by-side covered with one green bedspread. There are two doors in the side wall. When you open the first door you'll see linen displayed neatly. The other door opens to a wardrobe with its ceiling sloping to the right.

I'm afraid of this wardrobe. A while ago, before I was sick, I was locked up in it after I had been naughty. I cried, screamed, made a fist with my right hand and banged on the inside of the door. Nobody heard me.

I remember my grandmother pushing me in, my father's mother. I was afraid of her but she had to look after me because my mother was very sick. The day before I'd stuck my tongue out at her. She said if I did it again my hand would stick out of my grave for ever and ever.

Earlier my father said: 'Your mother is very sick and has gone to stay in a sanatorium to get better.'

I asked, 'What is a sanatorium?'

'It's a place where she can rest. She will be there for a while.'

'I want Moeke to be home again.' I wanted to tell him I didn't like my grandmother but I was scared she'd lock me up again.

Scarlet fever

But now I have to stay in bed. I wished I wasn't too sick to enjoy being downstairs and join in the singing. Sunday night is special, the night that comes after a holy day celebrated with two church services and quiet times at home. *You're not allowed to play games on a Sunday*. So most Sundays end with singing around the organ. Friends and neighbours come in and together they stand and sing to the glory of God. *What a friend we have in Jesus*. Even Monty, the black dog, joins in, howling.

SCARLET FEVER HAS COME TO THE VILLAGE. MY MOTHER SAYS those scary words as if they are written in capitals. My body, lying and twisting in bed that Sunday night, while downstairs they are singing hymns and Eef plays the organ. I listen to the singing and to Monty's howling. It makes me cry, but nobody hears me.

I might have to go to a sanatorium too. My body feels hot, and I'm very close to the ceiling – I can nearly touch the plaster and scrape off the ornate flowers on it. My friends can't see me for fear of catching Scarlet Fever. Yesterday Evie Bobbink from next door came to visit. He put a small plate with strawberries at the bottom of the staircase while I stood at the top, wishing he could come up and play. After he was gone I was allowed to pick up the plate. Strawberries, sweet and juicy. Tasting so fresh, like ice cream in summer.

I return to my bedroom and the small dormer window to the outside world that has to stay closed all the time.

Honeymoon decisions

While I've been writing my story, I have allowed my mind to wash up memories of events. In allowing those memories to come I've discovered stories I'd forgotten of events that happened so many years ago. Memories of more than 50 years come to me, just as the ocean collects shells and deposits them on a certain point of the beach, depending on incoming tides and prevailing winds.

BART AND I HAD A QUIET WEDDING, ATTENDED BY FAMILY and a few friends. We walked first to the Gemeentehuis for the civil ceremony and later to the church for the religious one. My mother had organised that Marika, a family friend with a beautiful singing voice, would perform 'Crimond – The Lord's my Shepherd'.

In that cool 11th-century church, on 11 July 1959, close to my home in Warnsveld I made a vow to God and Bart, promising to obey my husband, to follow him wherever he went.

The service concluded with the singing of Psalm 100. I could feel tears welling up, realised I'd forgotten a handkerchief and whispered to Bart, 'Give me your *zakdoek*!' He dug into the pocket of his black trousers, handed me

Honeymoon decisions

the grubbiest, dirtiest looking blue handkerchief I could imagine. I grinned, used it and gave it back to him.

After dinner, prepared by my mother and her friends, we left for our honeymoon in Germany. Within a year of arriving in New Zealand, I learnt what a 'wedding breakfast' meant. Girls at work would ask me, 'Did you have a nice wedding breakfast?' I'd say, 'No, we just had a dinner. It was very nice.'

A few days later we were camping in the hills close to Düsseldorf. We'd walked all day and were sitting outside our little tent near the Sorpesee.

Then I felt Bart's arms around me, strong and tight as always. 'Will you come with me to New Zealand?'

'You're joking,' I said, whipping around to stare into his grey eyes. 'Why are you mentioning this now? Why didn't you tell me before we married that you want to go so far away?' I became aware again of that choking, stifling feeling, as if my coral necklace was tightening around my neck.

Bart had just completed a diploma in tropical agriculture and was restless. He wanted to move as far away as possible – to leave the country of his birth and its restricted way of life.

'I'm fed up with the way things are here – the political situation, the poverty, the long waiting lists for housing. If we stay we'll have to live with your parents for at least another year. And even now I'm qualified I won't be able to get a decent job. We'll never afford a house with the country recovering from the effects of the war.'

I gazed at the river curling through the valley, glistenings of sun dancing on the water. It was so tranquil here, no noisy car-filled roads, only walking tracks. Not at all like crowded Holland. Perhaps New Zealand will be like this. But to emigrate and leave my family, my friends? Leave the village with its market square and pump? Emigrate to New Zealand? To be lonely again?

I remembered the picture of the world in my *Bosatlas*

that showed New Zealand's two uneven-shaped islands at the bottom of the page. I thought about having to return to my parents' house. Making love silently so that the bed wouldn't creak. My mother overseeing everything I did. And my father …

An image of white bread and sheep appeared in my mind. As a teenager I had read about New Zealand in a translation of Mary Scott's book *Breakfast at Six*. The title of the translation was *Wittebrood en Schapen*, which meant 'white bread and sheep'. I remember how I loved the book's description of wide open spaces and abundant food. The concept of freedom for everyone, not only the rich. But did we have to go to the furthest place on earth to find all this?

'I don't know,' I said. 'New Zealand seems such a long way away.'

During our engagement Bart and I had often sung together about going on a journey to a distant land. To me the words of that song didn't seem so romantic now. 'When the sun takes the place of the moon in the sky, we'll go on a journey, you and I.'

I would be lonely.

Would I still feel that tightening around my neck? Even without the coral necklace?

'How long does it take to get there?'

'Six weeks by ship.'

'Why don't we go to Canada? Lots of people go there. Some of my family are there already and it's not so far.'

'You married me, not your family. And don't forget, you promised to follow me.'

He took my hand. He was smiling but I detected a hardness in his blue eyes.

'Come on,' he said, 'let's go for a swim in the river.'

Bart pulled me up. We ambled down the hill, aware of

Honeymoon decisions

the soothing slurp of the river as we got closer, crickets chirping.

Later, as he kissed my lips, my face, my body, I thought, *I have to go with him.*

School

A German soldier is sitting in our kitchen. He takes me on his lap, strokes my back, up and down, and says he will send me a big, big doll from Arnhem where he will go the next day. He says he misses his children. I wait for the doll to arrive. 'Moeke, when is my doll coming?'

The doll never came.

During the war the German army took over everything in the village. They confiscated my father's trucks. They requisitioned bikes and cars. They took over bedrooms in family homes, including our home. Even the village school was needed to house the German soldiers. It meant I started school late, having had to wait until the new school year started in August 1944, once somewhere else had been found for us.

My first memory of school is sitting with a small group of children in the front room of the large house across the road from us. But in my eyes this wasn't proper school. Starting at the real village school didn't come until after the liberation. I have a memory, though, of going to a real kindergarten. On the back wall of the room hung a huge blackboard on which the teacher had drawn children playing in an enormous sandpit. The boys in the sandpit were holding spades while the girls held dolls. I played on my own with wooden blocks, pretending to build a barn where animals could shelter, and wished I could be part of that group playing happily together.

A YEAR LATER, MY FAMILY WAS LEARNING HOW TO LIVE AGAIN in a confused and searching world that was still coping with recovery. Men were returning from working as prisoners of war, and everyone had to make adjustments. There was a lack of work and food. A lack of accommodation. But we were all experiencing the most wondrous gift – the freedom to speak openly, share opinions and discuss our thoughts. I heard my parents talk freely with their friends without the terror of being betrayed by neighbours or people in the shops. The long summer evenings became a time of catching up, of standing in the tree-lined street and sharing news and companionship.

And I was going to a real school, not a temporary school in a house.

That long-awaited day, I was ready before my mother was dressed. After breakfast we set off, me wearing my new olive-green pinafore, Moeke in her navy dress with blue fabric-covered buttons at the front. The road was lined with trees in full autumn colours of gold and red, and in the backyards washing lines were loaded. For weeks I'd wondered what would happen when I started school.

'Moeke, do you think the teacher will be kind?'

'Of course she'll be kind. She knows what she's doing. But it's important that you behave yourself. You know God doesn't like naughty children.'

'Does God watch every child?'

'You know He does.'

I ran ahead, trying to get the fear of God out of my

ASTRIDE A FIERCE WIND

head while my mother walked slowly behind me. Turning around, I asked, 'Moeke, how many children will there be in the class? Do I know any of them?'

'You'll get to know them soon enough.'

'Moeke, who will I have to share a seat with? I hope I like her. What if she teases me?'

'Nobody will tease you.'

I held on tight to a small cotton bag, which contained a pencil and rubber. We reached the school gate and Moeke pointed to the door. 'That's where you have to go. I'll see you at lunchtime.'

The headmaster stood in the doorway. When I ran up the steps he shook my hand and I knew he had a direct communication line with God – he was gigantic and powerful.

He looked down at me from his great height. 'Come in, Huub, your teacher is waiting for you. Follow me.'

I thought, *His voice even sounds like God, deep and unfathomable*. Before I went with him I turned around to wave at my mother but she was gone.

Inside the building everything was big, with dark doors looming over the hallway. The rooms looked out on a playground where children were still running around – the noise was frightening.

The headmaster opened the door of my classroom and I stood in the entrance. Children waited in their seats for class to start. Why were they all looking at me? There were so many.

'Huub, this is your teacher, Juffrouw Bruin,' the headmaster said in his Godlike voice.

Juffrouw Bruin wore a pink dress with a bow at her waist and her black hair had lots of shining waves. She didn't look like a teacher to me.

She took me by the hand and said, 'You'll be next to Ans.' And she told me to sit on a wooden seat in the back row next to a short, chubby girl with blonde curly hair. I

School

liked the girl's tartan dress with its white collar but I didn't like her piercing eyes.

She looked at me when I sat down. 'You smell.'

'I don't smell – you do.'

'You've got funny clothes on.'

'So have you.'

'You're too tall.'

'How come you're so short?'

'You want to come and play with me after school?'

'I'll have to ask my mother first.'

Always that fear

The days were good when Ans and I played after school with other friends in the playground, hanging on the fence, climbing trees. In the early evenings we pulled doorbells, then hid around the corner. We giggled, planning our next move.

There were also cool mornings when Ans went to school on her own. I'd lie in my bed, my face turned to the wall. It was a headache, sometimes a sore stomach. I was hot, I couldn't breathe. A volcano inside me brought forth feelings of heat and pain. I wanted to tell Moeke about those whirling fears but I couldn't. Not yet. Even though I knew the war was over.

I try to push away the memories of the past years, hiding them in corners, covering them just as layers of different kinds of wallpaper cover the walls in some rooms of our house. I wake up and look at familiar things in my room, like the aquarium game on the table with its green and blue paper tanks in which I can fish for teeny paper fish. Every morning, with my eyes closed, I can catch each fish. This is normal; this is as it should be.

But my body has absorbed the terror. I still wet my bed. I still have nightmares. I'm afraid of the dark, so my mother puts a lamp in one corner of my room. But night after night, in my white cotton nightgown, I walk down the stairs in a

Always that fear

trance, holding my schoolbag. 'I have to go to school now. Will it be safe?' My mother takes me back to bed.

Lekker slapen. Nothing will happen tonight.
I'll be safe.

THE NEXT DAY A PLANE IS FLYING LOW. I RUN INSIDE, HIDE under the kitchen table, press my fingers in my ears. *No, no. Please, not again.*

Cabbage and cake

Moeke sits in her comfortable chair near the window. It's her favourite spot. I'm playing in the street and she waves at me. She's knitting a sock, using four needles. I don't know how she can hold the needles together.

'I have a surprise for you,' Moeke says when I come in, and she picks up a fallen ball of wool. 'You are going to a camp. You'll be with lots of other children and you'll play games. It is in a beautiful area and the leaders will be very nice. There'll be so much food and you'll get plenty of lovely, hot milk drinks. You are very lucky. Heli is going too – you both need a change of scene and good food.'

'I don't want to go. I want to stay with you.'

Moeke's face had that no-nonsense look. 'You'll be well looked after. After six weeks you'll be a different child. Look at you, you're as thin as a piece of wood – it's time you got some feeding up.'

'I don't want to be a different child,' I said. 'Let me stay at home.' I walked away, hitting my leg on an open drawer. I cried out, 'Ouch, that hurt!'

'That's your punishment for not wanting to do what we tell you to,' said my mother. I heard this comment many times as I grew up.

Whatever I said was useless. Together with Heli, I was put on a bus to go to camp. I cried as I climbed up the steps. 'Please, let me stay home, Moeke. I'll be good.'

60

Cabbage and cake

'Papa and I think staying at this camp will make you strong again.'

'But I'm strong enough.'

The first things I saw at the camp were straight rows of barracks in a barren field, with muddy paths between the makeshift buildings. Even the surrounding fields were patched with large puddles.

Sparse light filtered through the windows inside the barracks. There were no beds – just two lines of hard mattresses laid close together on the rough wooden floor, one on each side, divided from the middle space by a low wooden construction at the foot of the beds.

As I folded my knitted jersey and dark-green trousers on a shelf at the head of the bed where I'd been told to sleep, the other children started a pillow fight.

One of the girls said, 'Come on, Huub, help us,' and a feather pillow came my way. When I just stared at it the girl yelled, 'Grab it, Huub. What's wrong with you? Haven't you had a pillow fight before?'

I took a deep breath, and threw the pillow back.

The barracks were cold and damp and the grey blankets smelled of dirt. I said to Heli, 'I hate that smell. Of people and pee.' And I cried, using my pyjama sleeves to wipe my nose and eyes. Heli was fidgeting with her hair, scratching her skin. She cried too.

We had sums and history lessons in the morning. At 12 o'clock we ate barely cooked cabbage, tough broad beans and grey meat, all served in a grim and noisy communal dining room. The smells reminded me of standing in the queue at soup kitchens during the war. How was this food going to make me feel better and grow? We played ball games and went for long walks in the afternoon, and after an evening meal of bread and cheese, we went to bed.

I was afraid of the leaders.

'Here's a cloth. Wash the kitchen floor with it.'

'It's time to do the dishes, make sure they're clean.'

'You're not allowed to run around the barracks – you'll damage the grass.'

This wasn't the paradise my mother promised. Day after day it rained, and raindrops and tears mixed on our faces as Heli and I trudged through the empty country lanes in our wet clothes. I vomited every day. One of the leaders finally said, 'Huub, I'll ring your family and tell them to come and take you and Heli home.'

Heli grabbed my hand and whispered, 'What a relief.'

I was aware of Papa and Moeke's disappointment. My mother clicked her tongue. I could tell she was cross with me. 'Some health camp! I wanted you to put on some weight but you're still as thin as a lath.'

I yelled, 'How could I put on weight? I hated the food! It tasted awful, like dirt. It was like eating food from the soup kitchen again.'

'I still would have liked you to stay a bit longer.'

IN THE MAIN STREET WAS A BAKERY THAT BELONGED TO THE father of Janneke, a classmate. On Sunday afternoons we were allowed to play in the bakery where the warm ovens threw out the sweet aroma of bread and pastries. This was a safe place, watching the baker create the shapes for tomorrow's breakfast. I couldn't get enough of the taste and smell of those buns – they were nearly as good as the taste of the white bread at the end of the war. I knew I would be eating those buns at lunchtime the next day.

The shops were once again filled with groceries, meat and vegetables. Special treats of small decorated cakes appeared, and fruit from other countries – oranges with a bubbly skin that could be peeled in one long string, crispy apples, gold-

Cabbage and cake

skinned bananas. Mealtimes were regular, and Moeke said, 'At last your body is beginning to fill out.'

But I was still hungry. Always hungry.

When Papa was ready we could eat. He took a long time saying his prayers. In the meantime I was starving, my mouth watering at the smells from the covered porcelain bowls in front of me – cream-coloured cauliflower covered in white sauce and sprinkled with freshly grated nutmeg. Gravy and fluffy potatoes. Perfectly rounded meatballs, fried in margarine, waiting on a plate.

After we ate, Moeke took the dirty plates and bowls to the kitchen while Papa pulled the old black Bible from the sideboard and put it in front of him on the table. This went on for many years, day after day, while I listened to stories about people living in deserts. About them killing each other. David killing Goliath. God telling Abraham to kill his son Isaac. Would people still do that? Would Papa want to do that to Jan? He and Jan argued a lot. One night I woke up to a terrible noise downstairs – Papa so angry and beating Jan who was lying in a corner of the kitchen. Moeke screaming, 'Stop it! Stop it!'

Papa made rules for us to follow. I tried not to daydream while Papa read the Bible stories to us after breakfast and dinner. Each time he finished he insisted I repeat his last word back to show I had been listening to descriptions of David's mighty deed killing Goliath with one stone or, even worse, Abraham murdering his own son. Yet still I found myself thinking of bike rides with Ans through the narrow cobblestone streets of the village, pretending to be part of the Tour de France. Or playing hide and seek in the forest. But I couldn't allow myself to dream. I didn't want my father's dark eyes looking at me, not saying anything, just watching and waiting. Waiting for me to repeat the last word he'd read.

I ROCKED IN A SWING THAT HUNG FROM THE RAFTERS OF the open-ended garage where my father's Mercedes was tucked away during the night. Next to this space was a building that my father had offered to a friend in our village who wanted to start his own car repair business. Together with two employees, Oom Anton had begun to gather clientele around him.

As I moved slowly and rhythmically on the swing, my thoughts took me far away, over the rooftops of the neighbourhood, over the wide meadows outside the village. The smell of oil and the grease-covered overalls of the mechanics didn't hold any repugnance for me because I saw the vehicles they were working on as colourful magic carpets.

I observed the people who came to collect their cars. I saw the relief on their faces and imagined the distances they would travel now. In my eyes they were fascinating. There was the mayor, dressed in a smart grey suit. I imagined him sitting behind a wide oak desk making important telephone calls. There was the head of a large paper factory. He smiled at me but quickly walked away.

I never talked to them but I could tell by the way they wore their clothes that they had knowledge of the world in their veins, having experienced different habits and traditions in other countries. In the middle of winter they appeared with tanned faces from skiing in the Swiss Alps. One high summer's day a girl only a few years older than me drove away in an MG, the car roof down, a bright red scarf fluttering in the wind, exotic sunglasses on her face. Nobody in our family possessed sunglasses.

I wanted to travel too. I studied my big *Bosatlas* and wondered how long it would be before my special prince would come along and take me away to distant, exciting

Cabbage and cake

places. What would it be like to be on holiday? A holiday in a hotel near a beach?

I wanted to get away from the village. Away from my quiet mother who sometimes sat so still in her chair, a damp and crumpled handkerchief in her hand. Away from my father, whose eyes watched me intently as I was reading or doing my high-school homework at the dining-room table.

I grew up listening to my mother's stories about another world, a time from her past that she still dreamed about. It was a magic world where people had interesting conversations, travelled, gave parties and wore beautiful clothes.

Before she was married she'd worked as a nanny for a lady-in-waiting of Queen Wilhelmina. Moeke's face would grow soft and her eyes brighten. 'Mevrouw Bauduin lived in a grand and beautiful mansion here in our village. I had to look after her son Bobby until he started school. I started work early and finished late but I didn't mind; I really loved Bobby. Sometimes the Queen would visit Mevrouw Bauduin and I had to present Bobby to her. I'd dress him in his dark-blue velvet suit with a white collar, and each time the Queen greeted me by my name.'

'I wish I could have lived there too!'

My mother's face became very still. She put down her knitting. A cardigan for Lydia. Her hands rested in her lap and tears were in her eyes as she continued, 'Later Bobby became a lieutenant-at-sea, and he died when his ship was sunk in the Java Sea.'

Swinging away in my father's garage, thinking about my mother's exotic past and her boring life now, soon came to an end when there was a shout from the house: 'Go and get a pound of mince from the butcher!'

I dashed across the road, and heard the tiny tinkle of a bell as I entered the shop. There I inhaled the tantalising aromas of smoked sausages and bacon. As soon as the butcher had wrapped up the meat I was ready to leave the shop, but not before he smiled and said, 'Here, have a piece of smoked sausage. Be careful when you cross the road.'

Munching the small piece of sausage, I looked forward to that night's dinner. I loved Moeke's meatballs, fried in margarine – butter was too expensive – and I knew too that my brother Jan would offer 25 cents for my meatball portion. Though no way would I take up his offer.

Soon I was back rocking on the homemade swing, dreaming about the heroine of *Rebecca* – her struggles with life – and working out my own strategies of escape. Watching the mechanics at their work, I became determined to learn to drive as soon as I was 18.

One day a beautiful pale blue Hillman was in the mechanic's yard, waiting to be taken home by its proud owner. I imagined driving this heavenly car, wearing a smart navy suit with white gloves and white shoes, heading for a place where life would be wonderful, the big cities in the west – Amsterdam, Rotterdam, The Hague. After a while I'd stop at a grand hotel set in magnificent grounds, park the car and sit at a white table and chair on the huge red-tiled terrace overlooking the Rhine where barges laboured under their heavy loads. I knew that wherever I went I'd order a giant piece of butter-fried steak and exotic dishes from all around the world and then I'd return to a house that had a huge garden with soaring-to-the-sky trees and colourful flowers. There would be sophisticated people living in that house who would talk about books and music.

Living in a nicer world would be so different from my own home, where my mother would wipe her forehead and in her tired voice explain to her new friends, 'Oh, the doctor told me I should not have any more children after the first three. Huub and Lydia should never have been born. If only Huub had been a boy. My husband was so disappointed.' At that time these words didn't hurt as much as the bullying from my older siblings.

Cabbage and cake

Jan, Eef and Jo were constantly snarling at me, teasing and ridiculing me. One day, years later in Dunedin, I sat under the birch tree, watching my children playing and chatting happily in the sandpit, and I thought about the lukewarm relationship I'd had with my older siblings and wondered why they had pestered me so much. I know now that I didn't imagine that pestering, because on one of my trips home, Eef took me aside to apologise for it. 'I want to buy you something special to make up for what we did to you when we were young,' she said. 'We were very cruel.'

'You don't need to do this,' I said. 'I always thought that was just part of family life.'

Later, as a young married woman in New Zealand, meeting other families with children, I discovered that there could be different ways of communicating with your child or sibling.

I did travel in my teens. To Switzerland for holidays and, after I finished high school, I went to London to work as an au pair. Then a few years later as a young married woman I travelled permanently to the end of the world, 43° South, Dunedin, New Zealand.

A fleeting question has often crossed my mind. I have not dared to dig too deeply to find an answer to this question because facing the truth of not being liked, let alone loved, by my older siblings would have created even more problems. Yet if I had been closer to my family, would I have emigrated?

My beginnings

I grew up in Warnsveld, a quiet village in the eastern province Gelderland. In those days Warnsveld was surrounded by a forest and wide meadows that flooded in winter when the river IJssel went beyond its banks. The village was close to Zutphen, a city with a rich history of Spanish wars, old churches and a prosperous river trade since the Middle Ages. On my way to the Baudartius Lyceum I'd bike past the Spanish Gate through which the Spanish had entered the city in 1572. I imagined the ghosts of the persecuted people still floating above the wall.

Since Zutphen was only 30 kilometres north of Arnhem, 45 kilometres east of the German border and 125 kilometres from Amsterdam, it was a popular thoroughfare for trucks on their way to Germany. During the war it was also used by the Germans trying to reach England. They even put up a sign just outside the village that stated the distance to London. The Allies prevented the German vehicles from moving on by blowing up several bridges over the IJssel.

My father started his own transport business in 1924, the year he and my mother married. He bought a horse and a wagon, gradually acquiring more horses and wagons, eventually owning trucks to deliver sand and gravel to new building and roadwork sites. His business did very well until the Germans took control over the village and confiscated his trucks, so it was back to horses and wagons.

My beginnings

I remember opening the kitchen door in the morning to be greeted by Victor, a solid chestnut-coloured horse with an abundant creamy-coloured mane, wanting his handful of treats in the form of leftovers from the previous night's dinner. After the war Victor and the other horses were gradually replaced by more trucks, a Dodge being the first one. The big garage eventually held three trucks, and the chauffeurs became part of the business, their midday meal provided by my mother.

In 1924 my father employed a 14-year-old boy, Herman. Those two established an almost familial relationship, and when Herman celebrated 25 years of employment my father organised a professional photograph to be taken of our family, the drivers and the trucks. Even Monty – the dog we had then – is in the photograph, although Jan wasn't as he was on military service in Indonesia at the time. There were no 'green eyes' in our family when Papa gave Herman a brand-new car as part of the celebrations. He and his wife were special people.

In later years my father had a contract with the Rijkswaterstaat, an organisation comparable to the Ministry of Works, to ensure that specific roads in the area were spread with sand and salt during the winter months. There is a lovely story about one winter's afternoon when he got a phone call from Paleis Soestdijk, Queen Juliana's residence. The Queen intended passing through the village on her way to visit her mother-in-law, and the palace official was calling to ask my father to ensure the roads were free of ice so the Queen could drive safely to her destination. A few days later a letter written by the Queen herself was delivered to our house, thanking him for his contribution to her safety on a treacherous winter's day.

MY SISTER EEF HAD JUST TURNED 12 WHEN I WAS BORN ON 21 October, 1937. My mother had taken ill with pleurisy straight after my birth and needed bedrest. A string of women came to look after my mother and me and take care of the rest of the household. In between times my paternal grandmother helped out. I can't remember what I'd done wrong, but one day she locked me up in the wardrobe of my parents' bedroom. I was scared, banging on the door, *let me out, let me out*. I was told that after two months, on Christmas Day, my mother was finally allowed to go downstairs again, but soon after that she was admitted to a sanatorium 40 kilometres away. She could not cope.

Much to Eef's chagrin, she was told she had to leave school to help at home – hand-washing buckets of nappies, washing floors and doing other household chores, as well as taking a screaming baby for walks in the pram while her former classmates were playing games and hop-skipping along chalk patterns on footpaths. She told me she also had to take the neighbours' children sometimes as well: Heli, and Evie Bobbink.

One soft spring day, Eef bundled me into my pram and took me out walking. She pushed the pram along the road towards her old school. 'My friends were playing on the footpath,' she said. 'I joined them after putting the pram under a tree near the playground. You were asleep and we were fooling around and having fun. As we did, we slowly moved away from the chalk patterns on the footpath and along the street. When I got home I was asked what I had done with the pram!' And she finished, 'I felt so guilty leaving you there.' Eef was telling me this on a hot summer afternoon years later, while we sat in her beautiful garden, sipping a cold drink. She was worried, she said, imagining

My beginnings

I might have been stolen, rushing back to the playground, feeling relief as she pushed the pram home.

I cried when she told me this. I could see the young girl Eef was then, a bright mind, wanting to belong – she did not want to be an outsider – but having to be away from her friends and the classroom because she was looking after me.

I remember her as distant, gruff and grumpy in those days – the less said the better. But as I grew up, especially in my teens, Eef was always there, sitting at the dining room table, knitting me a dark blue dress or a swimsuit or several pretty white cotton jerseys to go with my green skirt.

Palm Sunday

My mother is kneading the sweet dough for our *paasbrood*, the cinnamon bread studded with sultanas and lemon peel that we eat at our first Easter meal. She is telling me the myth of the northern goddess, Frigga of Ostara. How she's often depicted as a swan, and has given her name to Easter and is part of the traditional Easter rituals.

I liked my mother's mysterious tales, especially the ones about strange creatures in mythology or the characters in fairy tales – pixies dancing under the trees or lonely girls finding a mound in a forest where ghostly white women handed out beautiful food. Best of all I liked stories about children who were strong and clever and could escape danger in the nick of time. At night I dreamed about being chased, wanting to escape. In my dreams my feet wouldn't move and my hunter – a wild animal, a stranger – was getting closer and closer. I'd wake, gasping for air and wait in the dark until my breathing was regular again.

The war was over, everything was back to normal, or as normal as possible, although some food restrictions were still in place, and today was the day before Palm Sunday – one week before Easter. It was going to be exciting. I stretched and ran downstairs to eat my buttermilk porridge.

After breakfast Moeke and I walked into the village. I

Palm Sunday

shivered in my moss-green coat and pulled my white hat a bit further over my cold ears. Easter was early and the trees were still bare, but daffodils and prunus blossoms promised summer.

At the drapery store the doorbell made a soft tinkling sound. Inside, the smell was like a new dress – slightly musty with a hint of dye. The woman behind the counter was sorting through a box of buttons. I said, '*Dag*, Mevrouw. I'd like to buy some fluffy chickens for the procession today.'

The shop attendant opened a shallow drawer under the counter. 'So, Huub, that's going to be a big day for you. Which ones do you prefer – the yellow or orange ones?'

I spotted a box with miniature chickens made from furry fabric and pointed to the orange ones. 'I'll take those.' Before the shop attendant could put them in a bag I was holding the chickens in my hands, turning them gently, not wanting to squash them.

Our next stop was the bakery. Freshly baked fruit loaves and small cakes were displayed in the window.

Janneke's mother stood behind the counter, filling a bin with delicious-smelling buns. 'Hello, Huub. I know what you've come for.' She left her space behind the counter, went through a door to the bakery and returned holding high a bread swan. 'I've saved some good ones for you and your friend Ans so you'll both have a chance to win a prize today.'

I looked at the bread swan with its raisin eye. The shape of its neck was long and exquisite and its slim body perched elegantly on a wooden stick. I said, 'Oh, she's just like Frigga of Ostara with her one eye – isn't she, Moeke?'

When I got home the decoration of the swan queen started. I surrounded her with laurel branches and ribbons. I strung several rows of sultanas and raisins and hung them between the green and yellow bows, and put the orange chickens between the bows too. Then I tied a narrow white ribbon around Frigga's neck with a double bow. I was sure to win.

After lunch I proudly carried my decorated swan to the church square. Ans was there to meet me, jumping up and down, shivering while waiting in the shadow of the houses surrounding the square. She wore a dark red woollen dress, and a large white bow was pinned to the top of her head. We giggled as we looked at each other. My dress was dark red too but my bow was pink. 'I'm so nervous,' Ans said. 'I really want to win this.' 'Who knows,' I said. 'We both might win.'

I admired the way she had decorated her swan with a circle of braided bread. 'We've got the same ribbons,' she said, 'but your chickens are orange and mine are yellow.'

In the warm spring sunshine we were told to gather near the church. We were a gaggle of children – six, seven, eight years old – who that day had briefly forgotten the wailing of sirens, the planes dropping their bombs and the craters left behind afterwards.

First our entries would be judged and then the parade would start. Tight as soldiers in a row we stood, heads high, waiting, holding our decorated swans and sun rings. Ans and I shoulder to shoulder. Everybody around us was chatting, laughing. A small girl in a pink dress said, 'I want to have a swan too.' Taking the child's hand, her mother said, 'Amelia, next year you can take part in the procession.'

Three important-looking women walked slowly around us, looking thoughtfully at each child's decoration. I noticed the frowns on the ladies' faces, especially as they looked at me and Ans.

I whispered to Ans, 'What are they saying? How many prizes are there?'

Ans whispered back, 'I don't think there are many. We

Palm Sunday

won't have a hope of winning anything.'

Then the band started to play, and our feet were already pretending we were walking. The important-looking women came closer to Ans and me. They stopped, one of them made a sign with her hand to the band leader and the band ceased playing. There was brief silence. We waited. Ans looked at me. The tall overdressed woman held up a piece of paper and called out two names: Ans Hof. Huub Visser.

'We've won!' we shouted, cross-linking our hands and dancing in a circling whirlwind, the swans forgotten on the ground.

The mayor draped satin ribbons over our shoulders and we stroked the smooth fabric as the band started to play again. The contestants formed into rows and we threw our bodies around to the beat of the music, waving swan queens and eternal sun rings high above our heads. Away from the church square we danced, through the cobbled main street, past the bakery and out of the village, along narrow lanes, beyond the windmill and the houses that were bombed.

And all the way we sang together the traditional Palm Sunday song about hand-painted eggs. The ones that were going to be abundantly available at Easter mealtimes – everyone eating at least three.

At one corner we passed the Romany people, or 'gypsies' as we called them then. The women sat on the steps of their caravans on the roadside and the men clapped their hands and yelled,' Good, good, good!' Little children in patched clothes darted around the adults, showing off their bare buttocks. I remembered the boys on the farm and my heart raced. I said to Ans, 'Come on, hurry up. I don't want to be sold to the gypsies.'

Ans' voice was strong. 'Why are you so afraid? Who would want to sell you to the gypsies?'

And then it was time to march back to the square, past old people waving from the windows of the rest home and past families waiting closer to the square. We smiled and waved back.

When we reached the square Moeke was waiting. I turned and said, '*Tot morgen*, Ans.' I'll see you tomorrow.

'Come here, *schatje*,' said my mother. 'I want to give you a big hug. Your swan looked beautiful. And so do you. You'll have to tell Papa you've won a prize.'

'Moeke?'

'Yes, Huub?'

'Were you sometimes afraid of your father?'

'Of course not. My father loved me. And your father loves you.'

'Moeke, I don't want to be sold to the gypsies.'

'What makes you say that? You're such a little worry-pot. Let's get you home – you're tired.'

'I'm not.'

Moeke said brightly, 'It'll soon be Easter and we'll have our sweet bread made with dried fruit and almond paste. And you can eat as many eggs as you like.'

I thought of Easter morning and of the basket of boiled eggs my mother would place on the breakfast table, each one meticulously hand-painted.

As we reached our home I thought of my other grand-mother – her white bonnets and loving smile. The safety of her home. 'I wish Oma could've been there today.' I said. 'Can we visit her later? I want to show her my swan. We can bring her some *paasbrood* as well.' I turned my head away. 'Do you think she'd let me stay the night?'

'*Ach*, Huub,' my mother said, 'you know by now that Oma is getting old. She can't cope with having you to stay. She's never been the same since Opa died. His death hit her hard.'

Palm Sunday

How can a death hit somebody?

I picked the fluffy chickens off the swan, squashed them in my hand.

Oma's bonnets

In our village of Warnsveld, not much changed after the war. The old water pump in the middle of the square continued to provide a meeting place for the villagers although it was no longer used, and the street that ran alongside had the usual shops. Food was still scarce and expensive, but the window display at the bakery – sweet fruity cakes and luscious mocha tarts – made my mouth water. And the greengrocer's colourful displays of fruit and vegetables were known to attract shoppers from other villages.

After all the traffic of the war, Warnsveld was a quiet place again with few cars or trucks, although Papa said there were more trucks thundering through on their way to Germany than before the war. On the outskirts, there were tree-lined streets with luxurious villas that led to the gloomy forest we escaped through when we were evacuated to the farm in Vorden at the end of the war. The forest with the old trees that sighed and sang in the wind. The forest that made me feel safe.

Everybody knew each other in our village, and people greeted me when I walked or biked around. 'What are you up to today?' 'How are your parents?' 'How's Oma? Give her my greetings when you next visit her.' Which I did often.

After my grandfather Opa Nijhof died in 1938 at the age of 65, Oma had moved to another suburb in the nearby

Oma's bonnets

city of Zutphen to live with my tante Mien, and Mien's husband, Jan. The suburb was on the other side of town, and so felt a long way from where we lived. My aunt and uncle had a small grocery shop there.

I felt comfortable with Oma and knew I could trust her. She made me feel safe. The two of us would sit in Mien's living room, talking and drinking hot chocolate. My oma would listen to me when something had happened at school that made me unhappy. She was old, but she still had a warm voice like the cream on a birthday cake, a gentle smile, and grey eyes that knew and accepted everything.

As Oma aged she started to wear dark gowns with lace on the front, but the most fascinating aspect of her appearance was the variety of bonnets and caps she wore. Her beautiful, strong grey hair had a parting in the middle, and she tied it up in a knot at the back, covering it with a cap. There were white cotton bonnets for daytime, black crocheted ones for the evening, and plain caps for sleeping in at night. Many of them she had made herself. Most special of all of Oma's bonnets were the ones for Sunday best. Oma's bonnets needed careful treatment and went to a woman in our village who was the local expert in washing the finely pleated creations, and ironing them with a goffering iron.

I loved visiting Oma and not only because of the comfort it gave me, but because I was also allowed to play with her antique dolls. I adored those dolls. One was brown-skinned with black hair and the other had golden hair, and both were dressed in dainty white gowns with lacy strips on the bottom, and delicate caps on their heads. Little leather shoes completed the look. I often asked in vain if I could take them home to sit on the bookshelf above my bed together with my favourite books.

I was 10 years old when I was given an assignment that would take me to Oma's every week.

'Huub,' said my mother, 'I'd like you to become the

bonnet bearer for Oma. You'll need to pick up the clean bonnets from the washerwoman every Saturday morning and take them to Oma's, and then in the afternoon give the washerwoman the other bonnets to be washed. Oma likes to have a clean bonnet every day as well as a good bonnet for Sundays.'

The washerwoman was a hunched, grey-haired lady with a deeply lined face. She lived in a tiny house with only a few rooms. Her narrow kitchen had a square wooden table with a gingham cloth over it and two low-backed wooden chairs that fitted right underneath. There was a blue granite bench in this kitchen covered with an old woollen blanket, and this is where she did her ironing. When the ironing was finished the woman folded the blanket and tucked it on the bottom shelf of a cupboard.

On my first Saturday as Oma's bonnet bearer, the washerwoman asked me inside and showed me the clean, freshly ironed bonnets.

'Now, child,' she said, 'I want you to be extremely careful when you take these back to your oma. Don't you go and make creases and wrinkles in the bonnets by squashing them too hard.'

My throat felt tight. 'What if I fall off the bike?' I said, my voice hoarse with fear, 'What if the bonnets get creased? My father will be angry.' I tried to clear my throat by coughing.

The washerwoman said, 'Your father would never be angry with you. He's such a good man. And you'll be fine. Remember, straight to your oma's house and no stopping on the way.'

With the tips of my fingers I held a special white starched cotton cap by two of its many tiny pleats. I was enchanted by the intriguing way the cap was made. Round the rim there was a thin strip of lace and I counted at least 22 pleats at the back. The starched ties were held in place by very small buttons.

Oma's bonnets

I tucked this precious bonnet and the other plainer cotton ones – meticulously wrapped in tissue paper –into the basket on the back of my bike, checked behind me to ensure the cane basket was snug on the bike carrier and set off.

Oma lived five kilometres away, and to get to her house I had to bike the two kilometres from Warnsveld to the city of Zutphen, cross the whole of the city and then bike over a long bridge built above the river IJssel. First I had to negotiate the narrow streets of Warnsveld. It was a cold day in early winter and children were playing on the footpath wearing colourful knitted caps while their mothers talked to each other in front of the houses, their arms tightly clasped to their chests, their feet constantly moving to keep the pervading cold at bay. There was so much to see on these streets, but I also had to be careful where I was going.

After a while I reached the city and cycled hard to get across it, reaching the bridge. The water was already half-frozen and great chunks of ice were being pushed downriver by the current. An arctic wind hit my face and I could feel the chill seeping through my woollen gloves into the muscles of my hands. The wind was so strong I had to stand on the pedals of my bike to keep myself moving.

At last I came to the lonely road that ran through paddocks where cows grazed in summer. Not far to go now, I thought, and told myself: *Keep going and soon you'll be at Oma's drinking hot chocolate.*

Tante Mien and Oom Jan's modest grocery shop displayed sweets under the glass, including balls that changed colour as you sucked. I loved the mystery smells, and the jute bags that bulged interestingly. What was in them? Who had delivered them? Who would buy such huge quantities of rice and barley? On one of the shelves was a glass jar that held broken pieces of biscuits. I knew I would be given a small paper bag with some inside.

My cousin was a sturdy young woman with amazingly long legs. She loved singing and was sometimes asked to perform at the town hall. I admired Maria when she stood on the stage, regally dressed in her red velvet gown with a fur cape around her shoulders – expanding her impressive chest and trying to produce the equivalent sound of the best coloratura in the world. Sometimes I heard her sing in the shop and then it seemed as if all the bottles and glass jars were moving in a unifying accompaniment. I loved the music but knew nothing about it. My imagination knew no bounds when I one day heard a cousin of mine say to her sister, 'Gert and I kissed right through Offenbach's "Barcarolle".' How could they eat a baker's roll as they kissed?

The first Saturday cycling to Oma's house with the clean bonnets, I found I needed to push harder and harder against the wind, weighed down as I was by the importance of my delivery. I had been biking for nearly half an hour, when I finally saw my grandmother sitting by the living room window, dressed in black and wearing a white bonnet. I waved, and Oma waved back.

It was wonderful getting out of the bitter wind and into the cosy house, resting my chilled, tired body. My oma sat across the table from me, her elbows resting on the red plush table cover. Oma's wooden chair had a high back with an upholstered piece in the middle made of more red plush, but my chair was an ordinary dining chair without any decoration. I became aware of how frail Oma looked in that huge chair. As if she would disappear with the slightest breeze from the south.

After Oma had opened the parcel with the clean bonnets she gave me the ones she had used the previous week, as well as the payment to take back to the washerwoman. Once the business aspect of the visit was completed it was time for the best part. My aunt placed a blue-and-white

Oma's bonnets

Delft chocolate pot with a strong cane handle on the table along with two cups and saucers, one for Oma and one for me. The two white cups were filled with steaming, sweet chocolate milk, and two petite biscuits were placed on the saucer on each side of the cups. When Tante Mien left the room she said, 'I'll leave the two of you together now so you can both catch up on all the things that happened this week'.

Oma held her beautiful long hands together and started on the usual litany of questions. How was my mother? Had I been good for my parents? Had I said my prayers every morning and evening? How was school? Did I do my homework? I didn't mind Oma's questions. I knew she listened thoughtfully to my answers. She really cared. At the age of 10 I had already learnt to reassure other adults who demanded to know answers to such personal questions and gave more attention to sipping the hot chocolate milk slowly and nibbling the biscuits. I gloried in the warmth of Oma and the hot chocolate milk.

I thought how lucky Oma was to be looked after by her daughter. The kindness of my aunt.

For a year my Saturday rituals continued, but one day when I arrived at Oma's house she wasn't in her usual seat. Tante Mien was waiting for me. She said, 'Please give the washerwoman my compliments. Here's also the money for her and one more of Oma's best bonnets.'

There was no smell of chocolate milk to greet me, and instead of talking to Oma at the red plush-covered table I now had to go up the few steps into her bedroom.

There I found a bird-like creature nesting in the wide bed between white cotton sheets with crocheted edges. Oma's head was on a large pillow and her grey hair was covered by a white crocheted cap that she'd made herself years ago. Her false teeth were in a cup on the table beside the bed and her greeting to me was as thin as the first layer of ice on the village pond. Oma smiled at me for a short time and then closed her eyes again, breathing lightly.

Biking home, I understood that Oma's special bonnets wouldn't frame her beautiful head any more, that my bonnet-bearing duties would probably be over. Who would listen to me from now on?

I turned around and looked at the cane basket behind me on my bike. Instead of Oma's bonnets, there was a bulky parcel. When I'd been leaving my aunt had said, 'Oma would like you to have the dolls. She knows how much you like them.' Crossing the long bridge, I thought about the place I'd put them. On the bookshelf above my bed would be best, next to my favourite books, because then I would see the dolls every day and they would watch over me at night. Perhaps it would be as if Oma were staying with me.

Pretending princesses

One thing that didn't change after peace returned was my relationship with Ans, my best friend since my first day at school.

The joy of running with Ans after school, like a whirlwind, our hair blowing in the wind. 'Let's have fun. Run. I'll catch up with you.'

There was the day I stopped still, looking at a caterpillar in my hand. Ans bowed her head over my hands. *How does it know when it's time to change?*

'Let's play dress-ups,' she said. 'In my attic after school today.'

I loved playing at Ans' house. She lived in a two-storeyed brick house with lots of rooms and an enormous attic. It was surrounded by a sprawling garden with old, gnarled trees. Her mother was much younger than mine and smelled like flowers, her clothes were flamboyant – a yellow swirling skirt, a frilly white blouse. Large printed flowers on soft fabric. Her blonde hair was shoulder-length and turned inwards at the edges. She looked like a girl, not a mother. I loved my mother. *But why does my mother look so old? Why is she always tired? Why does she always wear black?*

Ans' mother chatted with us: 'What did you do today? Have you learnt lots of new things? Do you have any homework?'

'We did tables. I hate tables. Can we have a drink, please?' Ans said.

'You must be starving after all that hard work.' Ans' mother went into the kitchen to make a fresh lemon drink. As she came back, she called out, 'Here are two glasses of lemon for my favourite one and a half cents. Ans, you're the half cent, and Huub is the one cent – she's nearly twice as tall as you.'

I loved Ans so much that I didn't worry about who was the one cent or who was the half cent. To be in Ans' house felt like swinging higher and higher on a swing.

We pretended to be fairies, or foreign princesses who danced in brilliantly lit rooms. We dressed up in royal clothes found in Ans' attic. A deep purple velvet evening gown with a delicate white lace collar, a gold moiré cocktail dress with a wide sash around its waist. There was an old carved oak chest up there that was laden with wonders – colourful scarves, glamorous shoes, and decorative hats trimmed with feathers and flowers. There were foreign princes too, clad in scarlet trousers and white plumy hats, who looked at Princesses Ans and Huub and held out cool hands, saying, 'Come dance with us.'

I understood that I wasn't the only girl to begin a normal life again when the war ended. Following the liberation of Holland the three real Dutch princesses returned to their home country after living in Canada during the war years. They spoke a few words on Dutch radio: 'We're so glad to be back in Holland again. We missed you all and have looked forward to our return.' Ans and I sat on the floor in her house, glued to the old-fashioned radio, listening with awe to the young royals.

We went up to the attic, took an old blanket and made holes in it. We tucked the blanket over the seat and armrests of an upside-down chair. Wrapped in an orange flag, Ans

Pretending princesses

whispered, 'I'll be Princess Beatrix and you can be Princess Irene.'

'Children of the Netherlands, we are so happy to be back in our country.' Ans' voice wavered with importance. 'We enjoyed living in Canada – it's such a beautiful country with its mountains and lakes. We had our own swimming pool. There's so much snow in winter. And we rode with the Mounties. But it's good to be back in Holland. Flying to Holland from Canada I asked a hundred times: 'Are we over Holland yet?'

Princess Huub chipped in: 'It's so nice to be back. Our grandmother will soon open Parliament and we will wear crowns and sit in our golden coach.'

After a while we forgot that we were speaking to the nation. 'I'll wear the golden crown and you can have the silver one,' said Princess Beatrix.

'No, I want the gold,' Irene replied. 'You'll be queen one day and then you'll have plenty of time to wear gold crowns.'

'Just wait until I'm queen! I'll do everything I like and marry the best-looking prince. And then you'll have to do everything I tell you to.'

Promises of heaven

I was 14. My mother told me, 'We've enrolled you for a youth camp in Ommen.'

I was going to be sent away again.

'Why do I have to go? I don't want to go to another camp.' That ghastly camp. The cold, wet bleakness of the barracks.

'You'll like this camp – it'll be so much better than the one you went to after the war.' Moeke stopped the ironing and pulled the plug from the socket. She walked to the corner where the radio stood on a low table, switched it on, and said, 'You must go. This camp will have lots of music and singing – you love singing – and all kinds of other activities, like games and walks.'

'I'm not going.'

'It's about time you learnt some discipline,' my mother said. 'You must learn to control yourself. If you're not careful, the devil will take over your life.'

'I don't care about the devil. I don't want to go.'

But my mother remained adamant; I needed to be reined in, she told me. 'Just be quiet and do as you're told – your temper will get you in trouble one day. You must follow Jesus as your example.'

I turned to face my father. I had to say it.

'Yes?'

I hesitated. 'Why don't you stay home with Moeke? She

cries when you leave her every night. If you are not here, how can I leave her as well?'

'Judge not, so you won't be judged,' my father said.

'What about your judgement?'

He took Moeke's hands, stroked them gently, whispering, '*Stil maar, stil maar.*' Be calm, be calm. He said to me, 'You're going. No more nonsense from you.'

AT FIRST THERE WERE WINDING RIVERS OUTSIDE THE TRAIN windows, looking like giant snakes trying to escape, and then they gave way to long rows of trees divided by sandy paths.

I hoped the campsite would be in a forest.

When the train stopped in a city I was met by leaders and other campers, and we got into a slow old bus that took us away from the suburbs and eventually back into the woods, along a straight road underneath tall pine trees that exuded their satisfying scents of safety and shelter. At the campsite I was pleased to see that this time we would be sleeping in real tents, which were dotted around a big marquee. I couldn't wait for the fun to start.

After the evening meal we lined up in the marquee, sat on the canvas floor and were told various stories from the Bible. Then there were prayers to be said and soon it was bedtime and lights out. I thought, Fun? When will it start?

In the dark, listening again to dogs on lonely farms barking in the distance, I counted the nights before I could go home. Again I assured myself, 'Tomorrow will be a better day.'

Before breakfast there was a long prayer meeting. The prayers seemed endless. Breakfast was followed by more Bible stories, with illustrations of colourful felt figures.

Sometimes Adam or Abraham fell off the board. With loud voices we sang, accompanied by guitar, about being in the Lord's army.

After lunch we were allowed to play. We ran around with balls, stretching higher and higher to catch them. Were we trying to reach the clouds and heaven? Then it was back to more religious information until it was time to eat.

I was taught how to make knots, learnt how to set up a tent and cooked on a small primus. Thoughts of the devil were far away when I ran around in a huge canvas sack.

On the last night one of the leaders played his shining guitar softly, and another started to talk, his words emotional. 'Now, children, you've all listened to the stories this week. You're going back into the world and now you have to remember them. Remember also to be good to your parents, your sisters and brothers. You know, if you give your heart to Jesus then you'll do all these things without any trouble. Are you ready for that? Come forward now and make your promise to Jesus.'

I didn't want to go. I wanted my freedom, wanted to experience what it meant to be alive and have exciting experiences. But the memory came of my father pointing to the full moon: 'Wait till it turns red, and you'll have to appear before your Maker.'

And so, together with the other children I trooped forward, crying, to give my heart away. Oh, I felt such a sinner, such a bad person. I couldn't remember what I'd done wrong but I knew I needed to have my guilt lifted. Kneeling in front of the leader, I prayed, 'Please, God, forgive me for having bad thoughts. I'll be good from now on.'

As I left the camp I promised myself that from now on I would be without sin.

My parents had many religious connections – Salvation Army, Brethren, Baptist and the Dutch Reformed Church – and in the early fifties they tried to obliterate their wartime

Promises of heaven

memories by a changed focus on religion. No longer driven by tenets and credos but by sheer charisma and plenty of words.

My father was respected by people in the village and, as a successful and popular businessman, he instilled in his employees a work ethic and an enthusiasm for the business. Firms that ordered deliveries of sand and gravel for projects around Warnsveld and surrounding villages could rely on his immediate service. This dedication demanded his full attention during the week but now there was a new goal for Sundays.

He became a lay preacher, and decided to open a church in his own home where he could preach on Sundays to all those who had been charmed by his charisma and his eloquent delivery of God's word. He especially believed in the healing value of visiting widows and orphans.

My mother didn't quite have that same belief. She sighed a lot and was always tired.

Every morning my father would bounce out of bed and sing 'Rock of Ages' *uit volle borst* – at the top of his lungs – and the whole Dutch version of the Moody and Sankey repertoire. His happiness seemed to lie in preaching, praying and singing.

Each Sunday the furniture in the living room was shifted, collapsible chairs were put in rows, and my parents sat down and waited for the 'parishioners' to arrive. My mother would take a bottle of eau de cologne and a clean white handkerchief out of her handbag, and as she sat in her red velvet-covered chair wearing a black dress with tiny white polka dots, she polished the lenses of her glasses. She'd smile politely to whoever came, asking how they were, what they had been doing during the week. 'Is your daughter feeling better? Are you comfortable in your new house?'

During Papa's sermons Moeke would sit with tight lips and a frown. Did the sweet, pure smell of cologne help her cope with Papa's verbal admonishments to be spiritually clean? I began to notice the difference: during the week there was often a silence, an atmosphere that could be cut with a chainsaw. Such a contrast to the smiles that went around on Sundays.

Once the service started my father's voice rose up confidently to beseech the wisdom of the higher authority. He shouted at his parishioners: 'Repent and be saved! Never shall you know what is waiting for you around the corner.' Wearing a freshly pressed dark suit with a starched white shirt and grey silk tie, he brandished his leather-bound Bible in the air as if to indicate that the closer he could get it to the ceiling the more impact his words would have.

But some days his words of doom overwhelmed me. 'Wait till the moon turns red and the Lord returns. Will you then be saved? Can you be sure your sins have been forgiven?'

At the sight of a full moon my heart trembled. I knew I was the most wicked sinner in the world.

Like the times I begged to be allowed to go to a film with my classmates. His reply: 'How could you sit there enjoying those worldly pleasures? What would happen if the Lord returned while you were in a cinema? Would you like Him to find you there? Would you like to end up in Hell?'

I felt an outsider when my classmates talked about films. I'd been told film stars were sinful, but even so I still hid photos of Doris Day under my mattress.

Ans asked, 'You're telling me you're never allowed to see a film?'

I shrugged.

'I'll ask them.'

'It won't work.'

'*Ach,* you are so timid. When will you learn to stand up for yourself?'

I didn't dare go against my parents' wishes. Where I

Promises of heaven

lived everybody knew each other; somebody would see me and tell. And I had learnt to fear what might happen if I disobeyed my parents. I would be sent away again to stay with strangers. I felt guilty for having worldly thoughts. Film stars. Popular music. I had to please my parents. But I also wanted to belong. I also wanted to go with my friends to the movies, and even to dances.

I asked my mother. A curt reply: '*Ach*, Huub, you know how Papa likes to have you around. It's important that his family gives a good example. It would be bad for Papa's reputation if you were to do things that made people talk.'

'Why can't I see films? All my friends are allowed to go. I feel left out.'

'Papa says no.'

Sometimes my mother stared out the window overlooking the street. She didn't answer when I asked, 'Why are there so many rules if you are a Christian?'

Then there was the night we had to babysit at Ans' house. Her sister, Ineke, was the same age as my younger sister, Lydia.

Ans looked at a wooden chair in the kitchen, which had a veneer seat with tiny holes in it.

'Let's experiment with these holes.'

'How?'

'What would happen if you peed through them?'

'We can't. We'd make a terrible mess.'

'Oh, come on, it'll be fun.'

'Why don't we use water?' I said. 'What if your parents come home early?'

'Don't be silly. We'll tidy up in no time. Let's get some old rags. It will be a really interesting scientific experiment. We have to test the flow of gravity. First we'll measure the pee and afterwards we'll pour water through the holes and measure that.'

'All right, let's do it.'

I performed the scientific experiment while Ans lay on the floor and observed the flow of gravity coming from above. We giggled until we completed our pee and water experiment, carefully measuring out and comparing quantities of fluid.

We did everything together. In summer we biked to Zutphen and consumed enormous quantities of colourful and delicious Italian ice cream. On warm days we crossed the river together, swimming diagonally against the fast-flowing current. But best of all were the days during the long cold winters when we sat quietly together in the attic, absorbed in our favourite books, only breaking the silence with:

'Let's go downstairs for a drink.'

'*Ja*, I'm starving.'

After our snack of milk and bread we'd go back again, sitting close to the warm chimney, surrounded by stacks of books and boxes filled with old clothes. We read so many books together in that attic, involving each other in the events of our favourites.

One day I saw Ans gazing at me.

'What's the matter?'

'You'll always be my best friend.'

Cold easterly winds blew in from Russia, and froze rivers and ponds. We skated on the big open-air ice rink. At night the large floodlights made mysterious shapes on the iced-over flooded meadow close to the village. The outside lanes were for the fast skaters, who swished by with tremendous speed, hands casually draped behind their backs. The inside lane was for slower skaters, and right in the inner sanctum was the place where glamorous figure skaters performed their complicated routines. After we had skated enough we sat in the canteen over hot chocolate or hot beef stock and felt our hands being warmed. We looked forward to the next day.

Promises of heaven

One winter afternoon we were skating in the meagre sunshine. Two jets were performing stunts against the clear blue sky. Close to the village was an air force base and we knew several young men from the area who were training to be pilots. We often told each other romantic stories about these gods who looked so strong in their blue uniforms. Henk, Ans' brother, was one of them.

That afternoon it seemed as if the jets were flying to the sun, leaving their white, wavy trails behind. From below, we watched them going higher and higher. Then we saw something we could not believe – two jets collided, and dived towards the earth.

Only one parachute opened.

The skaters yelled at each other: 'Look, look, the planes are coming down.'

'Will they land on us?'

Another skater yelled: 'Someone's going to be killed.'

Ans whispered: 'It won't be Henk, will it?

'No, it can't be Henk.' I took my friend's hand, held it tight.

She said, 'Let's go home.'

The next day Ans and I crept up to the attic and read about the accident in the local newspaper. The dead pilot had been in the same squadron as Henk.

'Do you think Henk will fly again?' I asked. 'He must be scared.'

'I don't know. He's very quiet.'

'Are you going to the funeral?'

'I'm not sure. Maybe – if Henk wants me to.'

'Was the dead pilot his friend?'

'I think so.'

'We'll always be friends. Nothing will happen to us.'

The organist

Even though I wasn't born a boy, I became the child on whom my father now pinned his hopes. 'You've got to learn to play the organ to support me during the Sunday morning services. It might make you do something else besides reading.'

That cold Sunday afternoon in February I was sitting with a translated *Jane Eyre* in a deep armchair near the fire. Outside icicles like tapered pegs hung from the gutter. I had no desire to play the organ but I supposed organ music was better than nothing. Or course a piano would have been better.

No hope though. There was something worldly about a piano. We didn't have worldly things at home.

But who would be the one to teach me? I hoped it would be somebody nice. I didn't want to have my fingers hit when I played a wrong note. This happened to my best friend. Her teacher had a false bun on her head. She barked at Ans during the lessons and bent down to whack her fingers. That's when my friend noticed the false bun. I wanted somebody who listened to me without letting false teeth drop on their chin, who would nod a dark but slightly greying head and make understanding noises. *Ja, ja, ja.*

A young man was found who would teach me. He had returned to our area after spending time at a music conservatory in Paris. I thought he must know so much, having

96

The organist

studied there for many years. He was told there was no need for me to learn frilly fugues and fughettas. 'Just teach her to play simple and solid basic hymns as fast as possible.'

The lessons were at his house. During that first long bike ride after school I wondered what my teacher would be like. Already I felt hot and sweaty. What would it be like when I got there? I hoped he wouldn't speak French to me. As soon as he opened the front door I knew I'd like him. Reddish hair, auburn moustache, dark eyebrows and very white teeth. He smiled with his eyes and with his mouth. Taking me into a side room he said, 'I'm sure we'll get on together.'

His teaching was clear and direct. He used simple words and I liked listening to his gentle voice. I learnt to play real music – first the long open notes, then the half open notes with a handle. The little black notes took longer to master. Eef and Jo learnt to play music by numbers, not by notes, but still they rubbished my playing. I was soon playing more pieces than they did.

My teacher's parents worked around the house as I demurely took my lessons on a real church organ with foot pedals and two keyboards, kept in the best room of the old farmhouse. A big clivia with a large red flower stood in front of the window, and solid furniture with plush beige covers filled the room. Little tables with white crocheted tablecloths held ornaments of china and brass, and white lace curtains hung at the windows. A completeness was locked inside this room. Nothing else could come in, nor could anything escape.

His mother would put her head around the door. 'Would you like a cold drink?' 'You are doing so well.' 'I hear you play.' 'Are you all right in there?'

I hoped she wasn't worried about what I might do to her son. I looked sideways at him. He looked fresh. The seat was big enough for two people. I kept my distance but I was sure I could smell his French soap. His arms looked strong.

I noticed the soft red hairs on his hands and wrists. He wore a starched white shirt with a striped tie.

But was he my type? I heard girls at school talking about types they liked. I didn't know what my type was. Dark, handsome, mysterious? Tall, blonde and athletic? His father was short and thickset, his mother short and cuddly.

My sisters teased me about him. 'He likes you. He told us so. He might want to marry you.'

They made it sound as if I didn't have any choice. I didn't want to think about those things right then. I was there to learn to play the organ.

The progress was slow, but my fingers got looser and wrists not so tight. The sound of the organ was beautiful. I moved from basic scales to elaborate finger movements. I couldn't be stopped. I quickly learnt revival songs collated by John the Gentleman. Playing them at home on the harmonium in our dining room.

Sunday after Sunday I played the organ, accompanying the regular hymn singing, including preludes and postludes as well as an occasional interlude. Before the service started I also had to carry 40 stackable chairs down the stairs and put them in rows ready to start. And I played when visitors came to our house, producing hymns for them on the highly polished organ with its green plush runner that had lots of photographs on it.

YET THERE WAS MORE TO LEARN. I LIKED PLAYING OTHER music. In the farmhouse along the riverbank I learnt to play a piece about sheep that may safely graze. Gentle minuets from Boccherini and Beethoven arose out of the pounded keys of the church organ. Happy and light. Cheerful.

I discovered a love for classical music.

The organist

One day I biked the 15 kilometres to Deventer in a biting spring wind to sit in an old church and listen to a performance of J S Bach's *St Matthew Passion*. Biking home in the evening, lilac on the air, I sang 'Erbarme dich' quietly to myself, and in my head were the words of the closing chorale: '*Ruhe sanfte, sanfte ruh!*'

But I could not sleep quietly; there were still the nightmares – being chased, my feet not able to move. And then waking up, my heart racing.

I couldn't talk to anybody – my sisters were busy with their young families, my parents' faith and attention seemed to be reserved for the people who came to our house on Sundays.

I'd learnt how to play Moody and Sankey hymns. 'What a Friend We Have in Jesus', and 'Blessed Assurance'. My repertoire didn't stretch far but I managed to accompany the small congregation, and whenever I didn't know how to play the chords accurately I increased the pumping of the pedals and sang as loudly as I could.

And so, every Sunday morning I did what my father wanted me to do. On warm summer days the windows to the street were wide open while the service took place. At school a classmate asked, 'What was going on in your house yesterday? It sounded like a church.' I walked away so she couldn't see my red face.

Almost as much as making music I loved reading. I devoured library books in the shortest of time – but in my family reading was still considered a waste of time. I was often told, 'Do something useful, especially when others around you are working in the house. You should be helping us. There's washing to be folded, ironing to be done.'

One weekend I knew I had to return a Dutch translation of Emily Brontë's *Wuthering Heights* to the school library on Monday morning and was desperate to finish it before I had to part with it. So on Sunday morning, before the service,

I carried my precious book into the living room and hid it between the cushions of the sofa, where I sat when I wasn't playing the organ.

My heart was beating fast when, in the middle of the service, I dashed back to my seat for the sermon. Keeping my head up, I focused on my father and pushed my hand under the cushions. I could feel the plastic cover of the book. Catherine and Heathcliff were waiting!

I grabbed it and slowly – very slowly – pulled. The book was in my lap. I opened it at the bookmark and began to read.

At first I kept an eye on the people in the row in front of me as I read, but after a while even though I was conscious of my father's voice and the people listening to him, my mind was somewhere else – with Heathcliff and Catherine.

And then I heard a rustle, a throat clearing. Katrina, an elderly parishioner, had stood up. She straightened her skirt and said in a voice like breaking glass, 'Preacher, how can you let this happen? There you are, preaching the word of God, and in the meantime your daughter isn't even listening to your holy words but is reading some filthy rubbish.'

I heard Papa's controlled words in response, 'Is this true, Huub?'

I looked at his face and nodded. This was serious. I hadn't seen him like this before. There was a moment's silence and then he spoke again: 'Let us all sing "Rots der Eeuwen, Troost in Smart".' 'Rock of Ages, Cleft for Me' was my cue. I put *Wuthering Heights* on the cushion and walked to the organ. I sat down, found the hymn and started to play.

A great many prayers for my soul were sent to heaven that day.

After the service my father said, 'Go upstairs to your bedroom. There's no lunch for you today. You must learn to be obedient.'

'But I had to finish the book, it was due back at …'

'Go to your room. You are an embarrassment to our family.'

I tried to catch my father's eyes. He didn't want to see me. Katrina was holding my mother's hands.

I stretched out on the bed while downstairs the congregation ate soup together. A fly zoomed several times around me, then disappeared through the open window. I peeked at my grandmother's dolls on the shelf above my bed, and that's when tears finally filled my eyes. *Can you hear me, Oma? I miss you so much. Why did you die?*

After lunch I was allowed to come downstairs. That afternoon, together with my family, I attended a ceremony at a quiet spot at the river Berkel. Katrina was one of several people being baptised by total immersion. Clad in a white gown, the older woman stood up to her waist in the slow-flowing river and looked adoringly at her pastor, my father.

Katrina's voice soared above all the other voices when we sang a hymn, and I heard her say to another woman, 'Now I feel totally cleansed. The devil hasn't got a hold on me anymore.' Then she turned to me: 'It's time you were baptised too, you sinful girl. You are a burden to your parents.'

I looked at my mother. Her eyes were fixed on the river. I asked her, 'Why don't you say anything? Do you also think that I'm bad?'

A FEW WEEKS LATER THERE WAS A KNOCK ON THE BACK door. It was Katrina, her hair a wild halo around her head, her eyes projecting disgust at Papa. 'I believed that when you baptised me everything would change in my life but it hasn't happened. This day has been the worst day ever – my bike is ruined, the potatoes are burnt, and it's your fault, only yours, because I discovered that the top of my head stayed dry when you baptised me. From now on I won't come to your house meetings. What's the point? You can't even control your own daughter. You can keep your faith.'

And Katrina rushed down the path, her skirts twirling around her, the back door left to bang in the wind. For a few seconds my parents looked at each other.

My father shook his head. 'Huub, it is time you were baptised by immersion.'

I stood up, faced my father, took a deep breath. 'I'm too young.'

Papa went out slamming the door. My mother took off her glasses and wiped her eyes with a minuscule handkerchief. I went to my room.

I dreamed of a black devil chasing me through a red-moon landscape.

And the next morning I said, 'I want to be baptised, Papa.'

A few months later Papa rented a small swimming pool in a neighbouring city and I, wearing a long white gown like Katrina, was baptised there by full immersion, along with five other parishioners. I'd hoped I would feel different afterwards but I didn't. I continued to have nightmares.

But I concentrated on music – singing hymns happily on Sundays and playing Bach and Mozart during the week – and gradually realising that my life was made more bearable by increasing my knowledge of classical music. I bought my first record: Beethoven's violin concerto with Herman Krebbers as soloist. Brahms' 'Alto Rhapsody' was next – Aafje Heynis singing about a lonely man losing his way in search of himself. The voices of the male choir begging for something to help him lift the sadness in his heart. I cried when I first heard the German words, then asked myself why I had that need to dwell on sadness. Until the day when I finally understood that the loneliness in my childhood had left a mark within me – one that manifested itself in feelings of insecurity and unworthiness. *I should not have been born.* But that I had also learnt to push those feelings deep down. From that moment I chose to learn other things. Deeper things.

SEVERAL SPRINGS AND SUMMERS LATER MY RED-HEADED organ teacher spoke to me after my lesson. 'I want you to play in the local church,' he said. 'You have to play an introductory voluntary and accompany the hymn singing. You've improved so much – you can do it now.'

What should I say? I was scared. I liked playing but this was too sudden for me.

'I don't think I'm ready for this. I'll make mistakes and feel stupid.'

'I'll be there right beside you. Don't forget, nobody can see you when you're playing. If you make a mistake people will think it's me!'

Gerrit was too nice. I had begun to like him as more than an organ teacher. I blushed when somebody mentioned his name.

How could I let him down?

Yet three days before the event I begged my mother to ring him. I heard her voice on the phone to my kind teacher, 'She doesn't want to play. She is so stubborn.'

I wasn't stubborn. Only full of fright and frenzy. I woke at night. Will I or won't I?

He was waiting for me as I came out of school the next day. Sunlight streaked through his reddish hair. The pale-green cotton shirt and rust-coloured cravat must have come

ASTRIDE A FIERCE WIND

from Paris. My feet didn't want to move. I felt awkward and I knew I had dirty shoes.

Girls from my class looked at him.

'Who's he? What's he doing here? Doesn't he look smart?'

I wished I'd never learnt to play.

'Can we talk? We'll go to the park.'

We walked slowly. My schoolbag hung between us. I knew I loved him but I'd made up my mind. I wouldn't play.

We passed the pond with the powerful white swans. Softly they glided over the water like a passing summer breeze. Thoughts in my head gave shape to music. I heard myself humming, *'Leise flehen meine Lieder, Durch die Nacht zu dir.'*

His voice was gentle and his blue eyes had a smile in them. 'You know you can do it, Huub. I wouldn't ask you if I wasn't sure.'

I wanted to grow up. One more year at high school. But I was frightened. Love was too complicated, its reality as spiked as a freshly sharpened knife.

I only wanted to hear music. I only wanted to sit at night behind the organ in a room that contained everything. Windows wide open I would play Schubert softly while I smelled the river breeze. As I sat alone on the large seat the lightness of the music would fill the room and I would dream about the mystery of a love that didn't have a cutting edge.

Greta's friendly visit

Greta was a young woman who lived in Amsterdam, having moved there from our village to work as a teacher. She was as much a friend of Moeke as of Papa, and before she moved to Amsterdam she used to help Moeke serve coffee to the parishioners after the service on Sunday mornings.

At regular intervals a letter from her would arrive, writing about how busy she'd been and asking if she could come and stay.

I thought Greta was nice. She'd bring me presents – a colourful scarf or sweet-smelling soap – though at times she would take it upon herself to educate me. 'I've looked through your French schoolbook, and I think I should help you with your composition.' If I'd forgotten to hang the washing, she would tell my mother, 'You're letting her get away with too much. She needs discipline.'

But my mother would reply, 'She's fine, it's her age. She's too big for a serviette and too small for a tablecloth. Just think back to when you were 14.'

Whenever Greta was expected Moeke scrubbed and cleaned the house thoroughly. I can still remember the combined smell of furniture polish and bleach. The guest room would be made ready, with freshly aired sheets on the bed and a tussie-mussie in pastel colours on the oak dressing table. There'd be a stockpot of soup in the fridge – vegetable-and-noodle soup made with blade steak and tiny meat balls.

Greta usually arrived just before lunch and there were hugs and I-missed-you declarations. On one particular visit, the morning after her arrival, my father said, 'Greta, it's such a nice day I thought I'd take you to the Drielandenpunt – you said last time that you'd never been there.' He looked at Moeke. 'You won't want to come?'

Moeke opened her mouth, then turned her head away. She got up from the breakfast table and took the plates to the kitchen, calling out, 'Huub, come and help me.'

She gave me a tea towel, and while she washed the dishes she said, 'I want you to go with Papa and Greta to the Drielandenpunt.'

'I've got homework.'

'You can try out your new camera. You're going.'

I wanted to sit on my swing and dream about my future away from the village. Instead I had to accompany Papa and Greta. The drive wouldn't be so bad, but what about when we got there? Should I take some homework with me? I packed my new camera and a book in my bag. I knew I'd be bored, stuck in the car having to listen to Greta talk about her teaching experiences and about the badly behaved children in Amsterdam.

We meandered through villages, wooded areas and narrow country lanes with trees on either side, and after we arrived at the point where the three countries meet – Holland, Belgium and Germany – Papa said, 'Huub, here's a rug. You stay here. Greta and I need to talk. We'll go for a walk in the forest. You'll be bored, and I know you'd rather read your book. We won't be long.'

I watched them walk away, Greta's red dress shimmering. Reading my book in the sun on the blue tartan rug, the sounds and warm scents of the forest around me, I waited.

Greta's friendly visit

In the distance I could hear cars, but I didn't hear footsteps until several hours later.

I saw their red faces.

Greta's crumpled dress.

As my father and Greta walked towards me I picked up the camera and took a photo. A black-and-white snapshot in which the skirt of Greta's dress shows a pleating at the point where her legs become her torso.

MOEKE WAS IN THE FRONT GARDEN WHEN WE ARRIVED home late from our outing to the Drielandenpunt. There were dead roses lying on the lawn. She waved, a bunch of roses in her left hand, secateurs in her right hand.

I watched her face. 'You look hot. Have you been working in the sun?' I asked.

'Dinner will be ready in half an hour,' my mother said. She turned to Greta. 'Do you want to freshen up?'

As Greta disappeared inside the house, my mother whispered, 'What did you do? Did you have a nice time?'

She knew. 'It was all right.' I felt as if my mother's piercing eyes had zoomed right into my thoughts when she asked the next question.

'Did Greta have a clear view of the three countries?'

'Why don't you ask her yourself?' And I bolted inside the house.

At the dinner table that night I watched Greta enjoying the meal my mother had prepared. I examined my father's face.

'Huub, you're very quiet,' he said, cutting his beef, placing some on his fork.

'I've got a headache.'

'Please pass me the gravy.'

I forcibly pushed the bowl towards him, spilling brown gravy on the tablecloth. Taking another helping of red cabbage and *appelmoes*, I said, 'Mmm, nice.'

'Huub,' my father said, 'there's no need to push the gravy bowl like that. Your table manners are appalling. What will Greta think?'

I faced Greta. 'What *do* you think, Greta? Are my manners appalling? Do you think *you* could improve them? Don't you think my mother has done a good enough job bringing me up?'

Was my father's face turning red? 'Huub, go to your room.'

I looked at my father, the preacher who put the fear of an unloving God into my heart, the man who cared so much about orphans and widows he visited them at night.

And what about Moeke? Where did she fit in? She must feel so awful. I vowed I would be nicer to her.

But why should I? Why didn't my mother protect herself, stand up for herself?

Why didn't she protect me?

YEARS LATER, AS AN ADULT GOING THROUGH A PARTICULAR difficult time, searching for a photo of my father, I found that black-and-white one taken with my little Kodak box camera when I was 14. He and Greta are close together against a background of tall trees. I pulled it out and put it aside. I again saw myself as a child, full of expectations, dreams. Even now I remember how I changed after that. A new hard core, like a piece of black rock, enabled my heart to survive the following years.

But at what cost?

Emotional famine? Should I, after our return from the

Greta's friendly visit

Drielandenpunt during that particular visit, have told my mother what had happened that day? I was so innocent. I'd genuinely believed my father when he said they were going for a walk. But when they returned I knew something was wrong, even if I didn't really know what had kept them occupied while I waited. Could I expose my internal defence system – just as a landslide exposes secret strata that have been covered for many years?

I picked up the photo, took a box of matches from a drawer in the kitchen and went outside to a corner of my garden. Under an autumn birch tree in a sunny suburb in Dunedin I stared at my father and Greta in the photo and felt again that betrayal, even if I hadn't been able to understand it or put it into words that summer day so many years ago.

There had been nothing I could do. That episode at the Drielandenpunt was repeated in various forms and under different circumstances, year after year. There were times when I wondered what would have happened if I'd said that I didn't love my father. Didn't respect him. Hated him, in fact.

I struck a match and watched the flame burn the photo, destroying the image of a sunlit day.

Burn it up. Get rid of it. Forget it.

Just a small spot of ashes on dry soil.

Move on.

The sea

We never went on a holiday as a family. No beach resorts for us where as children we could play with sand that free-flowed in our hands. No beach walks in stormy weather. We lived in the eastern part of Holland and the North Sea was in the west, nearly 150 kilometres away. Another reason was that my father, in post-war Holland, could not even leave his business for a week. But in our neighbourhood we had a river and a forest providing enough opportunities for the entertainment of children. Once a year we had an outing to a restaurant where we could play on swings and try to balance seesaws. We would sit outside in a garden on flimsy white seats and be given a glass of orange lemonade and a piece of apple cake.

When I first glimpsed the sea I was 10 years old. I'd seen photos of oceans in books, had received postcards from aunties who stayed in beach resorts. I'd read about the dykes that were supposed to keep us safe in our lowland but I hadn't seen one. I hadn't heard waves crashing onto a beach, didn't know what the word 'surf' really meant.

My class at primary school was to take a day trip to Amsterdam: not only would we visit the Rijksmuseum and Schiphol Airport, we also would be taken to Zandvoort, a popular beach resort.

I couldn't sleep the night before the big day. Would it be as I had imagined? Would the water be really salty? As

The sea

salty as the salted liquorice I loved so much? The sea was a mystery to me: where did the water come from, and why did it never run dry?

THE NEXT MORNING I WAS FULL OF ENERGY AND HAPPINESS, and as I came down the stairs singing loudly my mother said, a dusting cloth in her hand, 'I would not sing so early if I were you. You know what they say about birds that sing early – they make good prey for the cats.'

But her remark could not that day prevent me from singing.

The class was herded into the train at the station in Zutphen. Typically for postwar children, few of us had ever been away from the village let alone on a train ride. We inhaled the smoky smell, watched the huge wheels that would turn and bring us to our destination. Even the hard seats didn't bother us.

At the Rijksmuseum I stood in front of Rembrandt's *The Night Watch* and thought of that famous man whose paintings were full of images of light and dark. But would he have painted the sea? Observing the planes at Schiphol Airport, I felt I had waited long enough: planes were interesting but I wanted to move on.

At last we arrived at the beach.

As soon as I saw it – that immeasurable, infinitely stretching bowl of water – I left my classmates and ran straight into the surf. The softness under my shoes, the saltiness of the water, the constant movement of the waves – everything was as I had hoped it would be. It was beautiful to feel that waving mass of water around me. I felt light and happy. I splashed and swam a while, turning on my back, rolling over again, keeping an eye on my classmates watching me at the other side of the gentle surf.

The journey home was a stark contrast to my short time of freedom. Sitting on a wooden seat in the train with my clothes completely soaked, I was aware of the other children giggling as they looked at me, but soon I forgot about them, about the tightness of my wet clothes and my waterlogged shoes.

We arrived back in Zutphen. and trundled sleepily through the station's entrance hall. Outside my father was standing beside one of his trucks. He pointed to a wooden board leaning against the truck and said, 'You can all climb onto the back of the truck. I'll drive you to Warnsveld.'

There were shouts of joy from us all. I was proud that my father had thought of this surprise.

Que sera, sera

I must have been 13. Coming home from school in the late afternoon I switched on the radio. 'Hear that music, Moeke. Listen, that's English. I can understand it! "We'll meet again". "Some sunny day". I know what that means.'

Moeke put down her knitting needles, took two chocolates out of her knitting bag that was lying next to her. She handed me one and said, 'That is nice. Tell me what it means.'

I was so excited, dancing through the living room, hearing the slow rhythm of Vera Lynn's voice and the words about meeting again on some sunny day. 'I can understand what she sings.'

A few years later my mother and I sat together with a cup of tea, the radio playing softly. She'd taken up crochet, creating tiny scalloped edges around white handkerchiefs. I turned up the sound, took my mother's hands and pulled her out of her chair. 'Come dance with me and I'll tell you what Doris Day sings.' I shifted a few chairs, 'Listen, Moeke. She's singing about being a little girl and asking her mother, "What will I be?"'

Together we moved slowly around the room, my mother unsure of her steps, but she smiled as I translated the words. The power of words.

Que sera.

The yellow bikini

When I was 15, I was invited to stay with Eef and her friends, who'd rented a house in Noordwijk, a favourite seaside resort. I thought back to the first time I had seen the sea. How I had experienced the awe and wonder of that ever-moving expanse of water.

This time I knew what to expect. I packed my case: brown trousers that had belonged to my sister Jo, a woollen jersey for colder days, a red wind jacket and a cream blouse. I placed my swimsuit on top of the other clothes. The dark blue, almost black, swimsuit had been knitted by Eef. She'd said, 'It's a little big but it's better to have it that way. You don't want a swimsuit to be tight, to fit too tightly on your body.'

Early that first morning in Noordwijk I put on my knitted swimsuit, grabbed a towel, ran out of the house and headed for the beach. In the distance I could see a man walking his dog. The sea was still. Lanes of light stretched towards the horizon and a hazy sun covered the dunes. I bobbed on my back in the water, feeling the lift of the gentle waves beneath me. I'd arrived in my own heaven of deep blue sea and high sky.

Eef's friend, Yvonne, waved from the beach and I swam in towards her, and then stood up. I took a few steps in the surf, in panic. Next to me an elderly gentleman waded toward the beach too, turning his head, looking me up and

The yellow bikini

down. He didn't say anything but I knew why his eyes were focused on me. I wanted to cry. Everything was spoiled. My sodden swimsuit hung heavily down, reaching my knees.

After breakfast Yvonne said, 'Come upstairs. I want to show you something.' And there on her bed was the miracle. A butter-yellow bikini, so tiny and so perfect.

Yvonne held the two pieces out. 'Do you think this would fit you?'

'But … but what about you?'

'I've got others. I want you to have this. This will let you get a bit of colour on your body.'

I looked at Yvonne's suntan. Now that was something to admire: a combination of golden rays, olive oil and hours of the sun god Helios' admiration had produced a glow that seemed to reach far into her deepest pores. But my own body? How would I look in this bikini? So tall, so skinny. Oh, what if nobody ever thought I was pretty, ever loved me?

'Thank you, Yvonne. I love it.'

I ran to my bedroom and put on the bikini. I undid my long dark braids that were tightly pinned around my head and brushed my hair till it shone and tumbled around my face. Then I pirouetted in front of the mirror, stretching my arms out above my head like a sun worshipper on the longest day of the year. I was a film star! Oh, yes, in this bikini I could skim over the waves. In this bikini I could fly. All the way to England. All the way to America.

Now I belonged, proudly walking down towards the waves on that crowded beach in Holland. This bikini represented sophistication, excitement and, most of all, freedom. But what would my parents say if they could see me like this? Would they allow me to keep it? I knew my parents' opinions relating to things of the world – radio, television, films and dances. Playing a hockey game on Sundays. But I pushed those thoughts away.

There was much to do, running into the waves with the other girls I'd met on the beach, lying stretched out on fluffy towels in the dunes, absorbing the sun, taking sly peeps at the boys. On stormy days we screamed and giggled as the giant waves threw us off balance.

On the morning of my departure I tiptoed out of the house and made my way to the beach. One more dive into the surf, one more dream on my back, one more float in foaming turmoil before drifting onto the safety of land. I breathed in deeply. The salty air. The feeling of the light, warm sand in my fingers. When would I come back?

Afterwards I put on my brown trousers and cream blouse. I braided my hair, pinned it up neat and firm, and felt that tightness around my head. That night I arranged a private film-show in my head. The sky, the sand and the sea. All mixed up with that feeling I'd experienced during my holiday – freedom. It didn't matter that I lived in my family's world of rules, of fearfulness, of being different. One day I would be able to choose, and then I would travel by sea as far as I could go.

THE NEXT YEAR I WAS INVITED BACK FOR ANOTHER SEASIDE holiday. My happiness exploded even further when Yvonne gave me a black bra and black knickers, also her hand-me-downs. This was the ultimate in sophistication, allure and glamour. I stood in front of the mirror, twiddling and stretching since my lack of voluptuousness didn't quite fill the black cups.

There was another highlight during that holiday. As a special treat on the last night of my stay, my sister and her

The yellow bikini

boyfriend took me to see a film for the first time. Eef said, 'Don't you dare tell our parents that we took you!'

The theatre was small but it had a special atmosphere and appeared quite rich, with red plush chairs and luxurious wall decorations of golden figures. I had never been inside such an opulent and elegant space before.

Don Camillo depicted the comic adventures of a priest in a small village in France. I laughed and laughed, but at the same time a demon of fear made its way into my head. I became scared, looked around me in the dark. My father's voice: 'You would not like to be found in a film theatre when Jesus comes back to earth?' That evening I wished my sister had chosen a seat closer to the exit.

Before returning home I had been invited to spend a weekend with a friend whose father owned a Christian conference centre. There people of all age groups, but predominantly women with tight smiles on their faces and tight buns on their heads, came for regular spiritual nourishment. People slept in dormitories and meals were taken together. The day would start and end with long prayer sessions.

When it was time to go to bed that first evening I discovered that my little suitcase was missing. I had to sleep in what I wore. In the dormitory I took off my dress. I became aware of a sudden hush, looked around and was surprised to see 20 women with eyebrows raised. A few even turned their heads away. For there I stood, blatantly wearing my sexuality in a black bra and knickers as well as glorying in an unladylike deep-golden suntan.

Oh, I was too shy and timid to explain anything. I heard those older women whispering amongst themselves – one of them was Bart's sister, who would remember my display years later when I met him – and I felt uncomfortable, but

ASTRIDE A FIERCE WIND

I also began to feel a twitch of rebellion. Why did these people think that the outer covering of a person was the only thing that mattered?

I thought of the sea and the sand and felt that freedom again. I knew for certain now that I had to find my own path.

118

The windmill camp

Another summer holiday, another camp. This time it was a Youth for Christ camp in Giethoorn, the Venice of the North. My mother said, 'The camp will be in a windmill. It's very popular with young people. There are no cars in Giethoorn, only small wooden bridges over canals, and there are a lot of lakes.'

'How can you camp in a windmill?' Ans asked me later. She and I were sitting at the river's edge. We'd just been for a swim trying to cross the IJssel but there was too much wind. It was a dangerous river, full of eddies.

'I don't know. I'll tell you when I get back.'

The bus dropped me near the windmill, close to the lake's edge in Giethoorn. Those lonely first camps were a long time ago – I felt strong and able to cope with whatever lay ahead, and I couldn't wait to get out on the water with a sailing boat. I was hopeful this could be the best camp ever.

Inside the windmill I looked around the downstairs eating and recreation area. Large tables and long seats on old wooden floors. The walls were painted white, and there was a large dark-stained wooden cross above the dining table.

As I went up the narrow staircase my hands slid over the rough railing. Splinters came off the dry wood, like the little prickles of grass that won't give in to the mower. I went up another staircase and stood under the now motionless windmill vanes and looked out over the water-filled land-scape, imagining being a miller's wife carrying bags of wheat and rye to the waiting gondolas. I visualised myself shaking the finely ground flour out of my hair, just as the first soft snow is blown off a tree in a forest.

This camp was different. There was Bible study in the morning and at night, but during the afternoon we sailed on the lakes where the sun felt like a loving mother, its strong rays warming my expectant spirit in preparation for something that had nothing to do with religion or guilt. Lying back in the sailboat, I opened the buttons of my white shirt a bit further, allowing the sun to soothe my breasts.

Next to me was Bart, a tall young man. He had not only endlessly long legs but also grey eyes that had wide open spaces in them, wide and grey as the water around us. He was shy and didn't say much, but as we wound our way along the narrow water lanes between banks of golden reeds his long, thin hand reached out to touch my hair. He whispered, 'Meet me outside after the evening meal.'

I felt nervous. What if the leaders found out we'd sneaked away? What would happen?

I went anyway. Together Bart and I went for a long walk, crossing little bridges over the waterways of the small village. Everywhere people in boats were meandering along the waterways. Bart's arms were strong around me and his first kiss was tender with promises of passion. We sat at a canal edge, holding hands. There was no need to say anything, only treasure this feeling of another person so close by.

Later one of the leaders came over to us as we sat outside the windmill. 'We've been watching you. You know, just as a tiny match can light a piece of paper, so it can also destroy a whole building. You've got to think of the future. There's plenty of time to start a relationship later.'

We nodded in agreement. We knew that if we disagreed we'd be sent home.

The windmill camp

Sitting in a quiet place where the summer grass was beginning to smell like hay, we wondered how the leaders could say that our feelings were sinful. I loved the sensation of warm sun on grass, the sight of moonlight on water, the stillness of footsteps in a forest with millions of dried pine needles. I loved this new feeling of attachment.

During Bible study time a leader said, 'If you behave yourself and become a good person you will be rewarded in heaven.'

I thought that being in love was already like being in heaven. Why did these leaders have to make us feel guilty?

At the water's edge I threw a pebble and watched its effect. I understood what the task of the leaders was but I didn't have to leave this camp with a clean, freshly polished, silvery image. These leaders were spouting the same proclamations I'd heard for years and I knew their tenets had nothing to do with being a good person. All the same, I was dreading the last night with its promise of a snow-white soul. What was I going to do?

That last night we sat around an open fire in the still summer air. With the lake as a dark background I heard the urgent voice of the leader: 'Come forward now and promise you'll be a good sheep in the flock of the good shepherd. You do know what happens to people who don't believe in God, don't you? They go to hell.'

I didn't want to believe that any more. A tiny tree in a forest is protected in its early life by its companions and then grows strong and straight on its own. I knew that I'd grown and could trust myself.

Around me people moved forward but I walked back inside the windmill. Standing before the open window, I felt the gentle water-wind breathing over me with a freshness like the breath that precedes a first kiss. Later in my sleeping bag I listened to the water birds coo through the night. I

ASTRIDE A FIERCE WIND

wasn't a sinner. I knew that the sun casts a shadow when it shines, but I knew too that its shadow wasn't bad.

At the end of that summer holiday my dreams moved into another field – inside myself. After school I'd go to my room and read, absorbing other people's lives and experiences. The more drama the better. I'd learnt English, French and German and now could read books in those languages. I made notes as I read, and dreamed of their worlds. A magic mountain in Germany. The life of a doctor's wife in France.

I was more determined than ever to start searching for that other world, that place where I'd be free. Away from the conflicting messages I got at home.

Away from my father with his dark, brooding eyes.

I couldn't wait until I could meet Bart again.

Au pair

Fascination with the sea and the possibilities of reaching distant, interesting places made me realise that any boundary that divided countries was not really a boundary but only an extension of different atmospheres and attitudes. Ever since I saw the sea for the first time I wanted to be in that water, touching the waves, feeling the golden sand.

I imagined the combination of the dark blueness of the water and the pale blueness of the sky at the horizon to be an easy entrance to a heavenly world. But before I eventually got to that world I wanted to see more of the earthly world. The thought that on the other side of that enormous expanse of water was another country where people lived made me wish to visit those places. How would they speak? How would they think? Would they do everything the same way we did in Holland?

At high school each day we had lessons in French, German and English. On the first day of our English class we were told to bring a little mirror for our next lesson. The teacher explained to us that with the help of a mirror we might just learn how to put our thick Dutch tongues around that most horrendous of all speech complications, the combination of 't' and 'h'. To say the word 'the' required concentration!

We had to look in the mirror and observe how our tongue stayed behind our upper teeth. Slowly we had to move the tongue to the space between our upper and lower teeth. Once we had perfected this part of the technique we had to make sure the tongue was pulled back so it would lie resting with its tip just behind the lower teeth. Even after trying so many times, the best sounds we produced still sounded like *de de de*.

After high school I had the opportunity to work in London for four months as an au pair in a doctor's family, with four children under the age of six. Here was my chance to finally see how other people lived – those strange people on the other side of the mysterious water who spoke a different language, who just might be different from the people in our village, and who would certainly be more interesting. What would they wear? Would I be able to understand them after having learnt English for only five years? And what about the dialects? I lived in an area where 20 Dutch dialects were spoken within a radius of 20 kilometres. Again my teenage imagination was working overtime, trying to work out how these differences might manifest themselves and how I would cope with them. I looked into my little mirror and practised my THs that whole summer before leaving.

My suitcase was packed with clothes that I had been wearing for several years: an old blue corduroy skirt, a yellow jersey of towelling material, a thick duffel coat and several pairs of dull-looking trousers. I had packed only a few things because I hoped that my au pair pay would enable me to buy a fashionable Gor-Ray skirt and a Pringle twinset which had been the trademark of some girls at high school who 'belonged to the set'. Those girls were popular with the boys and I envied their free and happy existence. They were the ones who were allowed to go to parties.

I began to feel excited about the adventure that lay ahead of me. After arriving in Ostende I just followed the crowd when it was time to board the ferry to Dover. There were

Au pair

families with young children – how lucky these children were to experience travelling at such a young age! I loved hearing them speak in their native English language, understanding the questions they asked their parents.

While we were boarding the ferry the weather had begun to change. Most people stayed on deck to see the coastline disappear, but in contrast to the calm and sunny morning the winds started to roar around us, waves with their white caps increased in size and soon most people moved inside. The ship was heaving and after a while I began to feel seasick. I went outside and stayed close to the railing, hoping that the fresh air would make me feel better. The sky was grey, the winds howled and spray from giant, foam-capped waves hit my face. This autumn sea was certainly different from the summer sea I'd experienced at Noordwijk.

As I stood at the railing, a man appeared and began to talk to me in German. He told me how sorry he felt for me feeling so distressed but that I should not worry because we would arrive in Dover before too long. I lapped up the attention he gave me.

He moved a bit closer and told me he had a big, beautiful house in Hamburg, Germany, and if I liked I could go back with him on the next ferry and he would look after me. In his strong German accent he said, 'I will give you lots of money and you will have your own car.' He would buy me new clothes too, as many as I liked.

But I began to hear my mother's voice: 'It is all very well for you to go to the big city of London, but you have to be careful when you meet strangers. You never know what they might do to you.'

I was worried. If I declined the invitation of this stranger he might become so angry he would toss me overboard into the foaming waters. Slowly I edged myself towards the door of the main lounge and then, as if chased by sea serpents, dashed inside towards the safety of the other travellers.

Finally we were allowed off the ferry, and then the rush came to find a good seat on the train to London. It was getting dark and people around me in the carriage were commenting on the hop-burning fires in the meadows beside the railway lines. I didn't know what hops were, but with that memory of a train speeding through a foreign landscape I can still see and smell the experience.

As the train got closer to London I wondered about the people I was soon going to meet. I had been in correspondence with my host family and was told that I was going to be met at Victoria Station on my arrival. I had to look out for a tall, dark-haired man wearing a white sweater. But at the same time, in case things went wrong and we missed each other, I was also given instructions on how to make my way to the address in Forest Hill in southeast London.

I eventually arrived at Victoria Station at 10pm on a Saturday evening, and stood looking around for the man in the white sweater, but it seemed that in September 1956 just about every man at Victoria Station had dark hair and wore a white sweater. What would I do? Approach them all? I didn't like that idea after my experience with the German man on the ferry.

Trying to sort out a decision in my provincial mind, I noticed then that there were a number of men circling me and my suitcase, giving strange looks in my direction. This wasn't much fun, so I decided to find Bus 185 as instructed and make my way towards a more peaceful area away from the rushing crowd at the station. I found the right double-decker bus, in the meantime having practised what I would say to the bus conductor. Would he understand my English? Would he remember to warn me when it was time to leave the safety of the bus? Boarding, I remembered my THs and could hear my voice saying the words I needed

Au pair

in a heavy, Dutch-accented English. But, great wonder, he understood me.

I felt very grown up as I travelled through the famous city on that late Saturday evening. People strolled about in the mild evening air, young couples held hands. Around me I heard the foreign language being spoken. Would I be able to speak like that at the end of my au pair period?

After a while I began to wonder if the bus conductor had forgotten me. It seemed ages since we'd left the station. But he had remembered, and as instructed I got off the bus at Honor Oak Road and started to walk up the dark hill, lugging my heavy suitcase. In my hesitant English I asked a woman coming down the hill towards me if I was going in the right direction towards Hengrave Road. She wanted to know where I was going to stay and then kindly offered to change her own direction and take me to number 23. It turned out she knew the family I was going to work for. I felt as if I was in my own small village again.

Arriving at the household, explanations and apologies came forward – their car had broken down, and by the time it was fixed it had been too late to go to Victoria Station. Even after a short time I began to feel comfortable and soon I was given a large mug of steaming, milky Horlicks and told to go to bed. The next day I would meet the four children, who in their own way were to help me widen my horizons.

That first day of my experience as a world traveller had been a day filled with events such as I never could have dreamt about, and lying in bed I felt proud of my achievements so far. Arriving as an 18-year old in the dark streets of London, I'd known that whatever lay ahead of me, I would manage it. I had arrived in a house full of light, with a loving welcome, and I knew that I would experience freedom and excitement here. I could already feel the sophistication that life in London would give me.

TOWARDS THE END OF MY STAY IN LONDON I DECIDED THAT I would have my long hair cut, as befitted my new sophistication. Instead of having braids wound tightly around my head I would have free-flowing hair as a symbol that I had grown up. I could now ignore my father's words: 'I do not want you to cut your hair. A woman's hair is her crowning glory!' As the hairdresser began to unpin that crowning glory I reflected on my time as an au pair. On my free afternoons I had travelled into the centre of London and seen as many films as I liked. I had been to art galleries, museums and Nigel and Dinah had taken me on family visits to Canterbury and to Sheffield. I'd grown very fond of the children and hoped to stay in touch. By the end of my time in England I was ready to go home. To see Bart again. My knowledge of the English language had improved, and I had learnt that language and physical boundaries such as oceans and mountains do not separate people. The people I had stayed with had become my friends. The only thing I hadn't mastered was that pesky 'th'.

Courting

The return journey from Harwich to Hoek van Holland revealed another side of the power of the sea. The ferry rolled and shook, and even though I wasn't seasick I was glad to be on terra firma again.

Bart was waiting for me after I'd been cleared by Customs officials, and we sat close together in the train to Zutphen. We'd written letters to each other while I was in London and both knew we wanted to continue our relationship.

Time with Bart. Walking through forest lanes late at night. Time to be alone. Experimenting with love. Slowly, so slowly, then a gathering passion.

That urgency of wanting to belong to someone who cared. Someone to love. Someone who showed me love.

To feel safe.

To trust.

Brother

We'd had a good family time. Sitting together, drinking coffee and eating cake, jokes flying around.

I felt good. I had settled in my first job and enjoyed the challenges of learning about administration. Papa got up, said, 'I'd better do some work in the office before it gets late. I find I'm getting too old to do this.'

Picking up my empty cup to take to the kitchen, I said, 'I don't mind doing the administration. Actually, I'd quite like to get involved in the business. I know I can help.'

Papa turned around, 'Well, that might be an idea. We'll talk about it later.'

I decided to go for a walk, put my jacket on, opened the back door. Jan followed me. Grabbing my arm, he hissed, 'If you dare to do that, getting involved in the business, I will kill you.'

Spring 1959

One day a young couple with two children arrived at the Sunday morning service. My father welcomed them warmly and invited them to stay for lunch afterwards. They praised my mother's meatball soup and filled bread rolls, which were stuffed with a generous helping of cheese and ham, or thinly sliced salami and slivers of gherkins.

Helma's husband did everything she told him because she was special – she had visions, and she made us sit down and listen to them. Promises of greatness for my father, plus promises of a rich spiritual life that would lie ahead for all of us if we only listened to the message she conveyed.

She told us that the only way her vision voice could get through was by going upstairs and lying on my father's side of the parental bed. We sat around in that bedroom and waited to hear what good things lay in store for us. Afterwards there was much talk about the latest visions, of which she claimed no knowledge. But I wondered why she had to lie on my father's bed? Why could she not pass on her visions sitting in a chair downstairs?

One night in April 1959 after a prayer meeting, Helma started to tremble, and we followed her as she headed upstairs. The bedside lights with their golden lampshades created a holy atmosphere. My parents, Bart and me and another couple who had attended the prayer meeting, stood around her as she lay down on the bed. We listened to her words, believing that what she said was the truth we needed to hear to become better Christians.

But this time was different. In a thin, shaky voice, her eyes closed, she said that it would be good for Bart and me to get married. We could live with Helma and her husband – they rented a big house at the time – and we could have an upstairs room until Bart found a permanent position after his studies, when we most likely would have to leave the area.

While Helma's eyes were closed and her voice kept going, Bart and I looked at each other. We knew what the other was thinking. This would be the fulfilment of our dream – we could get married, which meant no more worries about falling pregnant. We went downstairs on a high, believing that this was God's will, that we could serve him in this way too.

My parents weren't worried. Bart was going to complete his tropical agricultural diploma in June, and he should easily find a job after he graduated. However Bart's parents had a different point of view: they believed that a man didn't get married until he had a proper job and could look after his wife. There were discussions by telephone, trying to find a reasonable solution, and in the end we decided to show our independence by planning a wedding in July, then live in Helma's house until we were ready to leave for that part of the country where Bart would find a job. At some stage the word emigration was mentioned but was never followed up. I was working as a secretary for a metal importing firm and Bart found a temporary job at a chicken farm on the outskirts of the village, close to the forest.

We were married 11 July 1959 in the St Martinus church. From our house we looked out at this church. It was a quiet wedding on a very hot day, the temperature reaching 36°C.

Earlier that morning my bedroom door had opened. 'Bart,' I gasped, remembering all the warnings of not being

Spring 1959

allowed to see each other before the wedding ceremony. We would have bad luck we if we did. 'You're not supposed to be here, don't look at my dress.' He edged towards my bed, kissed me passionately, and said, 'I left the railway tickets for our trip to Düsseldorf on your table. I might just forget them tonight.' He grabbed the tickets, kissed me again, and holding the door knob in his hand, he said, 'Will you come to bed tonight, Mevrouw Hellendoorn?'

'Oh, yes, I will.'

At first the arrangement seemed to work well; we were now together, and talked and dreamed about our new life ahead. My father regularly visited, and then would leave us to talk with Helma about her latest visions. Her husband was a travelling salesman and often away.

But I wasn't happy. The atmosphere in the house was tense, I had to bike a long way to work and sneaking suspicions had started to weave in and out of my thoughts. At the end of November I got a bad flu and my mother decided we should come and live at home until we knew where Bart's new job would be. She said, 'That means you can organise the chairs on Sundays and pick up the people from the station in Zutphen.' Later she said that we could again help with the lunch provided for the 'parishioners', who came from all around the province.

Slowly I felt as if I were back in that trap of family expectations.

I noticed that during the week my father would often be called to the phone to talk to Christine, a friend of Helma's. He told us, 'Helma has problems and she has asked Christine to clarify them to me.'

On a winter's afternoon in January a friend of my father's, Oom Jaap, was visiting us. He and Papa were talking in the living room when the phone went. I lifted up the receiver. It was Christine. We exchanged a few niceties and

I commented that her voice sounded like Helma's. I passed the phone to my father, 'It's Christine wanting to talk.'

But I couldn't help wondering – was this really Christine? I was sure the voice sounded like Helma's! What could I do? Had I then been right what I had suspected all the time, even mentioning it to my mother, who'd said, 'Oh no, Helma wouldn't do that.'

This time I became a different person. In the bright, frosty afternoon I grabbed my bike, put on my black duffel coat and pedalled at high speed to the other side of the village where Helma and her family had been given a house in a new subdivision. I knew they didn't have a phone so any phone calls had to be made from the grocery store at the corner of the street.

I put my bike against the back wall, went inside the store … and there at the end, where the telephone was, stood Helma. I heard her talking and knew she was talking to my father.

I raced back home, stormed into the living room where Papa and Oom Jaap were now talking, and shouted, 'That woman on the phone, that wasn't Christine – that was Helma. She is lying to you.'

My father got up. 'Quiet, child, that's no way to talk.'

I turned to Oom Jaap, my father's prayer buddy, and said, 'Oom Jaap, this woman is pretending to be somebody else so she can talk to Papa. This is not right. She is cheating Papa.'

He took my hand. 'I'll talk to your father. We'll visit Helma right now.'

They left the house and nothing was said when they returned, but from that time on Helma and her husband stayed away.

I didn't know any more about what was right and what was wrong. I had wanted to believe that my father didn't

Spring 1959

know anything about Helma's cheating. But that sunny winter's day I realised these phone calls had been planned.

Yet I still blamed Helma.

The next Sunday morning service started out like any other one. Bart had done the chairs, I collected people from the station, my mother greeted everyone warmly, I played the organ, my father preached, and prayers were sent to heaven.

Then Oom Anton stood up. In a strong voice he said, 'It pains me to say this, but I have found out that our preacher has committed a sin involving another woman. It is not right that we continue as if nothing has happened.'

Silence, silence, silence. My mother's sweet-smelling handkerchief came out of her sleeve; she dabbed her eyes, did not look up. My father stood silently behind her chair. He did not say anything. Slowly the room emptied.

That night I visited Oom Anton at his house. I said, 'What you said is not true – my father wouldn't do this.'

To this day I remember the way his eyes looked. He said, 'It is true, child. Your father is lucky to have a daughter who defends him.'

In 1995 Bart and I returned to visit Holland from New Zealand. While in Warnsveld we visited Oom Anton and his two daughters Grada and Stientje; their mother had died earlier. Before we left I moved close to Oom Anton and said, 'I now know you were right that time.'

He looked at me and said, 'He didn't deserve your loyalty.'

Official news

Yes. I said I would go with Bart to New Zealand. But we were married, and the New Zealand government did not accept married couples as assisted immigrants. We needed sponsors.

We counted ourselves lucky when the New Zealand migration officer sent us a telegram: *Work and accommodation now available in Dunedin. Please let us know your plans.* Through the initiatives of the Rev GW van Tricht and of the Opoho Presbyterian Church and one of its elders, a Dutchman named Dick van Barneveld, we could now emigrate. Our excitement became focused when we received Dick's letter, written on behalf of the Opoho church, which was in a Dunedin suburb of the same name. He wrote that this church had promised they would organise accommodation for us as well as create a temporary position at the Dunedin Botanic Garden for Bart. 'We will be at the Dunedin Railway Station when you arrive and take you to your place of residence.'

We booked our travel, and informed the New Zealand migration officer that we were leaving Amsterdam on the *Johan van Oldenbarnevelt* on 11 April 1960.

White bread
and sheep waiting

Bart walks towards me on the deck, a wide grin on his face. I open my arms. 'I love you.'

Our family is on the quay. Tomorrow I won't see them. Neither tomorrow nor next month. Nor next year. In future years their faces and bodies will be only images to be remembered as they are now. They will return to me like flashes in a silent film. I don't know this now.

I remember my last visit to Tante Riek. Her fearful expression as she clutched my arm, 'But do you really want to go so far away? What sort of a country is it where you're going? Are there really more sheep than people? Do they have streets there? Is it safe? Will you be safe?'

I had questions of my own. Is this how it would be? And is this really what I want? Would I ever see my mother again? If Bart and I have children will they ever meet their grandparents?

How will we be able to afford to make the journey home?

Goede reis, tot ziens. Bon voyage. Until we meet again.

A sliver of land

I stand at the railing
while the ship moves full steam ahead.
Behind me the dark sliver disappears
from the horizon.
I've left behind low-lying flat land,
wide rivers weaving through meadows.
poplars that will change colours
when I celebrate spring.

I imagine my mother's
crumpled handkerchief,
her tears,
her loneliness.
Her silent prayer to keep me safe.

I made a promise,
I'll be back.
I will work hard
so I can stand at the railing again.

The kitchen table

Go back to the 1940s. Just imagine a kitchen in an ordinary house in an ordinary street in a small village in Holland. There is a dresser with pewter plates and jugs, and a small TOD stove burning small pieces of wood and twigs. It supplies a steady warmth. An old wooden table has six chairs around it. Each chair has a plush cover, with stiles at the back. Normally the table has a plush table cloth on it, wine-red with subdued flower patterns. But this time there's no plush cloth. There's a child lying on the table instead. She might be four or five years old. She wonders why there are so many women at the end of the table – her mother, her grandmother, the district nurse. Why do they look at her body and at the way her legs are spread wide on the table? She sees their heads shake, hears words mumbling. She wonders why they look at her bottom and look at each other, and not at her, at her face, at her eyes. Can they not see she's afraid? She wants to yell out, Look at *me*. But she can't. Later, the only other thing she remembers about that day is that she had been sitting on her father's lap.

THIS MEMORY IS SO DEEPLY INGRAINED THAT IT TOOK A long time to conquer the helplessness I felt.

I don't have a context for it, but it has affected me my whole life.

In the late eighties I mentioned to my doctor I felt as if on some days I had a solid concrete wall in front of me. She asked, 'What would be the worst thing you could be told about yourself?' That comment finally provided a link and a pathway to healing.

I was told in 1995 that my mother, on her deathbed, had told a family member that my father had done 'naughty things' with me. I rang Eef, asking whether she knew. She didn't answer my questions. She just said, 'It all happened so long ago.'

Now it is a memory.

A memory that can finally be written out.

PART TWO

St Clair Pool

February 2015

I drive to the salt water pool, park the car and watch the waves for a while. Later, as my arms plough backwards through the water, I look at the towering clouds and wish I could still trust in the Sunday school God I grew up with. How simple it was for those who believed in God to accept everything worked out for the best. A purpose in life. Coming to terms with memories. Making better sense of difficult situations. Wishing I could do anything to help to make these difficult situations better. Allowing the thought of faith, hope and love when yet again something was happening in our family, something that was difficult to accept.

Accept light and shadow in life.

Surf pounds the rocks lining the outside of the pool and seagulls hover over the water before they settle on the sea-facing wall.

I buy an espresso, sit and stare at the vast expanse. It's like being on a ship, though White Island with its guano-heavy crust partially blocks my view of the sea. Memories of our voyage to New Zealand in 1960 weave their way into my thoughts.

When we first planned to emigrate we were overwhelmed with the anticipation of freedom. Freedom from fear. Being able to do what we liked: walk on lawns without being shouted at to *get off that grass*. Picnicking anywhere we wanted to. Freedom in Holland was simply not possible while the country was trying hard to get back on its feet after the war years. Only the well-to-do had their own homes, and housing was so scarce that young married people often had to move in with their parents. Only when a child was born did the young family become eligible for rental accommodation provided by the local council.

Attitudes were restrictive and it was important to conform. My family's rigid religious beliefs meant instilling in children a fear of God, of parents and of any authority. And then there was guilt. A word written in capitals in a child's brain and invading every thought. I had become afraid of the dreadful consequences if I didn't adhere to these beliefs. My parents, as did their parents, really believed it was good for the soul. The more a child suffered in its early years the stronger its character would be in adult life.

That April morning

Bart and I sailed to the end of the world, leaving Amsterdam on a cold April morning in 1960. Farewelling grey skies, a dull harbour and narrow canals with cobblestoned bridges. We stood close together at the railing on the highest deck. I said to Bart, 'See, there's Jan, on top of the hired van, waving with both arms.' Our families had driven to IJmuiden and waved until our ship must have been just a tiny speck on the colourless North Sea.

On that cold spring morning in April, we were sure that on the other side of the world paradise waited. We knew New Zealand was a place of abundance. A land of milk and honey. We did not mind leaving our Zion. *Johan van Oldenbarnevelt*, the ship named after a prominent Dutch statesman from the 17th century, would sail around the Rock of Gibraltar, through the Suez Canal and across the blazing hot Red Sea, with a final stop at Aden before the dry heat of the Indian Ocean. Six weeks of watching waves, each one bringing more distance to our old life. I buried my gnawing thoughts about that distance on the high seas, hid them in the ever tumbling water mass.

Life on the ship

We woke each morning to a brilliant light reflected from the waves. We adapted to living with hundreds of passengers who crowded the decks and lounges, shared the bathrooms and pounced on the scarce deckchairs. Everywhere we went there was the drone of giant diesel engines, providing the steady rhythm I now began to associate with security. My doubts about the safety of travelling to New Zealand disappeared.

'The Gulf of Biscay has never been so quiet,' a well-dressed elderly passenger said to his elegant companion.

I hoped the weather would remain calm. Stories by seasoned travellers circulated about the severity of storms in the Gulf. *Last year on this same ship we ran into such a storm. I've never been so sick in my whole life. The waves. The rolling and pitching.* The day a storm broke loose I stayed in our cabin to catch up on my reading while Bart went on deck enjoying the wildness of the elements.

At breakfast there were sturdy blue jugs of milk on the tables – creamy milk that swirled around my mouth – and the tables were laden with a luxury of choices. Bread in various shapes, made from grains grown in distant countries where sun filled the air. Cool juices pressed from pineapples, oranges and peaches. At lunchtime waiters brought out trays with salads, tender roast beef sliced thinly, and platters

Life on the ship

of cold tongue and ham. For us it was heaven after the years of food scarcity.

After lunch we would often go back to our cabin and to bed as the foam of the sea surged below the ship. I thought of my parents now so far away. Sitting with their coffee in the comfortable living room, absorbed in the newspaper, the familiarity of talking to each other in half-sentences, making comments about the daily news.

But I had moments when I wanted to cry. Cry for what I'd left behind: family and friends; the forest with its own smell; the *gezelligheid* – the Dutch concept of ambience. Yet life on the ship was good. We spent a lot of time on deck, playing tennis and croquet. Later we watched the drama of sunsets – orange and scarlet interwoven with pale grey and yellow.

At night we read in the massive lounge, its shining wooden floor featuring a dark red carpet patterned in white diamonds. There were large bright red leather sofas and creamy leather chairs around wooden tables. Above the panelled walls were sections with carved wood, intricate patterns showing the craftsmanship of the hands that created them.

We felt comfortable sitting in the white chairs and listening to a trio playing a variety of light classical music. One night the violinist took the microphone, looked around the room and said, 'Please let us know your favourites. We'd be delighted to play your choice of music.'

I walked up to them and said, 'Oh, I do like Boccherini's Minuetto.'

Within a few minutes the minuet filled the huge room. From then on, every time I entered the room the musicians played this piece of music.

And every time I blushed.

In the first week I'd become aware of a young woman

who appeared to be travelling alone. Often young men surrounded her, but most of the time she rested her arms on the railing and stared out over the ocean. She wore sunglasses, was tall and slim, and had long blonde hair that reached past her shoulders. On her feet were elegant white sandals with high heels, and the wide skirt of her red dress bobbed with each step she took. I wanted to get to know her, talk to her, but I was afraid. Shy.

I wished I could be more like Bart; I was envious of his ability to talk to everyone – not only on this ship with its many strangers, but in any situation. My own voice was thin, still in its childhood.

One morning Bart looked ill. 'I'll stay in bed today – I've got a headache coming on. You go and enjoy yourself.'

I climbed on deck, walked to the railing. Seagulls swooped as they waited to snatch any food thrown overboard.

A voice beside me said in clear English, 'Don't you think they're amazing, following us in the hope of getting something to eat?'

I turned round to see the young woman in the red dress standing next to me.

'Hello,' she said. 'I'm Andrea Pilkerton. I'm going to Australia.'

In my best English I introduced myself. 'My husband, Bart, and I are emigrating to New Zealand.'

I found out Andrea lived in London but was now on her way to visit her aunt in Sydney. She said, 'Where's your husband? I haven't seen him today.'

'He's not well,' I told her. 'He will be better tomorrow.'

That day we walked together around the decks, and discovered we both liked music and reading. Later I told Bart, 'I've made a new friend.'

I moved through the days as if in a dream. This new life was like the holiday I'd always wanted. My friends might

Life on the ship

have gone to the beach in the summer but they had never seen so much sea as this.

Each morning I looked out the porthole at the sun on the water, and at night, lying in Bart's arms in the narrow bunk bed, I dreamed about swimming in the sea in New Zealand, the country that came closer every day.

There were emigrants who would be leaving the ship in Australia. Most of them were meeting up with family who were already there. Listening to their plans, I was attacked by homesickness. I went quickly out of the lounge onto the enclosed side deck, my eyes raining tears as I pressed against the window, concentrating on the dull grey sea surging sullenly below. A large school of flying fish moved gracefully along the ship, their sleek shapes staying close together even as they jumped in and out of the water.

Where was I going? What would happen to us?

I felt a hand on my shoulder. Andrea said gently, 'Huub, you're allowed to cry. It must've been hard for you to leave your family.'

'I might never see them again, Andrea.' She led me to a quiet lounge, away from running children, away from the other passengers. Large palms in pots provided a filter from prying eyes, and Andrea kept her arm around me until my tears dried.

Then something occurred to me. I said to Andrea, 'At least I'll see my family in Melbourne for a day.'

In December 1959 my sister Jo and her husband, Johan, had left Holland on the *Waterman*. They already had four Dutch-born children and looked forward to starting a new life in Australia. I'd never been close to Jo, yet admired her greatly for undertaking this step since she and her family did not have any knowledge of the English language. I'd hoped to go to Melbourne too, but Bart and I preferred New Zealand as our new life destination.

Now, on our way to New Zealand, we were going to have an opportunity to meet up with Jo and Johan and their four children when our ship docked in Melbourne for a day. I had greatly missed the children and looked forward to seeing them again and finding out how they had adjusted to a new land, a new language, new friends.

The days merged into each other, day after day on the deck reading in the balmy sunshine, evenings talking with other emigrants, sharing dreams and hopes, making plans for future connections.

But it wasn't all perfect in paradise. Conflicting emotions were still rolling in my head which Bart found hard to understand. I tried to tell him about my anxiety for the future but he was happy and expected me to be the same. One morning I felt sick. It might have been the water. I clutched my stomach. *The scrambled eggs at breakfast? Oh, God, I might be pregnant. Please no. Not yet.*

Bart was getting his swimming bag ready. I wished he'd listen to me. 'Why did we have to leave Holland?' I shouted. 'Why did you refuse that job in Emmeloord? It would've been fun to live in the Noord Oost Polder.'

'You know why. I'm going for a swim. Are you coming?' And Bart walked away.

'I wished I'd never come!' I yelled after him.

Later, leaning on the railing at Port Said, I said, 'I can still go home if I want to. I can still go home overland without having to cross a sea.' I concentrated on the people in little boats calling up, 'Buy from me – cheap, cheap, really cheap. Cost you next to nothing.'

The sounds of bargaining surrounded us. Other passengers were buying wooden elephants, leather photo albums, cushions decorated with pictures of the Nile Valley.

'Come on,' Bart said, 'let's buy a photo album. You can put the photos of our journey in it.' He turned his head

Life on the ship

away, but I sensed his impatience.

That night we sat on the quiet top deck, holding hands, looking at the forever moving trail of foam following the ship. Bart didn't say anything. His grey eyes had a darkness to them.

I whispered, 'I want to go home.' I hated kicking up a fuss but I knew now that it would be a while before I felt really comfortable with the whole process of emigration.

'You'll be fine once we're in New Zealand.' His voice was harsh, as if forcing me to agree. 'We mustn't wait too long before we start a family. Then you won't have time to think of home.'

Still, I loved the leather album we chose, and that night carefully placed it in the bottom of our suitcase.

During the night the ship moved through the Suez Canal. Giant green palms lined both sides, offering sparse shade to people whose bodies were fully clothed to protect them from the burning sun and sand. I wondered how they could work in this temperature. I could hardly move my legs as I walked along the decks. What a difference from Holland with its frosty winters and the summers with cool forest lanes. Children wearing loose tops and shorts raced around on the dry sand, playing around their parents, who moved slowly in the heat.

Later the ship dropped anchor in the canal and a vicious sandstorm tore through the area. Behind the closed windows on deck I thought of the children playing by the canal. *What were they doing in the storm? Would they be safe?* I remembered hiding in the cellar during the war, listening for the gunshots, the bombs.

Travelling southwards, we watched the mountains of Africa to starboard, dark and mysterious in the golden evening light. I thought about the children who lived beyond those dark mountains. *What are their lives like? And what sort of life would our children have? At least they wouldn't have to endure war.* The heat of the Indian Ocean made me thirsty. Not only thirsty but lethargic and a bit stressed too.

'Can't we afford one drink in the bar?' I asked. 'It's so hot and I'm sick of the dirty water from the taps. It makes me feel ill.' Around the deck the other passengers relaxed in bars. We'd never been in a bar in Holland and this was an aspect of ship life that gave a tempting indication of how other people lived.

'You know very well we haven't got the money for that sort of thing,' said Bart sharply. 'Everything we have must be saved for our life in New Zealand. I thought you understood that.'

'But just one glass of fresh orange juice?'

'No, Huub.'

He talks to me as if I'm a child. A child who must be controlled.

I cried that night in the dark while in the bunk above me Bart slept solidly.

Tomorrow we'll cross the equator and there's no going back.

Heat was already simmering over the ocean when we came out on deck the next morning. I could feel the excitement over the imminent crossing of the equator. People stood about chatting, and for a short time the uncomfortable heat was forgotten and my lethargy disappeared. The swimming pool was ready to receive King Neptune. Banners and streamers were tacked up all around the walls and above the water.

The King arrived, surrounded by his supporters, his white beard reaching his knees. His upper body was naked, while the lower part was covered by a hemp skirt that looked as if it was made of coarse, brown, wavy hair. He wore a white turban.

Bart and I laughed while we watched some of the passengers being baptised by King Neptune, who sat in the middle of a greasy pole spanning the pool. The contestants slowly edged their way towards him along the pole, carrying a round, heavy bag that was to push him into the water, but the King attacked them with suds of slippery green soap. Trying to retreat along the pole – the audience cheering – most ended up in the water, leaving the King undefeated, a triumphant smile on his face. After a while he moved to his throne on the side of the pool and other passengers were invited to take their turn trying to push each other off the pole.

Andrea arrived at the poolside wearing a bikini. Her body was deeply tanned. She said to Bart, 'I bet you wouldn't dare to have a go, would you?'

'I'll go if you do,' Bart said. He turned to me, 'You don't want to have a turn, do you?'

I shook my head. *Schijthuis*, I told myself. Which means in English what it sounds like. I watched Bart and Andrea try to shove each other off the pole, their faces confident and joyous. I had no expensive bikini to wear. My little yellow bikini had long since disappeared – all my clothes now were sensible, serviceable. Everything I'd earned had gone towards our life together. This journey.

I wanted to run away, to go back to my cabin.

Andrea managed to push Bart in, and then dived in after him. They were both under water and as they came up she reached out for him. When they got out of the pool, they clung together for a few seconds.

BART AND I LAY SILENT TOGETHER IN MY BUNK.

'Do you like Andrea?' I asked tentatively.

'You don't have to worry.'

'What on earth did you see in me?' I said. 'I'm plain.'

'I married you, remember?'

All I could think was: *What if he leaves me alone in this strange country we are going to?*

Melbourne

Johan waited for us at the quay, took us via a train ride, a bus ride and a long walk ending with a hitch-hike to their old wooden house in a desolate area. A few months earlier my mother had been horrified by news in a letter from my sister Jo: 'There's a big hole in the corner of our living room and all I have to do is sweep the dirt and put it down through that hole.' My mother wailed, 'Oh, there will be mice coming up through that hole!'

We didn't see any mice, but Jo cooked us a lovely lunch with spare ribs Johan's boss had given them. I was impressed with how well the children had adjusted, telling us jokes about their experiences at school, chatting comfortably using the English language which Jo found hard to cope with. A few hours later we all made the return journey to the boat. It had been so lovely to see the children again.

We waved our goodbyes; my sister and her husband had a long journey to get home before dark, and Bart and I looked forward to the final leg of our cruise on the high seas.

Flight path

I envied them,
Australian girls on the ship returning
from their parents' old-world *home*.
Wide open spaces in their eyes,
an ocean around them,
they did things I'd only read about.
I watched them dance,
moving wildly, free to dare,
no need to hide
behind closed doors and heavy, striped curtains.
They knew their flight paths.

I knew that after a first sunrise in the new land,
I too would want to walk with wide open spaces in my eyes.

Palm Sunday procession near the damaged Leestense windmill, 13 April 1946.

My parents' wedding photo, October 1924.

Eight months old in a pink layette, 1938.

Four years old, 1941.

With Victor, a Belgian draught horse. (L–R) Lydia, me and Jan, 1945.

Kindergarten, 1944.

Damage by a V1 rocket at end of our street in Warnsveld, 28 March 1945.

After school, 1947.

Home for lunch, 1948.

Moeke with her beautiful smile, 1961.

Papa, 1954.

My first suit, 1958.

Walking through the village to our wedding, 1959.

Dancing in a field with Bart, 1959.

Our street in Warnsveld, the house is no longer there. Eef and Lydia visiting, 2007.

Showing off my new red skirt and red ribbons at our house in Warnsveld, 1955.

Our first Sunday in Dunedin, with the van Barnevelds. (L–R) Trudy, me, Bart, Adri, Dick and Rick, 1960.

Expecting Miriam, Signal Hill Road, 1962.

Taking Miriam for a walk in the Botanic Garden, 1962.

Dinner at 115 Signal Hill Road, 1963.

Talking to New Zealand on Moeke's birthday.
(L-R) Eef, Papa and Moeke, 1963.

Bart and I on an excursion
in our Ford, 1963.

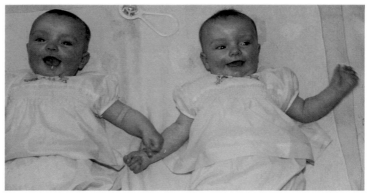
Our beautiful twins. (L-R) Foster and Ray, 1965.

Sunday afternoon at Taieri Mouth. (L-R) Mijntje, Bart, me, Miriam, Foster, Ray and Doodle, 1966.

Ray (left) and Foster checking their father's renovation handiwork, 1968.

Our first weekend away from the children. Picnic in Ashley Gorge, 1965.

Foster taking his first steps at Frankton on holiday. (L–R) Miriam, me, Foster, Ray (behind) and Mijntje, 1965.

Three-year-old Miriam on our holiday in Queenstown, 1965.

Visiting Holland. (L–R) Foster, cousin Marten, Ray, cousin Jeroen, 1976.

Skating at Oturehua, with Foster (left) and Ray, 1977.

Ray (left) and Foster ready for a tramping trip, 1978.

Taieri Mouth. (L–R) Me, Bob and Connie, Adri and Dick, Mijntje and Harry, and Miriam enjoying the sunshine, 1982.

All of us out for dinner before Ray went back to Massey. Foster with a beard, 1986.

Four sisters and a brother together again at Eef and Huug's 40th wedding anniversary. (L-R) Lydia, me, Jo, Jan and Eef, 1995.

At home with Bart, 2017.   Miriam and Ray, 2017.

Foster and Frances, 2017.

Madonna painted by Miriam in 1998, used for the cover of *The Madonna in the Suitcase*.

Welcome to
New Zealand

The night before we arrived in Wellington Harbour, word spread around the ship that the lighthouse at Farewell Spit was visible. On a starlit night Bart and I stood arm in arm on the top deck watching the flickering light, the signal of arrival at our southern hemisphere destination.

What would it look like in daylight? A lighthouse on top of a sand dune? Would New Zealand be as green as we'd been told by the New Zealand embassy people?

We had arrived in the new land!

We woke early, raced upstairs to the railing. So this was Wellington! So beautiful.

We knew it was an important city but finally, finally – we were getting closer to our new home. We hugged and danced on the deck, laughing and crying at the same time. It was a grey day, not the sunshine we'd imagined, even the water in the harbour was grey, but we were immediately fascinated by the houses on the hills surrounding the harbour. Yes, the hills were indeed green, so deeply green, and the houses were so white – and in a variety of architectural styles, some we'd not seen before – and they tumbled down those steep hills towards the harbour. It could not have been more different to the flat land we'd left so far behind.

Shortly after our arrival a message came through on the

intercom, asking us to go to the purser's office. A Dutch Presbyterian minister, Popko van der Velde, waited to welcome us to New Zealand. Dick van Barneveld and his wife, Adri, had organised this. We soon realised that such a gesture was part of their gift to us. How could we not feel comfortable here?

Bart's brother had an acquaintance who worked at the New Zealand Embassy in Holland, and he'd asked us to take some thick Dutch blankets to a friend in Wellington. This friend met us, and took us and the blankets home, where he provided a nice lunch. Then he dropped us back to the ship, where we waited until it was time to board the ferry to Lyttelton.

Later that night, on the ferry, there was a similar message on the intercom. Another Dutchman, Leo de Graaf, who was returning from Wellington to Dunedin after making sure his mother was on the right ship back to Holland, also met with us and welcomed us. Again this was lovingly organised by Dick and Adri.

Bart and I were in separate dormitories that night. Lying in a bunk in the women's accommodation I listened to people talking about the weather, *Thank God it's a quiet crossing*. I fell asleep immediately, and the next morning I was woken by a steward offering me a steaming cup of tea.

We disembarked in Lyttelton and on that late autumn morning were told to board a train that would take us to Christchurch. There we would be given our breakfast. Thick, glutinous porridge was served on our arrival at the Christchurch Railway Station then we boarded the train to Dunedin: hard wooden seats, coal-fired locomotives, grime and soot sifting into the carriage. We stared out at the snow-capped mountains in the distance, and then crossing the Canterbury Plains, we saw not only sheep but also little huts scattered in paddocks close to the railway line.

Welcome to New Zealand

'We might be sleeping in one of those tonight,' I said anxiously, yet trying to sound casual. 'We don't know where we'll end up.'

'We're experienced campers,' Bart said, shrugging. He looked so good in his new raincoat, hair carefully combed. He pulled me closer to him. It felt like a good beginning.

Closer to Dunedin we became aware of how much the train was groaning and whistling up the last hill. 'Isn't it steep!' someone cried. I looked down to the harbour entrance.

Smiling at us, one of the passengers pointed ahead. 'There's the Otago Peninsula, and that's Port Chalmers. It's the harbour for Dunedin.'

The train emerged from the last tunnel, winding its way along the harbour, readying itself for the stopping point.

'I've been reading about the peninsula,' Bart said. 'Apparently there's a castle up there. Larnach Castle.' He leant forward, pointing, a big grin on his face, which was lit up by excitement. 'I can't believe how green and fresh everything is.'

As we neared the town we saw houses with vividly painted roofs of all colours sprawled across the hills. I thought of the houses in Holland, every roof with the same terracotta tiles.

I turned my face to Bart. 'I think I will like to live here. But we must not have a noticeable roof.'

Bart squeezed my hand and laughed.

Welcome to Dunedin

A welcoming committee of our sponsors from the Opoho Presbyterian Church waited for us at the station. That welcome was warm, special. There was Dick van Barneveld, short and solidly built, a warm smile, and his young son, Rick; Barbara and Dick Calvert with one of their daughters; the Rev Belmer; the Rev GW van Tricht, who had been responsible for putting us in touch with the Opoho Church; and finally an acquaintance of Bart's sister Loura, who had sent us some initial information.

Dick van Barneveld said, 'You are going to live in Opoho.'

The Calverts took our luggage in their VW and we went with Dick and Rick in their 1947 Humber. The car reminded me of the cars I'd seen in England in 1956. Driving through town Dick pointed out the Octagon, St Paul's Cathedral, Knox Church, the Botanic Garden. Up the hill we went, past Knox College, up an even steeper bit of hill, and then turning left into Evans Street. Again, in our eyes, another steep incline … and there was number 76. A large green villa with a verandah.

We were overwhelmed.

'It's massive!' Bart said. 'And just for the two of us. I can't believe it. And it's got a garden.' We climbed out of the car and together with the Calverts, who had also arrived, carried our luggage through the gate and up the steep path to our new home.

Welcome to Dunedin

To the left of the long, wide hall was a large bedroom where the bed was already made up, and to the right there was a living room which we learnt to call a lounge. More bedrooms at left and right, and at the end of the hall was a kitchen.

'This house is used for missionaries on leave to regain their strength,' Dick Calvert said, opening a cupboard door and pointing to a baking tin filled with fruit cake. 'You can stay here for six months.' There was food and milk in the fridge.

It was a wonder, an unbelievable wonder, to receive these gifts and have a house to ourselves. Bart was to write home that we were overwhelmed on that first day. He said we could not have dreamed we would end up living in such a place.

We discovered that the previous tenants of our temporary home – known as the Missionary Manse – were Lloyd and Elaine Geering and their family, after Lloyd had accepted a position as Professor of Old Testament Studies at Knox College. They had just bought a property in Farquharson Street. Having lived overseas themselves, they understood the enormity of what we'd done and would come to visit regularly, keeping an eye on us youngsters.

'You'll be getting hungry,' said Dick to his son, and to us, 'I'll be back in an hour's time to take you home to meet my wife, Adri, and my daughter, Trudy.'

'We'd better go too,' Barbara Calvert said. 'See you soon. We'd like to take you to our holiday house at Taieri Mouth one day.'

After the Calverts and van Barnevelds had left, Bart and I stood speechless, hugged each other, unpacked our toilet bags, changed our clothes and looked again around the house. It had such views that we couldn't help looking through the windows at the beauty and natural splendour.

The hills were so beautiful, so clear. I kept hearing my

father's voice: 'I lift mine eyes unto the hills.'

That evening we felt fortunate to be invited to a house where strangers lived. A house where we felt at home immediately. Dick and his wife, Adri, were waiting with a beautifully cooked meal. Adri – tall and blonde, and with a warm personality – became a mother figure for me, ready with advice for a young and inexperienced homemaker. Their children, Rick and Trudy, respectively five and three years old, adopted us as an aunt and uncle. That night a very special and lasting friendship began.

Reality

The day after we arrived, Bart started work at the Botanic Garden as a gardener. This position was supposed to be a stepping stone for him, since the year before he had completed his diploma in tropical agriculture, but – as we soon found out – Dunedin wasn't exactly tropical.

That first morning after our arrival I decided to stay in bed and read. Plenty of time to get dressed later. I listened to the wind ruffling the cabbage tree leaves in the front garden and must have dozed off. I woke to a child's singing voice outside, 'Tante Huubje, *kom je koffiedrinken?*' Little Trudy had walked with her doll's pram from Dalmeny Street to invite me for coffee, a walk I was to discover was about half a kilometre. It was an astonishing experience to be met with such love.

Even after so many years we remember the kindness of the Opoho people. One day, shortly after we arrived, we were waiting at the Signal Hill bus stop when a car pulled over. A woman wearing a hat and gloves got out and asked, 'Are you the young couple from Holland? I saw you in church. Would you like a ride into town?'

Yes, we would, we said.

Coffee bones

All those years ago in a new country I set off to town to buy coffee.
Coffee meant home, coffee meant comfort.
They said there is good coffee at Stewarts in the Octagon.
You have to go down the stairs.
I didn't like stairs. I didn't like the cellar.
I had escaped from stairs that went into dark cellars.
I want coffee bones, I said.
You mean beans, the man said.
I went home and ground the bones in our new coffee grinder.
Beans and other magic words came later.

Always time for coffee

Adri and Dick had bought an old house and were in the process of renovating it. Our first year in New Zealand, we spent many evenings with them, Bart learning from Dick – a civil engineer with Dunedin City Council – how to do practical things to improve a home. Oh, yes, even at that stage we felt the attraction of 'doing it yourself', as so many Dutch immigrants did.

Adri and I would knit and talk. I learnt how to make shortbread and date loaf, how to make an excellent trifle laced with sherry, and where to buy ingredients necessary for Dutch recipes. We were told that Wardells grocery shop in George Street was a good place for foreigners to shop. My parents had supported many people who left the Dutch East Indies and settled in Holland after Sukarno came to power, and along with these friendships had come a new way of cooking. So apart from the standard Dutch fare, I also loved creating Indonesian dishes for the family – nasi goreng, bahmi goreng and opor chicken, spring rolls, satay and more. I could find most of the ingredients I needed at Wardells.

Apart from getting to know Adri and Dick, it was a delight for us to get to know their children, Rick and Trudy, better, and later to take them out to the beach or to watch a film while their parents were working hard on their home improvements.

WE MET ANOTHER DUTCH COUPLE WHO HAD BEEN SETTLED in Opoho since the early fifties. Bep and Dick Naus and their two children, Theo and Hanny, were enthusiastic people and interested in Bart and me as we were 'fresh from Holland'. Theo and Hanny's grandparents had just returned to Holland after a long visit.

Again we were taken out for a Sunday afternoon drive, packed tight in the Naus' Morris Minor, this time to Karitane. Hanny's little voice came from the back seat: 'Mum, can they stay for tea?' And so we went home with them after the drive and settled ourselves in for a tea of mousetraps and coffee. What a wonderful way to adjust to a new life.

Every Saturday night we played bridge with both Dutch couples and took turns in our 'hands', with one couple happy waiting to take part in the next game. Not only were there turns in hands, but also turns playing bridge at each other's homes. After midnight sleepy children were wrapped in blankets and carried to the car for the short ride home.

After the games of bridge we did a lot of *nakaarten* – a Dutch expression for talking about the games we'd played – but this also became a sounding board for how we were managing to live our lives in New Zealand. The two older couples had their own experiences to share, and Bart and I absorbed every detail. Dick Naus loved to tease and argue, and there was always plenty to argue about. We were never bored when we were with them. We wanted to become good immigrants too.

We didn't want to make mistakes.

Afterwards Bart and I walked back to our home. On clear nights we stood quietly, eyes up to the sky. Orion, Southern Cross, Milky Way. Observing falling stars in total

Always time for coffee

darkness. It was magic. But why then did I miss Polaris, Ursa Minor and Ursa Major, the Small Bear and Big Bear – the constellations of my childhood?

Bep and I shared a similar taste in reading and we discussed books by Dutch writers we both loved as well as the latest books we'd get from the library. One night Bep said, 'I do love to listen to the way you speak. You speak Dutch so beautifully.' I didn't have a clue what she meant, but a few years later I understood. Bart and I tried hard to keep our Dutch pure but gradually it became more anglicised, and whenever I meet people from our home country I realise how much we have modified our way of speaking. Though reading a Dutch newspaper now we notice the many English words that are interspersed among the Dutch.

We joked about our use of the English language. It was so easy to make mistakes. One day Bep had gone to the library and left with lots of books. On her way out she realised she'd left her spectacle case behind. Going back to the main desk, she asked the librarian on duty, 'Have I left my glasshouse here?' The woman looked at her. 'Your glasshouse?'

Bart and I felt great sadness when Bep, Dick and their children moved to Wellington for Dick's work. Visits to them became highlights.

When Bep and Dick were still in Dunedin we met Bep's sister, Connie, and her husband Bob van Raalte. The couple had arrived in Dunedin in 1950, and Bob – an industrial chemist – had set up a business together with his wife and his brother-in-law Dick Naus. Over the years they produced detergents, waterproofing for raincoats, leather softeners and wax for lawn bowls. They were also responsible for introducing yoghurt to the New Zealand market as well as cumin cheese and Gouda!

Connie and Bob took an interest in new arrivals from Holland. They helped find accommodation for them and organised events where Dutch immigrants could meet folk from their own country. Together with Bep and Dick they made dozens of folded white paper stars to be hung on the huge Christmas tree at Knox Church one year.

As young immigrants we enjoyed visiting Connie and Bob. Here was another home away from home for us – the van Raalte's kindness and warmth sustaining us during difficult times.

Sitting in the darkened church on Christmas Eve 1960, with Bart beside me, holding a candle and singing familiar carols in the words of another language, a feeling of contentment filled me. I knew I could cope with Christmas in the southern hemisphere.

Southern hemisphere Christmas

I place candles on the windowsill.
Their shape is safe,
until the sun contorts them.
Midnight is the best
time to burn candles here.

For tea we eat
thick slices of
weihnachtsstollen
laced with brandied butter
and icing sugar.

Then an image of closeness,
a forgetting of bright sunshine
and bending wax.
I come back to walking
my dog in thick snow
home, a roaring fire and aniseed milk.

What's in a hat

We acclimatised, we integrated and we were grateful to live in Dunedin, New Zealand. There was our awe and wonder at the natural beauty of the city, the green layer of native bush dividing suburbs, the lights at night surrounding a natural harbour, and we couldn't believe the hospitality of the Dunedin people. We'd left the country where we'd spent the first two decades of our lives to come to this place on the other side of the globe and, despite the difficulties, we were young and loved each other with a slowly growing strength. That love made everything an adventure. Even buying a hat.

During our first week in Dunedin Adri said, 'Women wear hats to church here.' In Holland we didn't wear hats to church and I wasn't very keen to buy one but yes, since the Presbyterian Church had sponsored us, I would buy a hat. Later I was told a story about a young Dutch woman who arrived hatless to a country church in New Zealand and was told by a matron in a flowery dress with a matching flowery hat: 'Young lady, if you want to worship in this church you have to wear a hat and gloves.'

The young woman was never seen again.

I bought a pretty red hat with a brim and a dark red ribbon wound around it. I woke up on our first Sunday in Dunedin, thinking about the red hat. Would it look right? We walked to church, Bart handsome in his Harris

What's in a hat

Tweed jacket and brown trousers, me wearing my dark blue woollen suit and the red hat. It fitted perfectly. Listening to the church bells, looking again in awe at the surrounding hills, I said out loud to Bart, 'I love these hills.'

We arrived at the Opoho Presbyterian Church and sat in a sunny pew. I listened intently to the sermon, which I couldn't follow, but it was pleasant to be part of the beautiful singing and to be feeling pretty. Feeling safe.

It was Bart who noticed first. He leaned over and whispered in my ear, 'We came here for peace and freedom, so why did you have to buy a hat? Barbara doesn't wear one.'

Sure enough there she was sitting in her pew with her husband, her brown hair shining in the sun. No hat. How I admired Barbara. *One day I can be strong like her*, I thought to myself. *Not care what people say*.

People were kind, asking how we were, what did we think of New Zealand? Yes, we loved it, and we learnt to say, 'Thank you for asking.' We learnt to use the word 'please' in every sentence when we did our shopping. We didn't want to be considered rude.

We were asked to visit. 'Come for supper.'

'What time would you like us to be there?'

'Come at eight.'

So we were there at eight o'clock. On the dot. We always arrived on the dot.

Our new friends began to call it 'Dutch time'!

Although it was hard – we thought it rude – we learnt soon enough to arrive respectably later than the mentioned invitation time.

ASTRIDE A FIERCE WIND

THERE WERE OTHER ACCOMMODATIONS TO MAKE TO BE considered a Kiwi. Ones that weren't quite as simple or as complex as putting on a hat. My sweet, elderly neighbour, Mrs Smith, couldn't pronounce my name and suggested I change it to an English name,

'Why don't we call you June from now on? It also has a U in it.'

I agreed. For three days I was 'June' and tried hard to be a June until the moment when I knocked on my neighbour's door.

'I'm sorry, Mrs Smith. I cannot change my name. I cannot do it.'

The incredible relief to hear the sound of my own name again, *to be myself.*

Was it the sound of acceptance?

Wonderful weekends

We became aware how much people in our new country enjoyed their weekends. In Holland we'd had to work on Saturday morning and Sunday was completely taken up with my father's religious activities. Imagine having two free days at the end of every working week. Wonderful.

Our first Sunday afternoon in Dunedin, after the church service with the red hat, we went with Adri and Dick for a drive in their Humber 80. Sitting with Rick and Trudy in the back seat, it felt as if we'd known the family for years. Rick reminded me of my little nephew Arjo, Eef and Huug's firstborn son. They were nearly the same age, Arjo four and Rick five.

After Anderson's Bay, we took the high road to the peninsula, with its green paddocks and clusters of trees. On our left was Otago Harbour, stretching out to Aramoana and the Pacific. A robust nor'easter swayed the trees in the paddocks. Creamy waves ruffled the water below ... but the surf seemed different from the Dutch sea, the rollers stretching out longer than the ones in the North Sea. We stopped where a cabbage tree interrupted the view towards the ocean and the road narrowed. Later we looked at the sandy beaches, the bays and inlets along the rugged coastline. We stopped again at the point where the Pacific stretches out to an unending sea and sky, got out and inhaled the fresh, windblown air. Such beauty to absorb.

Unfortunately, when we reached Portobello it had started to rain so Dick boiled the billy outside on his own, and we enjoyed an elaborate afternoon tea in the car with shortbread and date loaf.

Our second Sunday in New Zealand, Dick and Barbara Calvert invited us for an afternoon drive to their crib at Taieri Mouth. We'd already learnt that a crib was a simple holiday house.

Leaving Dunedin through Green Island, we drove along the coast road until we came to the long one-way bridge over the Taieri River. Here we turned left, passing the country shop that sold ice cream, basic groceries and vegetables. We drove through the village and reached another smaller one-way bridge. Turning right, we'd see the crib, close to a lagoon.

Simple indeed it was – bare concrete floors, an open fireplace with a chimney to the outside wall, roughcast walls and bunk rooms, and no electricity. I can still hear Dick Calvert's voice saying, 'I know what'll happen if we have electricity. The lights will never be switched off and our children will be reading deep into the night and want to stay in bed until lunchtime.'

The crib was surrounded by bush through which we had to clamber to get to the open dunny on a slight hill facing the ocean. There was so little to it, that, as my father would have said, 'a blind horse couldn't do any damage'. On rainy days we played games at the long wooden table with seating benches on either side.

Bart and I loved it, sitting outside, drinking smoky tea, toasting bread on sticks in the open fire, trying to keep our part of the conversation going, searching for words, explaining twice until we finally thought we'd got it.

It was the perfect holiday place. Close to the crib was a

Wonderful weekends

massive beach such as we'd never seen before.

The Calverts offered us and the van Barnevelds the use of this crib often, and we had some wonderful holidays together. In summer there were lupins in all colours, and even now I can recall their heavy scent that permeated the hot days and left a lingering reminder in the air at night. There were the early morning swims after a run along the beach which ended with us diving into the waves, and long walks at low tide to Moturata Island where we collected pāua shells and then sprinted back to the mainland before high tide. Towards the southern end of the beach were rock formations that were quite slippery when wet. At night we'd light a bonfire on the beach and sit around it with other holidaymakers in the little settlement.

Those holidays in Taieri Mouth couldn't be spoiled by anything. In my mind I see us sitting outside the crib on the freshly mown lawn around a red-and-white chequered tablecloth spread with pan-scones, pikelets and hefty sandwiches. We'd be talking, laughing and joking, and Bart and I felt we belonged.

Europa

In this new country where
kilometres are still miles,
we drive rural highways,
pass giant Europa boards.
Minimise Distance: Use Oil.

How can you 'minimise distance'
for connections with the heart?

Europa. A separation of six weeks by ship,
the heave of oily seas.
The sneaking awareness of hills,
new connections for the heart.

Sick for home

Oh, yes, there is happiness — a deep appreciation of all that's good living here — and those vistas, those hills. But always there is the gnawing homesickness, and my moods are like the sea I love so much, waves of restless feelings. Bart has settled well into his job at the Botanic Garden, working outside in the fresh spring air. He's away all day. I'm supposed to manage, but I don't.

The thought of growing old in this strange city frightens me. We pack a picnic and take the bus to St Kilda Beach. I hate the bleak hill staring out over this part of the ocean, which stretches to Antarctica. I am oppressed by the nearby cemetery with its lonely graves.

I say to Bart, 'Please don't bury me here when I die.'

He turns impatiently from me.

'I want to be buried in Holland.' My voice is a whisper.

I send long letters to Ans, complaining of not being understood when I venture into shops.

'Is the English language the only problem?' she writes back.

I write, 'I wish I could say it was. Bart is away a lot. I'm not very good at being a wife.'

Where have my ideas of adventure gone? Where are my dreams? But I am so homesick. Sick for the home I had desperately wanted to escape from. The way people speak is different here, not at all like the English I learnt at high

189

school or spoke and heard in London. A sweet is a lolly. A holiday house is a crib.

Meeting other immigrants helps. I have coffee with Drina who lives close by. Drina has never been homesick – her parents died in the war – but I listen to her. 'You'll get over it, if not this week then next year. For some women it takes a lot of time.'

I am in the Octagon one day on my way to the bus stop near the Savoy Hotel, and I hear an older woman speak. She is Dutch. I begin to cry. The woman is kind, but still she says to me, 'You've come here now. You must adapt. You must make the most of living in this beautiful country. You are lucky to be here.'

She escaped from a concentration camp.

WE CAME TO NEW ZEALAND TO EXPERIENCE ANYTHING NEW, to learn to speak like a Kiwi and behave like a proper lady or gentleman, wear gloves and a hat. When people asked us how we were, we replied with a thank you and not with a detailed account of problems we might be working through. I soon learnt that birthdays were not celebrated to the same extent as they were in Holland. Perhaps a card, a phone call, but not often on a grand scale, celebrating this special day by gathering friends around.

Adri and Dick introduced us into their circle of friends – fellow passengers they'd met on the ship coming out a decade ago. These kind people took us into their homes and supported us. They cared deeply about living in New Zealand and wanted to pass their knowledge on to us. Yet our new friends also made sure that the Dutch traditions from the early fifties stayed alive in their hearts and their homes. It was 1960 and still I was expected to follow the old

Sick for home

traditions. Even here. For instance one friend was horrified when I enrolled for an adult education class in German.

'Oh, how can you?' she said. 'You shouldn't leave your husband alone. He needs you when he comes home after work.'

But what about my own needs? I work too. I just said, 'I don't want to let all my knowledge disappear.'

These people meant so well, always looking out for us, assisting with advice on such things as how best to clean the kitchen floor and how to create a rich and comforting butter cake filled with a marzipan mix. *You must make it.*

I remember how worried I was when we gave our first birthday party. Taking the bus into town, I bought glasses, scouting Woolworths, McKenzies and the DIC for bargains. I still have some of the tall, thin drinking glasses I bought that day.

The day of the party I scoured the house from top to toe, polishing the furniture, making sure there wasn't a speck of dust on the tables or bookcases. I scrubbed the old bath, and polished the lino on my knees with a soft dry cloth. A woman only passed the test of being a good housewife when the bathroom was spic and span.

Years later I wrote a story about a typical Dutch birthday party and sent it to *Next* magazine, who liked it very much and promised to send a photographer. When they found out I was in my early sixties they cancelled the project.

The birthday party

I'm in my garden deadheading roses. I want to stay outside but it's Bart's birthday tomorrow and I must bake for my guests. But what? A Dutch apple cake? Which recipe? The one in the Dutch cookbook or the Dutch version in the English-language one? But Bart also loves a mocha cream cake – layers of sponge filled with a mixture of cream, brandy and coffee – and I know it'll be popular.

The weather is glorious, a spring haze covering Flagstaff and Mount Cargill. In the apple tree bellbirds practise their spring song.

I pick up a few cherry blossoms, their colours deep pink, and bring them inside to send to my sister in the northern hemisphere. There they'll be celebrating the arrival of autumn – masses of trees in colours of gold, brown and red. Here we don't have many deciduous trees. I miss the richness of the autumn colours I remember in Warnsveld. We often walk through Dunedin, trying to find a group of coloured trees. Near Olveston is the best place.

I am anxious. Such an important occasion for close friends to celebrate: another year in the life of an immigrant. Will the house be clean enough? Will my baking turn out all right? There'll be the usual male talk about cars and renovating, while the women concentrate on household matters and children.

The guests arrive. I greet them, then hurry to the kitchen.

The birthday party

I'm flustered, red-faced. No sooner has one thing been served than it's time for another.

This sacred ritual must never change. Two cups of tea or coffee, along with cakes. Milk, sugar and cream to be brought out on a side tray. *Always serve coffee and tea first, after that the cakes.*

But everybody has settled in for a good evening of talk and food, and so far all is well. Dick says to Jan, 'I looked at a car last week. You want to come tomorrow with me to look at it?' Jan's knowledge about cars is impressive. He helps us all when our cars need valve grinds.

'What year is it – as old as Methuselah?'

'Ja. There's quite a bit of rust, but I can fix it. The motor sounds good, the suspension's a bit shaky, but it should do us for a while. It's at least an improvement on what I've got now.'

Jan says, 'Just give me a tinkle. Are you ready to start the next part of your renovations?'

'*Ja*, I have all the timber in the house. Next weekend I take the chimney down between the living room and the kitchen, and then I can make one big room out of it.'

Bart says, 'I'll come and help – just yell when you're ready to start.'

And as I serve coffee and tea I think proudly that even in this short time Bart has learnt new skills, become even more clever with his hands, just like the other men who are so proud of their ability to repair things.

'The Labour Party is no good,' says Ko as he absent-mindedly takes a cup off my tray.

'*Ja*, but don't think National will give you the right treatment. These bloody politicians are all the same, all out to get something they want for themselves. They don't care a hoot about us.'

I take the tray over to the women, who sit closely together on the couch.

ASTRIDE A FIERCE WIND

Adri says emphatically, 'No, you must not use that soap powder, that is no good. I always use Persil, that is the best.'

'Jo, did you try the new mayonnaise?'

'No,' says Jo.

'I always make my own,' says Lenie. 'It's cheaper and much nicer.'

We all nod.

I sit down. Should I confess that I buy my mayonnaise? That I don't care what soap powder is best? These are good mothers who know how to take care of a house. They talk of their routines in housework. Washing on Monday, Tuesday ironing, Thursday baking day, and on Friday the house gets cleaned for the weekend.

'What is your routine?' Betsy asks me.

'I haven't found the right routine for my housework.'

'Don't worry,' says Betsy, 'you'll learn. You've just got to stick to it.'

How can I tell them that I've tried to adapt a routine for myself but it never works? I want to read.

Then clothes are discussed. Betsy says, 'I got a nice woollen remnant at Penrose's this week. I can make a skirt out of it.'

'What sewing machine have you got?'

'I have an Elna – it's the best.'

The discussion moves on to knitting patterns.

I ask, 'Have you seen anything of Joop and Japie lately?'

Leni's answer is quick. '*Ja*, I went there last Sunday morning at eleven, but there was nobody home and the beds were unmade.'

I look at Bart who winks at me. Later I say to him, 'I'm glad our windows are too high to see in.'

I admire these people who haven't forgotten their own language, although as they speak I hear Dutch words verbalised with an English ending. I wonder if I will still be able to speak my native language when I'm old.

I enjoy this time, sitting and listening to the voices, their backgrounds showing in individual sounds of dialect and origin. They've had to become strong to live in a different world, having made a conscious decision to leave their home country for whatever reason.

After the tea and coffee, it is drinks time. I gather cups and the plates of leftover cake, and take my time in the kitchen tidying them away since it is now Bart's turn to look after the guests. I can hear his quiet voice: 'What would you like, Dick? Jan? We have wine, whisky, brandy. A sherry?'

'Give us a *jonge jenever*.' A young gin.

Oh! Help! We forgot to get the gin! Can we ever live this down?

I flutter between kitchen and living room. Bring in bowls filled with peanuts and other nuts, heated smoked sausage chunks with mustard, fried meatballs, and small squares of pumpernickel with cheese.

The arrival of alcoholic refreshments is the correct time to start telling jokes in Dutch. Some of them aren't translatable. I think of how lucky we are to be able to keep our traditions and background alive by relating stories in our own language. Our language. From home.

After the guests have gone we yawn wholeheartedly, stretch our legs and say, 'That was good.'

THOSE MEMORIES. I WAS SO YOUNG. SO EAGER TO PLEASE. SO eager to fit in.

That birthday party, the first of so many. Always the same routine. But there was safety and order in that routine. The jokes changed. The food became more sophisticated. Red and white wine, even champagne, replaced the McWilliams Tropical Fruit Cocktail topped up with lemonade and the

ASTRIDE A FIERCE WIND

advocaat liqueur with its lashings of cream. Small meatballs were replaced with crackers and brie, blue cheese, smoked salmon. But Bart and I will never forget the warmth of the friendships we experienced during our years assimilating.

Now all those friends are gone.

Employment

There was so much to absorb. So much to learn about our neighbours, our new city, our new country. Going to work in a strange place and, as always, trying to do the right thing. We didn't want to stand out. We made sure to speak the English language when we walked in town and were surrounded by other people. We wanted to integrate. Not be enthusiastic. A real lady wasn't enthusiastic. She smiled, nodded and made you feel good.

I'd found a job at the Snow White Laundry in the North East Valley, where I learnt how to use a ready reckoner to write invoices for washed linen. The other young women working in the office took great pleasure in educating me. I still had to think when I used words in the English language, but I soon got a fast education in Kiwi.

One day the girls in the office told me I should ask the driver if he wanted a fuck. The driver knew what the girls' laughter meant and he didn't react. I got home that night and asked Bart why they had laughed so much. It took a while before I could bear to look the driver in the eye. I often felt like an outsider at the laundry, not being able to take part in any chatter. But I learnt how to eat 'pois' and chocolate and consequently put on a lot of weight, and I also got quite good at swearing.

Gullible? Oh, yes. But I still considered myself a visitor who couldn't possibly be rude. I didn't know yet how to joke in the English language. Later I learnt that a New Zealander showed acceptance of a foreigner by making jokes.

In October 1960 Bart started work at the Otago Catchment Board in George Street, initially as a chainman, later as draughtsman in the design office. A few months later I got a job as secretary at the Wool Research office, also in George Street. I felt at home there; people were kind. At night Bart and I had plenty to talk about, sharing and comparing our experiences. On Friday nights we often went to see a film, or visited friends.

Each day brought something new, either at work or through our relationships with new friends. The laboratory girls at Wool Research were friendly and some asked us to their home for Sunday tea.

All the bad memories of my childhood I put on the back-burner.

Yet did I really? I still woke with nightmares, a fast-beating heart. Dreaming of being chased.

WE ENJOYED OUR TIME IN THE HOUSE ON THE HILL IN EVANS Street but it was time for us to find another place to live. Missionaries on leave were ready to move in. For six weeks we rented a neglected flat in George Street, but then we moved into an old villa on Signal Hill Road. I sent letters home, letting the family know about the change of address. Reading these letters now, I am amazed at how happy and optimistic we sounded. Emigration was all we had hoped it would be. A new life, new friends.

No guilt.

This is an extract translated from a letter I wrote to Bart's parents on 31 January 1961:

Employment

Won't it be lovely to read outside in the garden, to pick flowers and again have that same beautiful view of the hills as we had in Evans Street?

We have been so fortunate to get this house and we are very happy. As immigrants we have been very spoiled but that doesn't prevent us from being grateful for small things. We are completely happy; my only wish is that there would be cheap transport between the two hemispheres. I would so love to see you again.

It is noisy here in this flat in George Street. We can hear the neighbour splashing in the bath next door. That means he can hear us too, and we always have great fun in the bath.

Now a bit about our day here. We close the door of the flat behind us at 8.25 am, Bart walks to the right and I go to the left. When we start walking we count to 20 and wave to each other, repeat the 20 steps and wave again and then go straight on to our work. We had said to each other before, 'Why didn't you wave?', and the other would reply, 'I did wave.' So this is a good solution and we have decided to keep to this routine for as long as we live in this flat.

Integrating

In February 1961 we rented a 100-year-old house on Signal Hill Road. The toilet was outside and the house was small, but we made our home here with the simple furnishings we'd brought with us from Holland in our container of one-and-a half cubic metres: blue cotton curtains, a gold cotton-covered high-backed chair as well as a rattan one with an orange cushion. Even though we had acquired a few things in the past year – a wooden table, a yellow tablecloth, four Swedish-style chairs, a grey Conray heater – the living room looked sparse.

Bart made a bookcase and on the top shelf we placed a pewter tea set given to us by Bart's parents and a beautiful Delft vase in hues of blue and gold. Not much, but it was enough for a good start.

During weekends we often took the bus to St Clair, sat on the beach and gazed over the sea, the South Pacific that stretched for ever, so far from villages with windmills. The horizon was sometimes blurred by oyster-grey clouds; other times it was as sharp as a pencil line.

We walked to Lawyers Head and at low tide crossed to the little island. This freedom, this space. We loved it.

We wrote weekly letters to our family, telling them that we were managing very well. We bought things for the kitchen, for the bedroom, for the living room. A vacuum cleaner, a Hoovermatic – a new washing machine on the market with twin tubs, and a spin dryer. Homemaking: so simple. We were content. Grateful.

WAS I CONTENT? YES, BUT THERE WAS ALWAYS THAT LONGING. A longing I didn't dare to express. Bart had made it clear he would never go back to Holland to live and that I had to work this out by myself. Our friends were settled and expected us to be the same. I pretended I was happy, but I cried a lot when I was on my own. Then an occasional irrational thought floated up such as realising that I would have to work 35 weeks to save up for the journey home. But of course I didn't want to leave Bart. We made a good team and a strong bond had been formed.

Going to the beach lifted my spirits for a while, but when I was there I always thought of the cemetery with its lonely crosses. So close to the beach, so near me. I thought of the families who visited those grave sites, flowers in their hands.

The other immigrants we met provided security at that vulnerable stage of adjustment. They gave the appearance of being strong. 'What happens when these friends grow old?' I wondered. 'Language, customs and manners of speaking will be gone. What if I grow old here? Do I really want to grow old here? Now I have a valiant knight at my side, but what if I end up alone? What if nobody can understand me? What if I don't remember the English words for things I want to say?'

I remember feeling inferior when I listened to the older women talking. Would I need 10 years to sound confident and at ease in this country like them? I admired the discipline they showed in keeping to the daily routine of housekeeping but it never worked for me. Books were more important.

ASTRIDE A FIERCE WIND

I could hide in them.

With Bart often away during the week, and my home-sickness coming and going, Adri offered to have me stay with them during Bart's absences. It was a lovely chance to get to know the children better, hear their stories and watch the loving relationship between these parents and their children.

And always there were those hills to look out to, the changing light and shadow, apocalyptic sunsets. Gradually fear was replaced by a thin layer of peace. And I worked hard on being accepted.

New life

During the final months of 1961 our letters home were full of an impending happening. Parcels arrived at the front door – fluffy blankets for a bassinet, sweet little jumpers in shiny cotton embroidered with pink and blue flowers. A nightie and Maya soap for the new mother. A shirt for the new father.

Our baby was due to be born at the end of March 1962.

Unto us a child

I remember the day of her birth.
Bright March sunshine.

The previous night we'd had a meal with Catherine and George, their first baby due soon as well. As we ate large, fried meatballs, red cabbage and apple sauce, we watched the late summer sun golden on the giant macrocarpa hedge of the little villa we were renting in Opoho.

One room was waiting for our baby. Brown-and-yellow-striped linoleum. Using my old hand-operated Singer I'd sewn white curtains with Mickey Mouse pictures. A friend lent us a cane bassinet. I draped yellow-and-white-checked fabric around its base and over the horizontal strip of wood at the top. We'd hung up the linen wall hanging Bart's sister Mijntje had sent us, a kaleidoscope of felt animal figures neatly hand-stitched: a wise-looking elephant, a brown and a black dog, a squirrel with nuts in its paws, a gigantic spider in its web.

Across the valley a gentle breeze pushed a long white cloud over Mount Cargill towards the west, leaving behind on the hill top a trail that looked like a tightly-packed wad of cotton wool.

That night our baby came into the world as a wave onto a beach; it was that easy.

But afterwards she was put into an incubator.

I cried when she was taken away. Her arms and legs were

Unto us a child

spread out like a frog and her eyes were closed but it seemed to me as if her face was plucked out of an Italian Madonna painting. A Giotto. A Raphael.

The next morning a nurse said I could see her. I was taken to the room filled with cots and small babies. There was a window. The nurse told me to wait there. I was allowed a short glimpse of our baby through the window when another nurse held her in her arms, tucking down the swaddling cloth so I could get a better view. But that wasn't enough. I wanted to put my arms around her, hold her close to me, press her gently against my breasts and feel her lips suckling me.

At first I didn't know what to say. There was something different about my baby. I had seen my sister's babies, they didn't look like my little one wrapped in cloth, held by a nurse. 'Is that distance between her eyes normal?' I asked. 'Is my baby all right? My daughter?'

'She's fine.'

'But why does she have to stay in an incubator if she's fine?'

'You'll have her in your room soon enough.'

Back in bed I looked at pictures of babies smiling out from the pages of women's magazines. I wondered, *Do all newborn children have such wide spaces between their eyes?*

During the day her breathing became normal and later that night a nurse brought her to my room. Bart and I stood close together, holding her. Our firstborn child. She felt so soft, so floppy, as if there were hardly any muscles in her body. So relaxed!

I whispered to Bart, 'Hello, Dad.'

'Hello, Mum.'

Everything was going to be all right. Her birth was a confirmation of our love and of our life in a new land, the beginning of an exciting new stage in our lives.

JUST BEFORE THE END OF THE VISITING HOUR THE DOOR OF my room opened. The doctor's face said it all. How could he find the right words? And what could he say?

There was no need. We knew enough about chromosomes.

My face felt hot, my breath caught up in my throat, my heart tumbled fast. Grabbing Bart's hand, I said, 'She's not all right, is she? Our baby? What's wrong with our baby? Her eyes!'

After he'd gone we held each other, silent and shaking.

The doctor had walked hesitantly into the room, accompanied by a nurse. There was no smile. He had walked past the bed where another woman had just been brought in. The nurse stopped at this bed and I could hear her voice, 'Would you mind coming with me, please?' They left the room together. The doctor stood by my bed, took my hand, looked first at Bart, then at me. 'I've called in a friend of mine,' he said. A paediatrician. She has looked at your baby and confirmed it's Down's syndrome. You'll have to make an appointment to see her in the next few weeks.'

Later that night the nurse sat at my bedside. 'Your baby's condition used to be called mongolism but now we call it Down's syndrome, after John Langdon-Down, a British physician.' 'I know about this,' I said. 'I had a friend in Holland whose brother had Down's syndrome.' (In recent years it has changed to Down syndrome.)

'Let's go and see your baby,' she said. 'She might be hungry.'

I tried to feed my baby but her lips were not ready. Another nurse came. 'It's often hard for a baby to learn to suckle. We'll give her a supplement and try again in the morning.'

'She'll be so hungry,' I said.

Unto us a child

'Try not to worry, dear. Would you like some information on Down's syndrome?'

Later there were so many questions. *Why, God? Why?*

Comparing statistics.

Health, education, life expectancy.

Dreams of parents.

Our families and friends in Holland, and now in New Zealand, had children who would lead normal lives. At that time I didn't think such a life would be possible for our baby.

Oh ye of little faith.

Miriam

We adored our special child right from the beginning. How could we resist the love that shone out of her eyes? Those blue eyes that soon followed our movements. Her soft blonde hair that gleamed in the early winter sun.

We decided to call her Miriam. A beautiful name connected with the strength of family love and survival. And in the quiet evenings in Queen Mary Maternity Hospital I whispered her name. A few days later I looked out of the upstairs ward window at the sodden grounds below, and over to the fog-covered hills. I couldn't even see Signal Hill that was so close to our little house. I don't mind admitting that at that moment I wished I was dead. The rain was like a waterfall, heavy and solid, and my overflowing breasts felt laden with bricks. Other babies were drinking life-giving breast milk, but my daughter's nourishment came in bottles – slow and hard for her until her mouth muscles strengthened. At least I knew how much her little mouth had swallowed.

I had panicky thoughts. How can I go on? How will I cope? I watched the faces of other mothers nursing their babies, how their heads bent forward as if trying to absorb every detail of their newborn children. I felt as if I were shut up in a square white tent, separating me from everyone around me, affecting everything I did or said. I listened to the other women talking about their newborns, laughing together, planning visits in the future. I noticed that whenever I entered a room they fell silent. I felt their pity. But I didn't want their pity. I wanted to talk, yet I didn't know what to say.

AFTER TWO WEEKS THE TIME CAME TO TAKE OUR DAUGHTER home to Signal Hill Road. I packed up her little things – bottles, clothes, nappies – and dressed her in one of the tiny cotton tops my mother had sent. Our child looked so content and pretty. I brushed her little bit of wispy blonde hair, took her in my arms and Bart and I hugged.

The three of us.

Dick and Adri had offered Bart the use of their car, so we drove our daughter home in style. When we arrived at 115 Signal Hill, I fed Miriam, told her how much we loved her, how special she was. I changed her nappy and then we carefully carried her to her bedroom. There was that indescribable feeling of happiness when we laid her in her newly prepared bassinet, covered her with a tiny sheet and the soft blue blanket my mother had sent.

We spent the day checking on our firstborn.

It rained for days after we brought our daughter home, but on the first fine day I decided to take her to the Botanic Garden. I walked slowly down the hill pushing the blue-and-white checked pram with Miriam inside, and through the gates of the upper Botanic Garden. Looking around at the autumn trees, the bright blooming dahlias in the large herbaceous borders, I inhaled deeply that little hint of autumn spice. There was a sense of triumph in the air, glad that another summer was past and now ready to embrace the chills of winter. I kept glancing at my child asleep in the pram, allowing feelings of pride to emerge, gentle and subdued.

My steps were made light by holding on to the pram, and as we walked home I met another woman I knew a little. I smiled at her and the woman stopped.

'How are you?' she asked.

'I'm fine, thank you.'

Was I imagining it or was there an awkwardness in her question? I stood quietly, waiting for her to say something else. But there was only silence. I wanted to say, I am no longer pregnant. What do you think of my baby? I have a baby in a pram. She looks pretty with her pink knitted jacket and hat. I love her. I'm proud of her.

I looked at my child, lying on her back, her arms spread out like a flat angel, but I couldn't say anything. During those early years as a young immigrant woman I was shy and afraid to say something that could so easily be misconstrued as being rude. Looking at the other woman, I thought perhaps she was shy too.

We nodded and said our farewells, and the woman walked quickly away.

The lightweight pram felt unbearably heavy to push.

During that first winter I knitted and sewed clothes for Miriam. My mother had sent books with Dutch knitting patterns and I sat in the pale sun being a mother, preparing my daughter's *garderobe*: a four-ply white woollen dress with blue stripes along the bodice and hem; a jacket with a matching bonnet, pink and soft.

And then it was time for her first official outing, her christening.

That day was special. I dressed Miriam in the christening gown sent by Oma Hellendoorn that had been used by generations of Hellendoorn babies. Long before the service started our Dutch friends arrived at our home with cakes and sandwiches, and coffee in thermos flasks. These people had been total strangers when we first arrived in Dunedin a few years before and now they took the place of our

210

families. We sat together and talked as if we'd known each other all our lives. The women oohed and aahed at Miriam in her gown of fine white cotton with delicate lace strips on the bodice, sleeves and hem.

I see a mosaic image of our friend and neighbour Lloyd holding her, sprinkling holy water on the blonde hair which is sticking out in all directions, Bart and I acknowledging our gratitude for her birth.

For her life.

EXTRACT FROM A LETTER TRANSLATED FROM DUTCH, WRITTEN by the Reverend GW van Tricht to Bart's parents after Miriam's birth.

A few weeks ago I visited your children in Dunedin. This was the first time I met Huubje and Bart, and their newborn baby. I knew the child had been born with Down's syndrome and, like most other people, I had made assumptions as to how the child would look, how it would behave.

When your daughter-in-law came into the living room with the baby in her arms, my first reaction was, No, this is not a Down's syndrome child, this is a normal child. I saw a beautiful, healthy baby whose eyes looked happily around from the safety of her mother's arms. Clear blue eyes, shining fair hair, the colour of milk and blood in her cheeks.

After a while I realised that this was the baby mentioned before. This child is different from other Down's syndrome children. It must be borderline. The only way I noticed a difference from other children was that this child had quite a movement in her tongue but this could be because she might have been hungry. She did everything expected from a normal baby, she babbled, she smiled, lifted her head and gave the impression of being a healthy normal baby. Your children will have written these observations to you and quite rightly you might have thought that they were not able to see the child objectively. The reality is that they most likely would not be able to do just that, that's one of the positive signs of happy parents.

This child is their own child and they will surround it with all the love children need to become healthy and balanced adults. But I do see their child objectively and the purpose of this letter is that I wanted you to know this. I have the highest hopes for this child. She might not become a high flyer – and that doesn't matter – but the future will show what possibilities will be available for this child.

I can only suggest to you as grandparents of this child that you can be proud of her because she is even more beautiful than in the photo.

REV GW VAN TRICHT
I AUGUST 1962

A family

Soon we stopped asking questions about the extra chromosome. We felt proud when we talked about Miriam's achievements, her ready smile. It took a while before the muscles in her back were strong enough for her to sit, but when she began to crawl she moved fast – one leg straight, the other bent at the knee. The grin on her face was the mirror of the freedom she must have felt as she raced across the lino.

The day before her first birthday I took the bus to town, the pushchair strapped to its front. When we got there the driver helped to put it on the footpath, caressing Miriam's wee head before he got back into his seat. He said, 'What a sweet kiddy, so bonny.' I glowed with pride: to me his words signified not only an acknowledgement of Miriam's beauty but also an acceptance of her way into this world.

Maybe it wasn't going to be as hard as I'd thought it would be.

That day my mission was to buy a huge teddy bear which I'd seen at Arthur Barnett's the week before. I carried it home on the bus, one arm holding Miriam, the other the precious teddy bear, wrapped up very carefully.

Shortly after that we bought a blue 1938 Ford, and with Miriam safely in the simple canvas car seat, its two metal hooks fitting over the backrest, we had lots of outings – picnics to Taieri Mouth, the peninsula and Long Beach. I have a photo of her sitting on a little beach on the road to Taieri Mouth. She's wearing red woollen trousers, a white jersey and a red hat with a white furry edge, and she's got her index finger up in the air as if she's testing where the wind comes from. I look at that photo and want to hug her again and again, as I did that time.

There were holidays in Cromwell, Queenstown, even a trip over the Crown Range, the old Ford huffing and puffing as we made it to the summit. But we did it, all three of us lapping up every moment of change.

From our kitchen I could keep an eye on Miriam as she sat in her highchair while I cooked dinner. Often when she was tired her tongue would stick out. To help her get control, I'd put my finger on my tongue and show her how I'd push my own tongue back inside my mouth. Soon she understood what I meant by this gesture and from then on I'd only have to point to my open mouth and she knew the score. As she grew, her tongue muscles grew stronger too.

Miriam's arrival steadied the homesickness that had surrounded me since we had come to live in this beautiful but strange land. Our Dutch friends were supportive: Bep offering to look after her if I needed a break, Adri popping in with cream buns for morning coffee. I admired the strength of these women – their knowledge, their confidence. But it also meant a lot when we met our neighbours Mr and Mrs Butler who were always ready with advice. Then there was Shirley Ford, the Australian woman with a generous heart who made me feel welcome in her circle of friends by inviting Miriam and me for morning and afternoon tea parties. Our other neighbours, Joan and Doug Christensen, offered to look after Miriam if I had an appointment in town. Their kindness became the basis of a long friendship.

And then I became pregnant again. Since I'd put on a lot of weight the doctor advised rest as much as possible, with

A family

my legs on a wooden stool Bart had made. Miriam wasn't walking yet but every time I sat down she pushed the stool ahead of her as she crawled on her bottom, arranging the footrest for me.

A few months before our second baby was due we celebrated our fifth wedding anniversary. I decided I'd show my improved skills as a cook and prepared an Indonesian banquet for our friends. I cooked rendang daging, nasi goring, bahmi goring, opor chicken, spring rolls, and all the other side dishes that were expected to be part of a *rijsttafel* feast.

A few weeks later we found out why I had put on so much extra weight. We were going to have twins. During that time Bart's sister Mijntje arrived from Holland to live with us and work here. We'd prepared her room with the same love we had given to Miriam's room, even though most of the furniture was makeshift.

I'll never forget Mijntje's comment as we showed her our very small living room: 'Is this where you live all the time?' Proudly we said in unison, 'Yes!'

This was home. And yes, we did live there. And how! Although our little house was full there was always room for more. Friends came and stayed too, showing the stretch-ability of that 100-year-old wooden villa with its two gables at the back and a beautiful fretted-iron edge along the front verandah.

And so we waited for the twins to arrive.

New arrivals

Before too long we would be a family of six, and so it was time to update our car. Update? The new vehicle was slightly bigger and at least 14 years younger – a beige 1952 Ford Prefect.

Bart said, 'It'll be so much more reliable when the twins arrive. We can't take any risks on our way to the hospital.'

Risks? How could there be risks? The maternity hospital was only a short drive down the hill and into town.

On a drizzly October night the babies decided to come into this world. At four o'clock in the morning we woke Mijntje and told her we were going to the hospital. Bart tried to start the car, but despite it being the new addition and supposedly more reliable, the Prefect wouldn't take. We freewheeled down Signal Hill Road but stopped on the flat stretch near the Presbyterian Church.

Bart got out of the car and yelled, 'Get behind the wheel and I'll push.'

I yelled back, 'Push? That's my job for the next few hours!'

I could hardly fit behind the steering-wheel, and visions of our babies being born near the Botanic Garden played in full colour in my mind. Bart pushed the car until we came to the top of Opoho Road, then he jumped into the passenger seat and, freewheeling, we moved quickly to the bottom of the road where there was a public telephone. A taxi soon appeared.

New arrivals

Foster and Raymond were born shortly after we arrived at Queen Mary Maternity Hospital. Seven pounds and eight pounds, they looked beautiful with their round little faces, blonde hair and dark brown eyes.

It was hard work looking after the three littlies. The daily washing of nappies and being organised to feed the crying babies on time.

Having had such an unusual religious upbringing I looked forward to the day when we could take our sons to Opoho church to be baptised. To make a declaration of gratitude in that church for the huge gift of two healthy children. In between the continuous tasks of looking after our family I'd occasionally say to Bart, 'It's time we arrange with Rod to have the boys baptised.' Or, 'The boys are doing so well, I can't wait to take them to church to be baptised.' Bart didn't answer.

One day Rod Madill, our minister, came to visit. After a pleasant chat I said, 'When can our babies be baptised?' He looked at me, and said, 'The other day I asked Bart whether you had thought about a date to bring the boys to church, but he told me he didn't want them baptised as he thought they should make up their own minds when they were ready.'

Rod's face was quiet, there was no judgement, but I started to cry. At that time in my life, so close to the birth of the twins, I didn't know what to do. We walked to the front door, and Rod shook my hand. 'You can bring them any Sunday,' he said. Later I pleaded with Bart, but he could not change his mind, and I lacked the courage to go ahead and make the decision on my own. I tried to forget the feeling of emptiness I had at that time but it wasn't easy. It was hard to attend a service where a baby was christened.

In their late teens Foster and Raymond joined the youth group at the Opoho church and then they wanted to join the church too. This meant the boys had to be baptised, so they made their own choice as Bart had predicted. When they were students, our sons went a step further and chose to become members of churches that believed in adult baptism.

The birth of the twins didn't change our weekend routine. On Sunday morning Bart or I would go with Mijntje to Opoho church, the other one staying home. And nearly every Sunday afternoon we'd go for a drive. We'd pack the thermette, water, tea, and a tin filled with a mixture of my attempts at baking: shortbread, a date loaf, cherry or caramel slices. Baking was still very new territory for me, but thanks to the help of friends, a bit of independent research and many mishaps, I was slowly becoming confident.

Unlike my New Zealand friends I'd had no training in this sort of cooking, because at home my mother rarely baked during those years when our country was still recovering from the war. Even now I use recipes in the original handwriting of my friends from those early days in Dunedin, and remember the good times we had together, talking as young mothers do, walking through the Botanic Garden, pushing prams and pushchairs, or sitting on the lawn behind our house sipping tea from locally made pottery mugs.

But how could we all fit into the Prefect? We wanted to show Bart's sister our favourite places: Taieri Mouth, Warrington Beach, Karitane and the Outram Glen. Bart, resourceful as Odysseus, made an iron-and-wood frame to hold a carry-cot which was placed above the other cot on the back seat. The babies took turns in sleeping in the 'top bunk' and Miriam sat on my knee or Mijntje's while we enjoyed the stunning Otago scenery.

We were a real family now: no longer feeling the loneliness of immigrants.

New arrivals

THREE BEAUTIFUL CHILDREN KEPT US ON OUR TOES. BART made wooden puzzles for them – intricate patterns and shapes we covered with coloured pictures of wildlife. I knitted animals. A large blue mouse with giant whiskers, a brown cat with smaller ones. But it was the golden teddy bear that went everywhere with Miriam.

The boys were growing steadily. Although they were fraternal twins, Bart and I recognised subtle differences between them. Raymond's head was rounder than Foster's, and Foster's face had sharper features. And each had his own way of reacting to things. However, they had their first tooth on the same day, and took their first steps on the same day when we were on holiday in Queenstown. Both boys had ready smiles and were solidly built, and when awake their legs and arms were never still.

Those years in that small house were busy. When Bart finished for the day, and Mijntje too when she was with us, then the meal was ready and Miriam was waiting and ready in her highchair with its yellow Formica tray. After that it was time to feed Foster and Raymond, always hungry for more food. The Plunket nurse rules of four-hourly feeding reigned, but it was hard to leave my hungry babies to cry until the next acceptable feeding time.

We had a playpen in the living room. Miriam loved chatting to her brothers, picking up soft toys they had thrown over the playpen's edge. To make it easier to lift the babies, Bart had installed a raised level, and soon they began to stay awake for longer, watching the daily happenings from their elevated positions.

I was always full of doubt about my ability to manage the household, expecting other women would do everything better than I did. Perhaps they did. I tried my best, and in retrospect I know I did very well, but it seemed as if it was never enough, never quite right. I was aware that my Dutch friends didn't think much of my housekeeping abilities. I always tried to snatch a bit of reading during the day when the boys were asleep – preferring to escape into the world of *Doctor Zhivago* rather than making the house spic and span. I had a motto that my house had to be clean enough to be healthy but dirty enough to be happy.

Once a regular routine had been established with the children, my feelings of not being able to cope were soon replaced with a deep gratitude and pride as I watched the children sleep at night. Even with three little children I sometimes still felt lonely, and when Bart and Mijntje came home I found it difficult to voice my loneliness. Again in retrospect, I now know I would have blossomed with some form of acknowledgement from Bart and Mijntje for the work I did, and acknowledgement of who I was in the family, my identity as a person. I loved caring for my family but longed for opportunities to find out more about life and living.

Growing shoots

One evening, when Miriam was three years old, there was a knock at the front door: a woman from a nearby street who had heard about our family. She hesitantly asked if she could talk to us for a minute. 'The IHC has started a playgroup in their building at Forbury Corner,' she said. 'It's a trial, three mornings during the week. Do you think your daughter would like to go?'

The following Monday Miriam was all ready to go to preschool – and looking so pretty in a grey pinafore and red jersey and tights. At 8.45 I put her in her car seat up the front of the Prefect, and the boys in their carrycots in the back, and drove from Opoho to Forbury Corner. It was hard to leave Miriam that first morning. I was a cruel, selfish mother. How would I manage without her? How would she manage? How could she make herself understood? Would she manage the toilet routine? But she smiled all the way home when I picked her up at 12 o'clock, and babbled to her brothers about her day. I knew I didn't have to worry.

We'd vowed that we would do everything to help our daughter. We wouldn't let her so-called handicap stand in her – or our – way.

One wintry morning we received a telegram. It read, *Moeder thuis bij Jezus* – Mother home with Jesus. I sat in my chair and looked at the brownish piece of paper that signified the end of my mother's life and for me the end of a key connection with my homeland. Feeling helpless, I cried out, 'I can't even go to the funeral.' And then Miriam came to me, climbed on my knee and hugged me. At that moment I realised that in her there was a continuity of my mother's caring nature, even across those thousands of miles. We sat quietly for a while, and then I sang to her the song my mother sang to me when I sat on her lap as bombs fell around our house towards the end of the war: 'Safe in the Arms of Jesus'. Miriam hummed along.

We'd enjoyed living in the little old house on Signal Hill Road and hadn't minded its outside toilet, but one Sunday night we noticed a For Sale sign on a 1920s house with a quarter-acre section in Warden Street. I said to Bart, 'The garden is big enough to put in swings and sandpits and other playing equipment. It would be so lovely for the children.'

But we didn't have much money. Two Dutch friends, Ko Roos and Bob van Raalte, came to the rescue. Both businessmen lent us a hundred pounds each, interest free, and with the little bit of money we'd saved we became the proud owners of an old, shabby-looking roughcast house. Ko and his wife Jo had started a fish-and-chip shop in Hillside Road, later moving to the North East Valley. They both worked hard, caring for their five children, yet they always had time for their friends. Their generosity, not only in supplying good fish and chips, was well known in North Dunedin.

I'll never forget that first winter in our own house in Warden Street. We were struggling financially, and when the church needed a new cleaner we gladly took this opportunity towards helping pay the mortgage. For a number of years we spent every Saturday afternoon cleaning the church and the church hall. During that first winter in the new house, the children managed to get the

Growing shoots

total cocktail of childhood illnesses – chickenpox, measles and rubella. Day after day I wiped running noses, listened to coughs and splutters, sat in a big old-fashioned chair reading stories, and regularly sponged their little bodies with a damp facecloth. Antibiotics. So often, so many.

It was a cold, wet winter, and each time the southerly hit the city the worn carpet and scrim-covered walls moved up and down like the swell of the sea at low tide. We used the only plug-point in the living room for the Conray heater we'd bought the first week after we arrived, but there was one drawback: it wasn't safe to heat it above 1200 watts! The kitchen with its old coal range was a mess, and the dark brown lino was torn in many places. I thought living in these conditions was enough of a challenge, but then Miriam became seriously ill with pneumonia as a complication of measles. We put her bed in the living room because her bedroom was cold, and as we watched her, holding her hand, we were reminded again how much she meant to us. The thought of losing her was unbearable. One particular day, even though I sponged her every few hours, the high fever continued and that night was the longest and loneliest ever. But the next morning she woke and said, 'I have orange juice, please?'

The run-down house with three bedrooms became our home, and before we could do anything else to it the piles needed to be replaced. At night, while the children were asleep, Bart would disappear through a door in the outside wall and set everything up. He'd yell, 'You can start mixing the concrete!' And so I shovelled and mixed the slurry, filled the wheelbarrow, and wheeled it to the side of the house so that Bart could fill cardboard boxes and set them in their places under the house. I admired the way he tackled the demanding tasks. He had learnt a lot during our first year in Dunedin when he helped Dick van Barneveld with the renovations of their first house.

Once the basic groundwork was done we began to work hard to change the inside of the house. After a full day at work Bart became a carpenter at night. He looked the part with a tool bag held up with a belt around his waist, and wearing an old blue-checked shirt and comfortable trousers. Bart was a hard worker, totally focused on what needed to be done, and in no time at all he was an expert – cutting up timber, measuring each four-by-two carefully until it fitted into its ordained place, as part of a kitchen or bathroom wall. I would paint whatever needed painting, starting with an undercoat and gradually moving on until I had completed one part of the house.

Slowly, room by room, a transformation took place.

Bart and I often talked about the changes we intended to make to our home. We painted the inside walls palest cream and added warm colours to our makeshift furniture. We were told our house looked like a Dutch home, with pewter plates and vases reflecting a satiny glow. On the living-room wall was a Dutch clock with Atlas bearing the whole world in his hands, and in the kitchen hung a well-used Douwe Egberts coffee grinder that I'd bought with points I had saved buying Douwe Egbert coffee.

'We must replace the rotten windowsills and doors.'

'Yeah! And I don't like that chimney. It looks wobbly. What if there's a storm and it falls through the ceiling of the children's bedroom?'

The list was endless: the roof needed replacing, the bathroom was archaic. An electric saw-bench became part of our bedroom furniture, and the children slept through its roaring noise while night after night we worked on the latest project. On the mornings when there was no playgroup, I cleaned sawdust off the threadbare carpet and turned the radio to Kate Harcourt's children's programme, 'Listen with Mother'. The children and I danced and sang around the mulberry bush and felt sorry for Dr Foster who had to go to Gloucester in a shower of rain. And there was always the grand old Duke of York with his 10 thousand men. We marched, we chanted and – yes! – we were content.

By this time Mijntje had celebrated her 25th birthday in Dunedin and was making her own friends. She was tall and beautiful with her short dark hair and pale skin. A gentle person, caring and friendly, she loved observing the children growing. We knew we would miss her company but were delighted when after 16 months with us she decided to go flatting in an interesting two-storey house in High Street. We hoped she'd stay in Dunedin. Bart's sister had trained as a librarian in Holland and worked at Otago University's central library. She would often bring home books that I could read as well. It was a good feeling to have a family member in Dunedin, even if it was in another part of town when she moved, and we still saw a lot of each other.

LIKE MOST OF OUR IMMIGRANT FRIENDS, WE CONTINUED working on our house, the creation of a comfortable living space becoming part of the process of settling in. I loved the back garden, which was surrounded by a fast-growing hedge. Close to the house was a chestnut tree with colours of palest green in the spring and dazzling gold in the autumn. Each spring I waited for the white chestnut candles to open up and reach to the early morning sun. Further down the garden were apple trees, one of them supplying an abundant yield. Many years later we found out that the name of this particular apple was Freyberg and that it had been planted in 1937. In autumn we preserved 40 jars of apple sauce.

The lawn stretched out beyond the kitchen window and I kept a close watch as the three children and their friends ran around with Doodle, our dog, and Mittens, our cat. I listened to their calls, their shrieks as they climbed the apple trees. Bart made a swing in one of our strong trees, and a sandpit with beach sand that held red, green and yellow buckets and spades.

We planted shrubs and trees and flowers that gave an intensity of colours – yellow, pink and red. I placed a climbing rata against a bank, thinking of the day when I would see its fluffy red flowers amidst the dark glossy leaves, and a witch hazel in a corner, where it displayed yellow tendrils in the middle of winter, just before spring flowers pushed through the winter earth.

I knew that whenever I planted a tree or a shrub a small part of me secured a stronger hold on the new land.

By moving to 51 Warden Street we became close neighbours of Lloyd and Elaine Geering. Our back section bordered the garden of the house they'd bought in 1960 just before our arrival in Dunedin. There was a hole in the hedge and Elaine and I climbed through it regularly when we met for a drink in the late afternoon. I felt helpless when I listened to Elaine relate how church people treated her family during the build-up to her husband's 'heresy trial' in 1967 and the subsequent wave of hatred towards him by those who said they believed in God's love. Lloyd was tried by the Presbyterian church for daring to agree with widely held theological thought that Jesus' resurrection had not been an historical event. I missed Elaine so much when they moved to Wellington in 1971.

Gradually my circle of friends grew and I thought that my loneliness had vanished, just as a wave on the beach dissolves into foamy bubbles. But why did I still make trips to the letterbox in the hope that somebody would pass our gate and say hello to me in our quiet street?

I was always waiting for letters from our families, and

Growing shoots

wanting to make phone calls to Holland to hear the latest news about family events, but overseas telephone connections back then were distorted and expensive. When I tucked the children in at night it felt so right to live in New Zealand, surrounded by good friends and beautiful scenery, yet my thoughts were often with our family at the other side of the world. I still had feelings of being torn in two. Of having one foot in my home country and one foot in New Zealand.

My father and Bart's mother and sisters sent parcels with clothes for the children, a remnant for me to make a new dress, a book for Bart, strong tea towels, salted liquorice and Douwe Egberts coffee. Each time a parcel arrived I could feel the love that had gone into the selection of its contents and the careful packing and posting. Those mornings when we found a parcel from Holland on our doorstep were a highlight of our early years in Dunedin.

I often thought of my mother, her round face framed with greying hair. Eyes with a mischievous sparkle. How she had sat quietly in her chair, reading, knitting. Her kindness towards strangers who inevitably arrived on our doorstep in those days of my childhood, having been invited by my father. One wintry morning he arrived home with three gypsy women wearing long black dresses. My mother had to wash their clothes and arrange bedding for them for the three nights they stayed with us. And she had to cook for them too, of course. 'They were sitting at the side of the road,' my father said. 'They were cold and hungry. I couldn't leave them there.'

Moeke never complained.

I thought of my sisters who had experienced the closeness of my mother's death. I felt left out, unable to take part in the grief, but I was able to share my feelings in letters. I pictured the cemetery in our small village, surrounded by old trees, meadows and quiet country lanes. I imagined how my family had stood there. I thought about the words I had wanted to say to the woman who had borne me. I'd never talked to my mother as a person, never asked her questions about her life as a woman and a mother, about growing older, being old.

It was during those days that awareness of the transience of human life slowly filtered into my thoughts. Filling the garden with plants, my hands crumbling the soil around the fragile roots. Our lives were fragile too, yet so strong. I wanted to make a success of my life here. Be a good wife, a good mother. A good friend. This was the now.

People were kind. They brought plates with scones and jam, invitations to morning tea parties. Slowly I allowed feelings of safety and trust to emerge, bringing with them a shielding balance.

IN 1967 WE CELEBRATED MIRIAM'S FIFTH BIRTHDAY. SHE invited her neighbourhood playmates – Jane, Eileen, Steven, Mark and Stephanie – as well as other friends from the playgroup. Miriam glowed as she sat in her decorated chair in our balloon-filled dining room, sharing hokey pokey ice cream and red and yellow jellies with the others. How she loved the raspberry lemonade, saveloys, 'mousetraps', Mallow Puffs, and hundreds-and-thousands biscuits. And as she breathed in deeply to blow out the five candles on her birthday cake I put my fears aside for the next stage of her life. I felt so proud of her.

I knew we would manage.

Each morning during the week a taxi picked Miriam up to take her to Sara Cohen School in Rutherford Street, and returned her home in the middle of the afternoon.

Growing shoots

I'll never forget that first day – she was ready long before we were. By that time she could read a few words. During the past year we'd made cards of white cardboard and covered them with huge letters of the alphabet: A, B, C ... The next stage was putting the letters together to make a word: CAT, DOG, HOUSE. Each night after dinner we produced one new word and gradually we chanted a language together.

Watching Miriam with the children in her class, I noticed she liked to work on her own. I also began to be aware that she liked regularity in her life – not always easy to manage with a household of five people and lots of renovating work going on.

Miriam was happy at Sara Cohen School and we gradually established a good routine. The boys by that time were attending Kelsey Yaralla Kindergarten, first in the afternoons and later in the morning. Miriam came home wanting to show off her new writing skills. She'd sit at the table, tongue between her teeth, concentrating on the task. Grammar and spelling mistakes didn't matter – the content was always exactly right, whether it was for a birth, birthday or bereavement. What a thrill it was to receive the first birthday card in her handwriting: *Love you, Mum.*

It became harder for Miriam to accept any change in routine. It was tough on her to get used to our irregular lunchtimes over the weekend. For her lunch was at 12 o'clock, dinner at six. But when we were working hard in the garden or using the saw-bench to cut timber for studs and dwangs we'd wait until a task was completed and then think of meals.

We were quite tough with her on those occasions: 'We'll have lunch soon. Go and do some reading. Just wait.' And she'd run away, throwing her arms up in the air, her face dark. We knew but could not really understand the extent of her need for routine and I often felt frustrated at being put in this spot: having to face her needs that were a result of her extra chromosome, but also coping with the pressure of jobs that needed to be done. Where was the fine line between her needs and wants? I don't think I ever got quite used to it.

IN 1969, FOSTER AND RAY TURNED FIVE AND STARTED AT Opoho School, which was at the top of our street. It was a popular meeting place. While I waited for the boys at the end of the school day, new friendships were formed like the first side shoots of a newly planted tree.

One frosty winter morning after the children had gone to school, I made *oliebollen* – special Dutch doughnuts made with warmed milk and yeast, dried fruit and white flour, deep fried in hot oil. I phoned my friends: 'Come over.' And they did. Catherine, Val, Sheila, Gwen.

They began to say to me, 'You're just like one of us.'

Bart and I were very much involved with the Opoho church. On Sundays we sat and watched the spun-gold rays of the sun penetrating the coloured stained-glass windows. Bart was a deacon and fixed the leaking church roof. I played the organ to the best of my ability, though often my tempo was pushed along by extremely competent older women turning in their seats and waving a hand up and down. Faster, faster. But with my feet pumping the pedals and my fingers wandering loosely over the keyboard I happily sang along with 'I feel the winds of God today; Today my sail I lift' and 'The strife is o'er, the battle done'. The words were different but the melody was the same as the hymns I played in Holland.

But was the battle done?

Would I ever belong here?

Would my memories ever be replaced by the necessary

Growing shoots

mental and physical energy needed to cope with the daily activities? I wanted those memories to diminish at least, but they were too strong.

Visitors

That winter we got a letter from my father: 'I want to visit my southern hemisphere family.' He would visit not only us in New Zealand, but also my sister Jo and her family who had settled well in Melbourne, living there since January 1960. Two more children had been born – Australians! The youngest, Connie, was only a month older than our sons.

Opa Visser was to arrive in early December and stay for four weeks. The children were excited – a real grandfather arriving on a plane from Holland! I was trying to feel pleased too. My friends said, 'How nice for you to have real family with you again: your father.' I was worried, but also hopeful. Perhaps the simmering anxiety I'd felt for so long might be solved. Might finally be cleared.

We cleaned the house and tidied the garden and did the baking, and we couldn't wait to introduce my father to his Kiwi grandchildren. The morning of her opa's arrival Miriam twirled around and skipped through the house after she'd put on the dress I'd made for this occasion, my own design of a pink, waffled-cotton top, with the skirt and short sleeves made of dark-blue cotton. I'd even put pink pockets on the dark-blue skirt.

Foster and Ray looked lovely in their newly knitted green cardigans and checked green trousers. They were two years old and running around in anticipation of seeing the

Visitors

aeroplane that was bringing their grandfather.

'Plane, plane, plane,' they shouted as they chased each other in the long hall, flapping their arms.

We climbed into the Ford Prefect and set off. But as we neared the airport, all excited and nervous, I noticed my father sitting on a rock. I yelled to Bart, 'Stop!' We got out of the car, ran up to him kissing and hugging and spouting questions. 'Have you waited long?' I asked. 'What happened and why did you come early?'

My father said casually, 'I wanted to surprise you and thought I could take a taxi to your house, but there were none!' It turned out Papa had arrived early in Christchurch from Melbourne, and finding a plane ready to leave for Dunedin, decided to take it! We smiled and hugged again and drove home, where the first thing we did was to drink coffee and eat Dutch apple cake.

Opa had arrived just in time to take part in the Christmas rush. He became Father Christmas for us because, thanks to him, we could buy a fridge – something we'd done without until that time. As we had done with Mijntje, we took him to our favourite places, and on New Year's Eve took a picnic to the Waipori Power Station and Lake Mahinerangi. That night we celebrated the arrival of a new year at Adri and Dick's together with Connie and Bob and other friends, eating *oliebollen* and *haringslaatjes* and singing 'Auld Lang Syne' at midnight.

After Opa's arrival I was aware my father was sad he couldn't talk to the children. 'You should have taught them Dutch,' he said.

'I know it is sad,' I said, 'and I am really sorry but we wanted to make sure Miriam would at least manage to communicate with others in the English language.'

One morning we were having coffee under the sprawling birch tree in the garden, and my father said, 'I'm going to marry Tante Jo.' A friend of my mother's. I needed to take a deep breath. I spoke slowly, spacing out each word, 'I am glad for you, Papa. I know it must be lonely for you on your own.' He took another sip of coffee and looked towards Flagstaff. 'She and I are getting on well.'

At that time it was hard to accept that my mother would so soon be replaced by one of her friends, but how could I judge the loneliness of an older man? Yet during my father's visit buried memories had resurfaced. I was again aware that his attention towards me was not that of a loving father. The ambiguous relationship I'd experienced in my childhood, that had been brought to the surface after I was married, was still there.

OPA LOVED TO TALK, AND AS LONG AS PEOPLE LISTENED TO him he liked them. However if they dared to voice their own opinion the flaws in their character would be analysed.

He also liked to pinch and slap my bottom. 'Don't do that, Papa.'

Most days he sat under the silver birch in the quarter-acre garden, keeping a diary, writing his religious thoughts. He'd say, 'How quiet it is here. There's hardly any traffic.'

I said to Bart, 'Let's take Opa to Queenstown – he will love the scenery there. So different from Holland where the green meadows are divided by straight canals and you only see church spires in the distance. He will love the mountains.'

So we set off, leaving our little toddlers for the weekend in the care of good friends. I felt guilty but there was no way we all could be comfortable, sitting in the Prefect for such a long way. And I knew that the boys would be well looked after. Miriam could come – she and I sat on the back seat, holding hands as we drove along the rolling highways. I

Visitors

pointed things out, 'See, darling, the sheep in the paddock, and see the lambs? They've grown so much since they were born in spring. And look, there is a horse and a rider. How beautiful they look together.'

I leaned forward so Opa could hear better in the front seat, 'Remember the horses we had, Papa? Remember Victor, Papa?'

'Yes. It was good when the horses were replaced with trucks. We could get on with life.'

Queenstown in those days was a quiet town, even in the Christmas rush. We went to Cecil Peak Station and sat at the lake's edge, having brought rugs and a picnic. So beautiful, so peaceful. Eating fresh, juicy peaches and apricots.

That night Opa had to sleep in a different guesthouse which was next door. We had a meal in town, and after we got back to our accommodation I tucked Miriam in. 'Opa,' I said, 'it's time you went to the guesthouse.'

He looked at me. 'I want you to come with me. You need to come.'

His eyes were dark and strange. I didn't like that look in his eyes, that look I had remembered all those years. I turned to Bart, my own eyes fearful, a question.

Bart took my hand, 'Come on, Opa, we'll all go together. After all, it's only next door.'

'No,' Opa said, his mouth tight. 'I want Huub to come with me. By herself.'

'We go together. *Now*. We will have a long drive back tomorrow.'

Later I lay in my husband's arms. He passed me a handkerchief. 'You are safe now.'

'I never thought I would become grateful for that distance,' I said.

Finding a balance

I couldn't help thinking that since we'd now had two visitors from our home country perhaps more would follow, but first we had to say goodbye to Mijntje. She'd enjoyed working two years at the University of Otago library but decided to return to the Netherlands to continue her studies for head librarian.

We may have had many friends but losing Mijntje was a sad time for us. She was family and we missed her. Before she left she said, 'I know how and where you live now, and that will make our contact much easier.'

At the beginning of 1970 we were expecting another visitor from Holland, my tante Gerrie.

> *You'll be so pleased to hear that I will be visiting you. I have decided to come by boat and will stop on the way in South Africa where I have some friends. I hope you don't mind, but I thought I'd tell you that I'll wear my Salvation Army uniform when I arrive. I find people are far more helpful to me when I wear the uniform and at my age I can do with all the help I can get.*

GERRIE

Before her retirement, my aunt, Tante Gerrie, had been a brigadier in the Salvation Army and had been in charge

Finding a balance

of an old men's home. After arriving in New Zealand she decided that my housekeeping wasn't up to the standard she was used to. She sent me to town to do the shopping, and while she had the house to herself she took the furniture from the living room into the hall and gave everything a good spring clean. The sideboard was shifted, the sofa turned 180 degrees and the cushions shaken. All the rugs were taken outside and beaten with a *mattenklopper*.

Tante Gerrie adored food and drink. She told me that she wouldn't touch alcohol, but one day she arrived home with a bottle of advocaat, which she emptied within a few evenings. She loved my trifle – especially the sponge cake that was soaked in a cup of sherry – and insisted I made it regularly. My aunt decided what I had to cook, what the children needed and when things needed doing. She didn't like leaving the supper dishes on the kitchen bench at night.

'We never know when the Lord might come back to Earth,' she told me. 'It could happen tonight, so we can't have a kitchen sink with dirty dishes waiting for Him.'

And Bart could do nothing wrong in her eyes.

After a while I felt as if I were a guest in my own home.

I had become a confident housekeeper with a daily routine centred around the children's school times, which gave me a feeling of achievement and security. But Tante Gerrie disrupted things. It was like a mat had been pulled out from under my feet.

Yet I did like my aunt. She was my real family.

I also admired her independence and her *recht door zee* attitude, a straightforwardness that I lacked. Why couldn't I be more like Tante Gerrie, who pleased only herself? Who didn't worry all the time about whether she might hurt others?

I wished I could assert myself when I knew I was right. That I could let others know how I really felt.

But that might mean an argument. A fight.

Laten we het maar fijn houden, hè?

Let's keep it nice, eh?

And that's what I did. I 'kept things nice'. And not only in my household. Ruffles in relationships were for other people. *Laten we het maar fijn houden.*

After three months we said our goodbyes to Tante Gerrie at Dunedin Airport, and on the way home Miriam asked, 'Mum, why are you sighing?'

A working wife

A working wife. That's what we called ourselves in those years. Was being a mother and a housewife not work? Were we not experts in multi-tasking?

In 1971 I was offered a job as part-time secretary in the political studies department at the University of Otago. My first job since Miriam was born, apart from some temping jobs the year after the twins started school. I loved working with young people and sympathetic staff. I remember especially Professor Jim Flynn's kindness and respect. As head of the department he decided I'd need an electric typewriter. There was one problem though. I'd never learnt to touch type, but while Jim dictated letters and other material my fingers would dance over the keys of the manual typewriter and there were never any complaints about the results. The system worked. It worked perfectly. But now my fingers refused to dance on the keyboard of the electric typewriter no matter how hard I tried. I practised in my free time to build up speed but it didn't work.

There was only one solution: at the beginning of the following year I enrolled in a typing class. I parked the car, walked to the building and got a shock. Standing in the doorway, waiting for the 'new entrants' was my colleague from the mathematics department. She was the tutor!

'What are *you* doing here?' she asked.

'I've got to learn to touch type.'

We laughed and laughed. And I did learn.

I made new friends. We were invited to parties. Other doors were being opened.

A new staff member, Craig Conly, arrived from the USA with his wife, Ute, and their two children. Shortly after their arrival my family went swimming at St Clair. Just before we were ready to leave I noticed Craig and his family standing at the edge of the surf. They looked so forlorn and I remembered how I had stood there once: watching the waves and feeling homesick.

I went over to them. 'Why don't you come home with us?' I said. 'We have enough food.'

I cooked Wiener schnitzel with a paprika sauce, and we soon became friends. Bart and Craig played chess while Ute taught me to play the guitar. Together we played and sang the early seventies songs. We both enjoyed Joan Baez's music. We talked about books, and Foster and Ray played with the Conly children, Michael and Debbie. We had our first ever barbecue at their house. It was a feast!

The extra income from my university job provided opportunities for more renovating. More trips to Fletcher's to get supplies for refurbishing bedrooms. The electric sawbench worked overtime on Saturdays.

A trip to Holland

Then my father took ill. Confused feelings had the upper hand. What should I do? Would I ever forgive myself if I didn't make the effort to see him once more? To talk with him as I knew my friends talked with their fathers?

By that time I'd settled into my work at the university and felt confident that we could take out a small mortgage to pay for my fare. An idea popped into my head, and after talking with Bart we decided it would be good for me to take Miriam with me.

So in the Christmas holidays of 1972 Miriam and I took off from Momona to travel to the other side of the world. I still see her in my memory, walking ahead of me towards the plane carrying a green Air New Zealand bag over her shoulder and wearing the yellow cape with dark blue edging I'd made from a Penrose's store remnant. She was excited, and marched ahead, not even wanting to turn to wave to Bart, Foster and Ray.

We must have been flying over Oamaru when she wanted to go to the toilet. Afterwards, wobbling back to our seats, she said, 'I want to go home now!'

All the way to Holland, she kept asking for the time. She didn't have a watch, and how could she understand time zone changes? Of course it was confusing for her. But when I told her the plane would have a short stop in Athens she said, 'Nana Mouskouri lives in Greece.'

Waiting at Athens Airport, people milling around, she looked at every woman, expecting Nana to join us.

I was proud to introduce her to the 20-plus family members waiting for us at Schiphol Airport. My father was much better by this time and had driven to the airport to be there. There was also Bart's mother – Miriam loved meeting Oma Hellendoorn – and aunts and uncles from both sides of our families plus their children. When Miriam saw Marjolein's dark hair and dark glasses she said, 'Like Nana Mouskouri!'

We walked through the airport to the carpark, talking, gesticulating. Such a crowd. Arms linked, smiles, grins. 'Glad you are here.' A feeling of belonging.

My father drove us to Warnsveld in his Mercedes but in Holland seat belts hadn't been introduced to the driving public. It felt strange and scary not to 'belt up'. Silently I longed for our safe little Humber 80 with its seatbelts, especially when the speed dial got up to 150 on the *autobaan*. Miriam didn't notice – she was fast asleep on the back seat. We crossed the wide rivers whose bridges were bombed during the Second World War. Some of them had recently been rebuilt and seemed to float in the air, reminding me of giant cobwebs held together by thin filaments of metal.

At that early time of the day there was always a thin haze over the meadows. It wasn't quite sinister, but there was something about the vagueness of the landscape that contrasted sharply with how I perceived Holland when I was far away. Everything was normally so defined. So straight and linear. But not at this time of the day.

I loved seeing it again, reacquainting myself with the lowlands country, the place where I was born.

After an hour the landscape changed. On either side of the *autobaan* were thick forests. As a child I was fascinated by those straight lines of trees – how the ground under

A trip to Holland

them was soft and spongy when we went to look for wild blueberries on hot summer days, how the warm scent of the pines made me feel sleepy after a while.

And suddenly there was the turnoff to the village where I was born. I recognised the giant oak tree at the intersection of the main road, the smaller road that led to the street where I lived. And there beside the road was the 11th-century grey brick church with metre-thick walls, where Bart and I got married one hot summer morning. Once when I was a child, the church's foundations needed reinforcing. I'd watched with interest as holes were dug around the old building and archaeologists excavated skeletons that could no longer be identified. Would any of those bones have belonged to members of our family?

The car stopped. We had arrived at my father's house. So different from New Zealand where we had our wide front and spacious back gardens. Here there was only a metre or two to the front door. Tante Jo, my father's new wife, welcomed us.

Inside the house everything looked familiar. The small hallway had the *kapstok*, where we hung our coats. On the tiled floor was the same Persian rug. In the living room with its shiny parquet floor, was the profusion of pot-plants on the wide windowsills, a substitute for greenery during long winter months. The plants looked healthy and well fed, not even one wilting leaf hid amongst them.

Those weeks in a wintry Holland were very special. Not only because we had snow at Christmas but also because our families got to know Miriam. And they all loved her. It was so good to meet up with my sisters and with Bart's family, spending time at their homes, getting to know their children. Miriam soon had a lovely connection with Bart's mother.

And as for me, it was a true reunion with my sisters Eef

and Lydia, our relationship until then having been quite superficial. I'd left Holland as a young woman of 22, and since then I'd been totally focused on making a new life in New Zealand. We'd written letters during the twelve-year gap but that couldn't be compared with having sisterly chats and laughs. Together we visited my brother, Jan, and his wife, Lily, who now lived in the house I'd grown up in.

Opening the door it felt as if I hadn't been away for 12 years even though there had been changes downstairs with a new kitchen and fireplace. There were different curtains, different furniture, but I wasn't prepared for my reaction to arriving again at the house where I'd grown up. Setting foot inside made me suddenly realise that I'd never see my mother again. The grief I had felt all those years opened into expectation. I expected to see her coming down the stairs, or sitting in the corner near the window from where she'd wave to me when I arrived home from school.

We spent Christmas and New Year's Eve with Lydia and Wim and their children. Coming down on Christmas morning and seeing lit candles on the decorated breakfast table reminded me of the Christmas mornings at home. That night Lydia cooked a delicious dinner. On New Year's Eve I offered to make *oliebollen*, the traditional New Year's Eve treat, and in the afternoon of the last day of 1972 we went skating in the winter sunlight. We laughed as we fell on the ice, surrounded by people enjoying themselves too – laughing as they fell, getting up again and moving off at a fast speed. I watched how Miriam too kept moving, not afraid to hold Jan Huib's hand as he skated slowly with her.

Later my sister Eef, her husband, Huug, and their two sons, Arjo and Jan Hugo, arrived, and we celebrated New Year's Eve together. Strong memories: the phone call from Bart who was waking up to summer sunshine after celebrating the last day of the year with our Dutch friends;

A trip to Holland

my daughter sitting between my sisters on that wintry New Year's Eve.

Although my father had recovered from his illness, he was quiet and would sit with his eyes closed. He didn't say much and I could not find the courage to bring my issues to the table, aware at the same time of time ticking by. His new wife was kind to us but I could sense an underlying frustration and anger.

Wherever we stayed Miriam and I had to sleep in the same room, and often in the same bed. But from a young age onward Miriam had needed a light during the night, and it was the first thing she said when we arrived at a new place: 'I want a light.' I couldn't sleep with the light so resorted to sleeping pills.

We visited Dr Thate, our now retired family doctor. One of his sons, Henk, had been in my class at primary school. In 1960 Dr Thate had invited us to visit him the day before we left Holland. He'd said, 'What are you going to do on the ship those six weeks?'

We hadn't known what to say but knew we wouldn't be bored. After all, it was our honeymoon.

He said, 'I'm going to ring the art shop in town to open up so you can buy some drawing materials. You need something to do.'

I was so touched. A busy man like him to think of us and care for our wellbeing. Now, in January 1973, it became a special occasion to see him again. I remember having a fleeting thought: *If only I'd had a father like that.* Overridden by guilt, I pushed the thought away.

One night my father organised for me to visit one of my teachers at the Lyceum. Papa wanted Miriam to stay at home, but I said, 'Of course Miriam comes!'

From the moment we entered Meneer Kamperman's house it was obvious why my father had wanted her to stay at home. My teacher's guarded look at her, at me, then his questioning look at my father made me realise that my father hadn't told him about Miriam's extra chromosome.

I was so angry. Why couldn't he have accepted her as she was, been proud of her? I was a lion, a tiger, a wildebeest – all three in one. She was my daughter, and she was special.

I knew by then that there would be no heartfelt talk between us. It wouldn't happen, that breakthrough in communication I'd hoped for. I would have to go back to New Zealand and come to terms with that.

We left Schiphol on a cold wet day. Miriam tenderly holding a Christmas present doll and wearing the lovely yellow coat with brown edgings Lydia had given her. She looked forward to seeing Dad and the boys again and I felt the same. I had missed Bart so much and vowed I'd never go on such a big trip on my own again.

Producing an abundance of tears I waved to the dear family members who had been so good to us. When would I see them again? I hoped it wouldn't be too long. I'd promised Miriam we'd visit Disneyland on the way home. As we boarded the Boeing Jumbo she said warmly, 'I like Donald Duck.'

Sounds and words

I held my breath as the plane gathered speed along the runway of Schiphol Airport and took off into the icy winter air, the sound of its engines roaring. I took Miriam's hand in mine. She looked tired. Down below, the canals, motorways and bicycle paths had become invisible. Safe journey. Safe landing.

Their sound is gone out into all lands and their words unto the ends of the world.

This chorus from Handel's *Messiah* floated through my mind as I thought of the steady sound of the plane being heard in so many lands. Through the still dark night we went, towards our destination in the southern hemisphere: Aotearoa, the Māori name for New Zealand, the land of the long white cloud. Aotearoa, my home for more than 10 years, the green land of mountains and lakes, the land of plenty I was promised as a young bride in the low country I had just again farewelled. Yes. Yes. The land of plenty. Even now. Because for me *plenty* did not hold images of luxurious homes, the latest gadgets and designer kitchens. Plenty meant feeling safe. Feeling safe and belonging. Having enough food on the table to feel satisfied. Feeling warm, contented. Belonging.

Yes, belonging.

Friends and family.

Their sound is gone out into all lands and their words unto the ends of the world.

But oh, I thought, as we flew, this sound – this deep thundering sound of modern technology – cannot muffle the pain of saying goodbye to loved ones: sisters, brothers, nieces, nephews, friends.

The passengers in the plane settled down for the long journey ahead, the continents to be crossed – flat lands, snow-covered mountains, luscious green jungles. Inside the plane the atmosphere had settled too, the humming sound of the big jet engines a companion to the small, quiet voices. There were mothers with young children on their knees, soft voices encouraging them to close their eyes.

I whispered to my Miriam, 'Hush, darling, hush. Sleep, try to sleep. It's going to be a long, long night.'

She looked at me. 'Night, night, Mum.'

There were elderly people reading, their books relaxed in their hands, grey heads bent under the glare of the spotlights.

A stewardess pulled a trolley with snacks, handed out peanuts and crisps. She emptied colourful little bottles into glasses: gin and tonic, whiskey and soda, brandy and Coke, each glass inviting the passenger to sip … slowly … another sip. An enticement to gradually forget the last few hours of farewell, the images of people and places left behind.

Farewell, my country, farewell, my low-lying land. Farewell, my family. Write soon.

Words to the ends of the world.

I adjusted Miriam's blanket. She looked sleepy already. I opened my cabin bag, took out a paperback and concentrated on my reading.

While I was reading I was aware of the people around me, but didn't feel I had to talk to them. At that moment I didn't want to know about them, didn't feel like talking. There would be many hours ahead for getting acquainted with the people next to me.

As I read the words in the paperback I'd brought, I thought about the village where I was born, with its legends, its history and the lonely graveside I had left behind. I thought of the legacy of stories my mother had left me. Not only her stories about Queen Wilhelmina but also tales and legends that were supposed to have happened in our area.

The plane glided through the night sky, while thousands of metres below people lived, loved, had their dreams.

I would soon be back in the land of my choice, the land I had grown to love despite its different culture, different language.

More memories of the past emerged. Memories as strong as a mighty flowing river with its origin in a high mountain. I couldn't turn off the flow when these thoughts came, thoughts that kept searching for calm, for peace of mind. I was glad that now I could accept them, but I remembered the early years when I rejected them, wishing I could turn off the flow with its overwhelming tributary of recollections.

Turn the tap, turn, turn. I did not need those memories flowing into areas where I didn't want them.

Let me go on with my living here in this world.

I watched Miriam as she slept next to me, wrapped in her blanket, her beautiful face as still as an angel. I was proud of her. She'd done well, adjusting each time to staying in other homes. Family and friends loved her.

I thought back to a Christmas legend my mother told me years ago – and its tale of love.

THINK BACK, CHILD, MY MOTHER HAD SAID WHEN SHE SAT ON my bed one cold Christmas Eve. *Think back to the days when there was no electricity, no running water, only wild morasses*

and forests around the small huts in which people lived. There were landlords but they were a law unto themselves; they had servants to do the work. There was one family who were set as an example for the other villagers. The father and mother went to church, the children attended school and they all did their tasks in the house. Then one day the mother died, and however hard the father tried to keep his family together, he found himself wanting. There was the washing, the scrubbing and the cleaning – how could he do it all and work so hard on the land as well?

He found a woman to marry him who turned out to be a bad stepmother for the children. But on Christmas Eve one of the daughters escaped from her stepmother after she'd finished her duties in the house. Stella had polished the furniture, washed the floors and peeled the potatoes for the evening meal. Now she wandered over the fields, far, far away, all the time dreaming about her real mother, talking to her in the cool frosty air, her breath coming in small fog bubbles from her mouth. As she approached a mound in a clearing of the forest she heard the sound of Christmas bells ringing beneath bushes and trees. Stella could hear her heart beating, and then she heard a voice: 'Come closer, Stella, do not be afraid. We bring peace.'

Slowly she moved forward until she stood in front of the mound. Oh, but then she saw something she could not have imagined in her dreams. Through a wide-open door she saw a long, long table decked with a white damask cloth on which stood silver candelabra, their candles flickering so softly, so gently in the quiet winter air. Around the tables she saw women dancing, floating in white robes, a pure and heavenly radiance around them.

With their hands they invited Stella to enter, and together they all sat at the long table with its pure white cloth and golden cutlery and ate the most beautiful meal she had ever tasted. There was tender, white, roasted pork, its crackling glistening in the candlelight; there were the freshest of green vegetables on gold dishes; the juiciest of bright orange carrots; roasted chestnuts and more. They laughed together, and though the outside air was cold, inside the mound it was warm, cheerful and merry. When it was time to go, the women gave her a silver candelabrum with three candles to light her on the way home. Stella walked carefully, clutching the precious silver in her hands, and hardly dared to breathe for fear the flame would be extinguished. As she walked she remembered the words of the women in white: 'You will find peace.'

AND AS MY PLANE MOVED THROUGH THE STILL NIGHT, CLOSE to the silver stars, close to the white moon, I remembered my mother's voice all those years ago when I was a child listening to the words of the Christmas story. Even now my mother's words were with me, unto another end of the world.

I sat up straight, becoming aware of the voices around me, some softly talking, some raised in excitement and anticipation of a reunion. I thought of the story I would tell the children, a story from the other end of the world about a girl finding silver and gold beneath a plain-looking mound and taking the treasure home.

Their sound is gone out into all lands and their words unto the ends of the world.

I thought about the riches my mother gave me, the wealth of silver and gold stored within me that I now took home to treasure and nourish. A wealth created from inner richness found in the darkness of death and loss.

Back to Dunedin

We had left Schiphol Airport on a wet afternoon, heading for Los Angeles via Chicago. I'd utilised all our combined luggage allowance, and when we got to Chicago we had to go through customs. Miriam's name was on my passport, as it was in those days, and we stood in the queue, shuffling our bags and suitcases, my passport at the ready to show the authorities. There were so many people around us, so different from Momona airport back in Dunedin. Having flown eight hours, our internal clock warned us that it was midnight. Miriam was tired, I was tired.

When it finally was our turn the formidable woman behind the counter asked in a harsh voice, 'Where are you going now?'

I managed a smile. 'We're flying to Los Angeles tonight, and tomorrow night we will return to New Zealand.'

She looked at me, looked at Miriam, then at me again, 'You realise, of course, that you could never live in the United States!'

I wanted to strangle her. I wanted to tell her that I did NOT want to live in the United States – that I wanted to go home to New Zealand where we felt safe and weren't singled out as being different. But of course I didn't say anything. I just put the luggage on a trolley and moved on to catch our plane to Los Angeles, where Miriam met

Back to Dunedin

Mickey Mouse and had a wonderful time.

But people looked at us in America and I wondered why. Did we look so different? Later I mentioned this to Ute, my American friend, and she said, 'People like Miriam are usually kept inside by their families.'

I looked at Miriam's bright eyes and I wondered: *How could they?*

Although we'd had a special time renewing our family ties, I was glad to be back in Dunedin. Those hills, those blue skies, the expanse of it all. The sharpness of colour a contrast to the dark of a European winter.

A divided heart

The plane glides through the night
leaving continents behind.
Thousands of metres below us
people live,
love.
Have their dreams.
And people eat *oliebollen*,
skate on rivers,
dream of parliamentary peace.

I've learnt to live
with memories of the past.
I have shelved the trill of the nightingale in May.
The bells of the carillon in the market place.

Soon I will be back in the land of my choice,
the new land I've come to love.
A different language,
chime of bellbirds, tūī,
a university clock tower.

Renovating (again)

Bart and I were no experts when it came to house renovating but we knew we wanted to have an open-plan look in our roughcast villa. So while Miriam and I had been gallivanting in the northern hemisphere Bart, Foster and Ray had pulled down a chimney that had been between two rooms in our house. Even now they still talk about the skip that was filled to overflowing with chimney rubble and old timber bits from the two rooms. In the car on our way to the airport Bart had said, 'This is a good job to do while you and Miriam are away. Us men can do the rough work and when you're back we'll concentrate on easier stuff.'

'I'll do the painting when I get home,' I said.

They'd worked so hard but Miriam and I returned to a mess. What a contrast to the neatness of the Dutch houses. Our walls had psychedelic splashes of Polyfilla, there were four-by-twos lying on the floor, sawdust covered all the furniture, and the electric saw-bench was now standing in the dining area. For one moment I wanted to turn round and fly straight back to Holland. But praise was due and it came with superlatives – they really had done well.

WE HAD ENJOYED THE RENOVATING PROCESS AND WERE feeling proud of our achievements, but after my return from Holland we decided to have a new house built at the back of our quarter-acre section. During the long winter evenings we browsed through home-and-garden magazines, trying to decide what sort of house would best fit our section. We got to work, and were delighted when our old house sold within a week after we'd put it on the market.

In September 1974 we moved into the new house. With its dark-brown, cedar-stained timber on the top part and solid, white-painted concrete blocks as a base, it had been built to last a long while. During the shift from the top house to the bottom house we walked down the drive into the garage, holding boxes of clothes and small possessions in our arms, and Miriam and I sang the John Lennon song 'Imagine', including the line about having *no* possessions. And I thought how lucky we were to have this opportunity to start afresh in a sunny house with lots of rooms. These rooms felt a little empty for the first few years, though, despite all the things we'd carried down the hill! While we were juggling mortgages and normal household expenses, carpets and curtains had to wait, and our simple furnishings didn't go far.

Bart and I worked hard now to develop the garden while the children played around us, forever finding games where they could chase each other. Miriam would often go inside and dance to her records – the Bee Gees, Cliff Richard and many more.

Surrounded by bags of cement, sand and a pile of grey, uneven-shaped rocks, we created rock walls close to the house. Water and a fine mixture of cement and sand bonded the stones together. I remember thinking that nothing on earth would make these walls move once the mixture between the rocks had dried.

Learning to fly

I had been anxious when I started work in the Department of Political Studies about thinking in and using a second language during work all the time. And what about the people I'd be working for – would they make me feel inferior.

I couldn't take part in the discussions, but I loved being in an environment where challenges were discussed, arguments bounced around and people kept finding new ways to continue discussions on the same topics. I started to read different books: B F Skinner's *Walden Two* and *Verbal Behavior*; Hitler's *Mein Kampf*. Searching for a better life. Regardless of consequences. My reading was slow but I wanted to learn. I also enjoyed typing articles the academics had written, even though I hadn't got a clue about the political situations being examined. Absorbing, learning, learning, absorbing. Trying to find even the tiniest bit of understanding of what made people want to go to war.

I began to think about my own life from a different perspective. My childhood, my teenage years in Holland. Coming here to Dunedin. A wife, a mother, a friend. I kept my dreams of freedom close, tried to be the person my husband and our Dutch friends expected me to be. Organised. House-proud. Devoted to my family.

The freedom I wanted wasn't associated with the hippy movement of that period, though if I had grown up in a different family I might well have wanted to join. I wanted to find out about life, and enrolled in courses on personal development run by a local church. I loved Bart dearly and people would forever comment what a strong bond there was between us, but that didn't mean we had a peaceful existence. I was often sharp and impatient. Bart took time to find a reply, sometimes walked away.

But where had I been? Immersed in novels, autobiographies: different lives in different places.

Dreaming.

In the seventies I read *Man's Search for Meaning*, psychiatrist Viktor Frankl's book about how he survived his experiences in a concentration camp by finding meaning in small things – showing the ability of a human being to choose opportunities. *Make the right choice.*

From my mid-thirties I began to look for meaning in my life, tried to guide my thinking along the lines Frankl advocated. But where could I find this Meaning of Life? In cooking, cleaning and baking? In voluntary work? In the mixing of concrete for retaining walls in our garden? Being kind to my neighbours wasn't a problem and I was generous with my affections, but I felt diminished when I couldn't talk about my homesickness, my longing for our family in Europe.

Why don't you go home if you don't like it here?

Some days I was close to understanding what Meaning encompassed, imagined that the barriers were disappearing. I tried to talk of Meaning to Bart, but his concentration focused on our day-by-day living. Electricity bills, car maintenance and petrol, and of course there was the running of a household.

'You'll have to watch the housekeeping money – we need more timber for the next lot of renovations. We'll get up early on Saturday. Finish the kitchen sink.'

We were deep into the rebuilding by then. Every Friday

Learning to fly

lunchtime we visited Fletcher's, acquiring more building materials to be slotted into their right places over the weekend. Working hard until late, often finishing with a midnight supper of bacon and eggs.

But there were relaxing times as well. One winter a white frost lay for days around Dunedin, and on a Sunday morning while it was still dark we filled the car boot with picnic things – a Primus to heat a huge pot of *erwtensoep* or pea soup, bacon and egg pies, and the thermette for coffee.

On the Pigroot, the wonderful name of the long drive towards Central Otago, we watched the sun on the hills. At the skating dam in Oturehua the children rushed down the slope on their hired skates, with Bart and me following on our old-fashioned Dutch skates, long and slender. We relished the freedom as we glided over the ice, watching the other skaters flowing in and around each other in the crisp winter air. We went to the area where curlers were throwing their massive stones made of granite, tense with determination to choose the right way to hit their own curling stone. Faces guarded and hard as the curl itself, as hard as the landscape they lived and worked in.

Miriam wasn't keen to try out the skates but pretended she was skating when she moved into the middle of the dam and started to turn round and round, moving forwards and backwards, arms outspread, hands bright in red gloves. Then coming back to us, looking as happy as the boys.

We heated *erwtensoep* on the Primus. The bacon and egg pies were divided up, the water in the thermette heated enough for instant coffee. And it was so good to be there, to be part of this. The crispness of the day, the bright sun, warmed by the food, with the fresh air around us.

We drove home in the dark, the children quiet on the back seat.

Memories. Skating with Ans. Meeting Bart on the ice all those years ago. That excitement of attraction. All the good things I, as a young girl, hoped would happen.

And they had happened.

Bart took my hand as we stopped outside our house. 'It's been a good day, Hubel,' he said.

IN 1975 I STARTED WORK FULL-TIME IN THE DEPARTMENT of Surveying at the university. I loved working with young people, and felt comfortable with the level-headedness of the staff. Discussions in the staffroom were a highlight – being more based in reality than the esoteric world I'd entered in my previous position. Those years were among the best in my life. For the first time I began to feel a sense of 'self', I began to like who I was. I realised I wasn't just a pesky young sister who needed to be punished or a rebellious daughter or an immigrant with an accent and a different past regardless of how hard I tried to suppress those differences. The time had come when there was no need to suppress them any more. A time when I became myself.

Another journey

In the autumn of 1976 an invitation came from Bart's family: 'We'd love you to be with us when we celebrate Vader and Moeder's fiftieth wedding anniversary later this year. We will help you get here.'

I said to Bart, 'Why don't we take the boys with us? It'll be an opportunity for them to meet up with real family, to see the land where we were born. Perhaps learn a bit of Dutch?'

After Miriam's birth we'd decided to speak only English with her, not wanting to confuse her, yet years after our trip to Holland she still remembered the words her family spoke to her in Dutch.

We were grateful when Joan and Peter Gardner offered to look after Miriam while we were in Holland. We knew she'd be well cared for.

Now here was our family again at Schiphol Airport. Though not as many as that first time – some had passed away, others had had to sell their family homes and move into retirement complexes. Cameras came out of handbags, and as they clicked I thought, *It's as if I haven't been away.*

I saw Foster and Ray's confusion as they were over-whelmed by strangers whom they were told were family. The members of Bart's family and mine had waited a long time for this moment, and while their arms were moving and their heads shaking they bombarded our sons with indecipherable, 50-mile-an-hour Dutch.

I introduced everyone slowly in English. 'Here are our sons, Foster and Ray. They're both so excited to finally meet you all.'

'I want to take a photo of the two of you,' Mijntje said. 'You look very different from when I saw you last.'

They bent down and hugged the boys, one after the other – the grandparents first, and then all the aunts and uncles from different towns and villages in Holland. Their cousins approached them. Six of them. One said in English, '*Dag*, I'm Jan Huib. We've found bikes for both of you and when you visit us we'll go on a bike ride.'

Bart's mother took their hands. Using the English language she said, 'I am Oma, your father's mother.' She glanced at me, then said to the boys. 'I feel sad your other Oma is not here any more to see you – such beautiful boys from the other side of the world. She loved you too. But enough of sadness now. Tell me. You liked the flying? You were not afraid in the plane?'

Bart's mother was a stately woman, pepper-and-salt waves framing her long face. She wore a navy blue suit with a straight, well-cut skirt and a jacket that looked as if it had been moulded on her. I remembered how proud she'd always been of her clothes – her silk shirts, and shoes and bags that matched, and how one day, before we left Holland, she'd said, 'Never buy rubbish, Huub. It won't last.'

Their hands joined, grandmother and grandchildren walked ahead through the airport to the carpark, talking, gesticulating. I heard Bart's mother's voice: 'You think we are funny, *ja*? Don't forget, we have love for you. Lots and lots of love, as deep and as big as the ocean.'

Ray chuckled. 'I liked your parcels, Oma.'

'I'm so glad you're here, *schatje*. We make a good time *samen*. Together. I have more presents for you at my house.'

Walking beside my father, I said to him, 'I wish Moeke could have been here.'

Guilt. Guilt about the promise I'd made the day we left for New Zealand: 'I'll be back.'

Always that guilt.

My father didn't reply. I wondered what he was thinking. He was pleased to see me. Did my appearance bring back his own feelings of guilt?

No. I won't think about all that.

Yet I could never love my father. Not even feel pity for him, now he was an old man.

In the gigantic carpark Wim lifted our luggage into the boot of his car. We drove through long, flat meadows divided by straight, narrow ditches. I felt a tug in my heart when I glimpsed church spires in the distance, looking as if they were sprinkled into those meadows. Some of the spires were in familiar towns, others I couldn't place any more.

We stayed with Lydia and Wim for our first week in Holland. On our second night we were sitting at the dinner table and I looked around at the happy faces – the children sharing jokes, the adults enjoying the lovely meal Lydia had prepared, and I thought of our Miriam. *She would have loved this so much. I hope she's all right. Will she manage to go to her special class at Intermediate?* And then at once, as I was thinking of her, knowing she was far away, it was as if a powerful load was lifted from my shoulders. *I don't need to worry, I can't do anything here. Enjoy your time. You need this break.*

BART'S SISTER, LIEN, TOOK THE BOYS TO EAT *POFFERTJES* – small puffy pancakes sprinkled with icing sugar. Mijntje and I talked about our different lifestyles while the boys read *Asterix* in English – my sister-in-law still worked at a library and had met Harry, an obvious soulmate. I met up with my childhood friend, Ans. She and her husband had a photography shop in Zwolle but they lived in Wijhe, in a rural area south of Zwolle. We didn't need any preliminaries to start talking about our lives. It was like old times.

We visited Volendam where we admired the traditional dress of the women. Striped skirts. Black aprons. Coral chokers. 'Look, Mum,' said Foster. 'Those orange chokers are like your necklace.'

We visited Tante Gerrie in Rotterdam. 'I'll never forget my visit to see your country,' she said 'If I were younger, I would come to live with you forever.' Then there was her next question: 'And you – would you like to live here again in Holland? And no lies.'

I had asked myself the same question during the past few weeks. Would I? 'I don't know,' I said. 'I love our life of freedom in New Zealand. I don't think anybody criticises the way I hang out the washing now. Or comments on the way I dress. But I do miss our families.'

While in Rotterdam we took the boys to the Euromast, an observation tower specially built for the 1960 Dutch flower show, Floriade. We went up in the lift, Foster and Ray anxiously watching the lift attendant. From the observation deck we looked at the panoramic view of the city, which had been totally rebuilt after the war. We stared down at the massive harbour, at ships in many different sizes and colours, ships with foreign owners. The harbour was opened in the 14th century, and it was the world's busiest port until Shanghai took over. I felt small at the thought that so many people left this harbour, returned, and then left again, never to return.

As we descended, the lift attendant noticed our green Air New Zealand bags, looked at Foster and Ray and said, 'Because you've come so far you can go up again – a free

Another journey

ride! Your parents can come too.' I felt so proud to say we now lived in New Zealand.

I LOVED BEING BACK IN HOLLAND, VISITING FAMILY AND OLD school friends, popping in at the neighbours, now old and grey but still interested in me. 'Every week we ask your father about you and your family. He tells us your news. His eyes are sad when he talks about you, so far away.'

Guilt. Always that guilt.

I was aware of a strong bond between my sisters Eef and Lydia. I felt an outsider when they talked together about things they were interested in and that I hadn't got the faintest clue about. Even though most family members laughed that my letters were like newspapers, the return correspondence from Holland had been sporadic and superficial, and it was only now that I heard all that had happened while I was away. So much that I hadn't been part of, so many changes in the village, and in the city where I went to school.

A strange thing occurred to me. While I was in Holland I still felt homesick, but not for Holland, because here I was, but for New Zealand. Whenever I thought of the wide views from our house in Dunedin, the garden with its abundance of green foliage, I felt homesick *for New Zealand*.

'I'm torn between two worlds,' I said to Bart. 'Will that ever change? I don't fit in here now. Every shopkeeper asks me why I speak Dutch with an accent, yet my accent in New Zealand still classifies me as an outsider.'

Surprising ourselves

'Before we go back to New Zealand I want to see the Delta Works', Bart said. So we drove south to Zeeland crossing one of the big rivers on a motorised pontoon. Behind and in front of our car other people waited to drive away into the rural countryside once the pontoon had docked.

Standing outside the car, I looked at the fast-flowing river around the pontoon. I straightened my back to resist the fierce wind blowing through my hair. I wanted that wind to blow my head clean, free from the destroying thoughts of what happened in my past. Would I ever experience that? Above us seagulls screamed, flying high yet waiting to be fed.

Driving through the province of Zeeland with its many waterways I was reminded of Abel Tasman's travels. In his lifetime only shipping vessels were used to link these waterways but now the Delta Works enabled easy travel between the northern and southern parts of the province. And then I couldn't help thinking how easy it was now to travel between hemispheres compared to the days of long voyages endured by the 17th century's navigators.

'Nearly 2000 people drowned in the 1953 North Sea flood,' Bart told the boys, trying to keep his wind-blown hair away from his face. 'Soon we'll see the flood protection project – the Delta Plan. This was sped up by building primary dams as well as secondary dams, and in October 1986 the Eastern Scheldt Dam storm surge barrier was completed. It's a tidal dam that can be closed whenever an extreme high tide is expected.'

So much water around us. Caissons as high and long as apartment blocks, built as a framework that, at the flick of a switch, became a solid barricade to protect the land from the damaging effects of a roaring North Sea.

Holding my arms around my sons' small shoulders, I said, 'The people in Zeeland often had to cope with floods that caused a lot of damage. Imagine always living with that threat of water. No wonder the motto of the province is *Luctor et Emergo – I Struggle and I Emerge.*'

'I suppose as emigrants we've had to take that motto as our guide,' I continued. 'Struggling to hold our heads above water during the times when we've felt like lambs but had to be lions to keep our own identity.'

Bart was looking at me. 'I'm glad we kept ours,' he said.

But had we? Had we?

WE SAID TO OUR SONS, 'BEFORE WE GO BACK TO NEW Zealand we'll take you to the *bedriegertjes.*'

They looked at us. 'What's that?'

How could I explain? 'It means Tricksters. Or perhaps, Deceivers.'

'Who will be deceived?'

We drove to Castle Rosendael in Velp where the *bedriegertjes* are. Together we walked along lanes with centuries-old oak and beech trees, along paths that divided planted areas. There were roses everywhere as well as rose-covered arches, and annuals in pink and red. In the middle were large ponds with fountains.

I remembered my mother taking me here after the war. My stomach nervous with excitement after first travelling by train, walking next to her to the castle, seeing the sun shining on her dark hair. My mother's voice in my head: 'Small fountains are hidden everywhere and you never know when they will be turned on. You'll be suddenly surprised with sprays of water.' I didn't like to be suddenly surprised. I wanted to know what would happen.

Now I watched our sons running ahead, darting and dancing on the tiles, constantly aware of the fun of being tricked by the unexpected sprays. What would they do when it happened? *When, when?*

I saw again the round tower with its four-metre-deep walls. I thought about how prisoners had to await execution here. *What had they done that was so bad they had to die? What about the earls and dukes who lived here all those centuries ago? What about the women dressed in beautiful and elaborate clothes?*

As a child I expected magic as I walked past the shell-studded sculptures and fountains, past a waterfall with two marble dolphins at the top that suddenly caught me unaware – *Moeke was right!* – with sprays of water: the *bedriegertjes* playing their trick. But always with me, whatever the magic or excitement, there was dread and fear.

Will he come to my room tonight?

Will there be another war?

Now I watched our sons stepping over stones in the little creeks, egging each other on: *Let's try the tiles where the fountains are hidden, see if they work.* Confident, free, able to speak out. Yelling to us, 'Mum, Dad, come and get wet!'

Around us people laughed, children squeaked. Make-believe waterfalls gushed, and fountains exploded their sprays high up in the air, creating rainbows in all sizes.

It was not my fault. The war. My father.

It was not my fault.

Surprising ourselves

When it was time to leave and we were assembled at the airport's departing point, surrounded and held by our families, it wasn't only my coral necklace that felt tight around my throat.

Lydia cried, 'Come back soon. I miss you both so much.'

Turning to Bart, I whispered, 'Let's go. Now. I can't bear it any longer.'

While our passports were being checked, Foster said, 'I don't know why you had to leave Holland. It's great fun here.'

Singing

I've always loved singing. When I was 10 years old I joined a children's choir. One night the conductor said, 'We're going to have a concert in a few weeks' time. I want you to sing a few songs by yourself.'

I blushed, and with a beating heart, I stuttered, 'I can't do that. I can't.'

He rang my parents. They tried to persuade me. I refused.

At high school I joined the school choir and loved it. I can still remember what we sang during our school performances. I learnt about other types of music, so different from the Moody and Sankey hymns and the Doris Day songs.

In 1961 I met a young woman in our Dunedin suburb who told me about the choir she had joined. 'Why don't you come with me?' she said. And so I went with her to a rehearsal of the Dunedin Choral Society and joined the sopranos. Professor Peter Platt was the conductor. It was a wonderful experience for me, and I continued singing with the choir until just before Miriam's birth, when I stopped for a few months with all the demands of being a mother. Then the twins came and I resigned because of too much work on the home front. When we returned from our trip to Holland with the boys, I joined the choir again, this time with Bart. It was now called the Schola Cantorum, with Peter Warwick as its conductor.

Singing

They were rehearsing Johannes Brahms' *A German Requiem*. Sir David Willcocks was going to conduct the performance. Bart was a good tenor, always welcome in any choir and I joined the sopranos again.

Those months were special. While we were in Holland we'd learnt that Bart's mother, who had greeted the boys so excitedly at Schiphol airport had become ill, and we'd been told to prepare ourselves for the worst. We felt helpless but were very grateful all our children had met her.

Brahms wrote *A German Requiem* after his own mother died, and both Bart and I both found tremendous solace in this music. We knew that any time we could expect a phone call from Holland, but when it came, it was still a shock. Moeder had been a wonderful mother and mother-in-law. Our thoughts at that time were constantly back in Holland with Bart's family

At a choir rehearsal later that year I met a woman who had come from the UK with her husband and three children. Her husband was also in the choir. We sang, they sang. They had three children, we had three children. And so I invited them for Sunday afternoon coffee and cake. We talked, the children played games and a wonderful friendship started with Sue and Robin Harvey and their family. We shared a love for music, for books and for the outdoors.

We often went for walks on Sunday afternoons to beaches at Taieri Mouth, Murderer's Beach, Doctor's Point – the children running ahead and having fun, all of us returning to our house or to their house for a meal. Over the years we've shared much sadness and much joy, and their family has increased with in-laws and grandchildren.

Meeting up with these friends and the friends we'd made over the years was a highlight for us. Many of them had also experienced learning to live in this new land and accepted us as we were. Whether they were born in New Zealand or

ASTRIDE A FIERCE WIND

anywhere else in the world, we were aware how much their friendships enriched our life.

Without family in this country, we have had so much to be grateful for with our New Zealand friends.

How to deal with grief from a distance?

Lydia and Wim had moved with their two sons to Loosdrecht, while Eef and Huug lived with their two in the southern province of Limburg. The families still met regularly, and even though they lived in different parts of the country and there were age differences among the cousins, the boys got on well.

It was 2 January 1980. Wim's birthday. Eef's younger son, Jan Hugo, aged 22, had just bought another car. 'I want to go to Oom Wim's birthday in Loosdrecht,' he told his parents. 'I want to show them my new car. I'll stay overnight and drive back tomorrow.'

He left the house, excited to take the car for a long spin.

Later that afternoon in Loosdrecht he showed off his treasured vehicle, excitedly pointing out all the advantages that this car had compared to his old one.

After the birthday meal Jan Hugo said to his cousin Jan Huib, 'I want to fill the tank up for the trip home. Do you want to come? See what my car's like?'

And off they went. Two cousins. Joking, laughing, having a good time. Jan Huib, captain of a soccer team. Interested in photography. Interested in so many things. A good friend to many. Jan Hugo – jovial, caring. Loved cars. Always popular.

Family.

It was a rainy night. The petrol tank was filled and the boys were on their way back to Lydia and Wim's home, where coffee and cake were waiting for them. The narrow road was lined with trees, as Dutch country roads often are. On that dark, wintry night Jan Hugo drove carefully. On one narrow road there was a truck in front of them. A truck that had to brake suddenly. A truck with power brakes. Jan Hugo slammed his foot on his own brake.

The car hit a tree, spun off the road.

We got a phone call. 'Jan Huib is seriously ill. Jan Hugo will be all right.'

Oh, that distance, that awful bloody distance. I wanted to be there, I wanted to give love, share love and sadness. Be there to listen.

Three weeks of anxious waiting. Then another phone call. The loss of a much loved son. We shared intense grief about the passing of that lovely bright boy – cheeky, impulsive and daring.

On the morning of the funeral I rang Lydia. We cried. Later she wrote, 'Your phone call gave me peace to get through that day. You were so close to me.'

I rang Eef. 'How is Jan Hugo?'

What did I expect? A young man with a warm heart, proud to show off the car to his cousin, how would he deal this?

Eef's voice so quiet, so slow. 'He doesn't know what to do. It will take time.'

Two families closely connected.

Connected by inner scars that would take a lot of healing.

A FEW MONTHS LATER THE UNRELENTING RING OF THE TELE-phone in the night.

How to deal with grief from a distance?

Lydia's voice, breathless: 'Our father has gone to meet his maker.'

'Should I come?'

'We can manage.'

I listened to Brahms' *Requiem*, written as a consolation to the living. The soprano soared, '*Ihr habt nun Traurigkeit …*'

But for me there was no consolation for that sadness. Not yet.

I thought of the conflicting messages I'd received from him over the years. Couldn't forget my suspicions of him and his ambiguous behaviour, and even though I felt sad for my sisters I was quietly relieved when he died. That relief overrode any guilt I might have experienced for having those thoughts that came forth from my shadow. Thoughts I often couldn't voice, but could now accept.

The apple tree

Close to the back of our new house were apple trees. There was one tree whose fruit had an intriguing flavour – tart, yet sweet when yellowing. At the beginning of each autumn Bart picked all the apples off the tree and I preserved them, producing dozens of bottles filled with apple sauce. We'd always done this since we moved into the house in February 1966. Apple sauce was a favourite in any Dutch family, eaten not only as dessert but also often as a second vegetable to go with meatballs and red cabbage. Or with green beans, or cauliflower topped by a white sauce sprinkled with nutmeg.

There was another apple tree closer to the back of the house. It grew apples nobody liked, and so they rotted on the ground during autumn, occasionally being pecked by birds. But it was so good to sit under this tree and read on a summer afternoon, safe in its protective shadow. The apples might not be any good but in spring the blossom was luscious and promising, and I loved its dramatic shape.

In the eighties I learnt a lot about hospital life. Each time I left home with my bag packed for a stay in hospital Miriam said, 'I pray for you, Mum.' After each operation she brought letters she'd written and I was always surprised at her skills – not only in typing the beautiful letters, but also how good her spelling was. Her words showed her caring nature.

Do not worry about the Sisters they are friendly looking after the patients and try to made friends with you. I hope you get more new friends at the Same Ward.

I am a good helper around the house because if my mother stay at Hospital I could peel the potatoes for Dinner at night. On Monday I will do the breakfast dishes and the Lunch dishes and I laid the table ready.

IN SEPTEMBER 1980 I WAS AT HOME RECOVERING FROM A hysterectomy, still feeling tired and listless, reading under the tree laden with pink blossom. I'd planted a New Dawn close to the trunk and in summer I'd thought about how we'd have white roses with pink edges trailing the branches.

The phone went. I went inside to answer it. It was Bart. 'I'm going to cut down the apple tree tonight,' he said.

My heart rate jumped, my mouth went dry, my tongue numb. I stuttered, 'No, you can't do that. I love that tree. Its leaves in autumn, the shade ... the birds singing. The blossom right now. And I've planted the New Dawn.'

'Doesn't matter, that tree has to go.'

'But why?'

'It looks messy.' The phone beeped.

I lay down on my bed and cried for my beloved tree. I tried to see the reason for Bart's decision but couldn't. The scars in my belly hurt with all the crying. That tree wasn't in anyone's way. I knew that when Bart wanted something done, it would be done. He was still the autocratic Dutch head of the family. But I wasn't taking it this time, even though I felt weak.

Bart came home at 5.30. He slammed the front door, stormed into the kitchen, where I was putting together a meal. 'That tree will go.'

'No, that tree stays. We get told not to sit in the sun too long, so this tree will stay and give us a safe place to sit.'

'It's an awful-looking tree. The apples are no good.'

'That tree stays.' I switched off the elements of the stove and said, 'There! You can do the rest. I'm going back to bed.'

A few hours later I changed my soaking pillowcase. I felt sore, tired.

But I didn't hear the sound of the chainsaw.

Later that summer we asked an expert for suggestions to improve our garden. He followed us downstairs, and when we went outside through the sliding door he looked up at the apple tree and said, 'That tree must definitely stay.'

In the process of finding photos for this book I was amazed how many photos we took of people sitting at that spot under the apple tree. Initially around the big barbecue table that Bart had so beautifully made, always a barbecue close by, and later, at a table gifted by good friends from Holland. Cocky and Gideon Janse had been visiting their son Vincent who was doing his student elective on a farm in Gore and we invited them to spend time with us. They showed their appreciation for our hospitality by organising the delivery of a beautiful round wooden table. We bought the chairs to match and it became an even more favourite place.

MY HEALTH CONTINUED TO BE A PROBLEM WITH OPERATIONS and a new illness loomed. It had already become necessary for me to reduce my working hours after several operations. But now I needed a further operation for breast cancer, which would take place in the week before Easter 1981.

The apple tree

This was the year I decided to make my Easter bread early. The rich, yeasty mixture needed to rise several times before it could be shaped into an oval, then filled with almond paste and folded again. Children especially enjoyed the melted butter and brandy icing.

Wandering into the kitchen, grabbing a handful of raisins, Ray asked, 'I hope you're going to make *weihnachtsstollen* again at Christmas time?'

'Oh, yes, I will. And I'll use the same recipe I always do.'

I needed to concentrate on a tradition. It would make me feel better. While I was kneading, shaping and folding the sweet, almond-flavoured dough I thought of the preparations our families would be making towards Easter in a European spring. And as always memories returned of the yearly performance of the *St Matthew Passion*: its dramatic music, the chorales. The words of Bach's oratorio repeated in my mind, '*Wenn ich einmal soll scheiden, So scheide nicht von mir.*' 'Be near me, Lord, when dying, O part not Thou from me!' I didn't want to die. Not yet. I would fight.

Yet as the oven filled the kitchen with the warming aroma of our traditional bread, I felt scared. What *if* I died? What would happen to the children? I'd always had a vivid imagination but it was hard to imagine I might not see the children grow up into adults.

I took the Easter bread from the oven, so beautiful, so rich. I dribbled a mixture of brandy and melted butter over the hot surface, poured myself a glass of redcurrant juice and went out to sit on the balcony in the fading afternoon sun.

The leaves of the apple tree below were showing signs of gold. I was glad the tree was still there and tried to forget the angry row of last year. The hills still had that late-afternoon sheen, and a long white cloud hung over Mt Cargill. A lonely bellbird fluttered around the apple tree, trying to find the right branch to perch on.

I thought back to the last few weeks. To when I was told I needed the cancer operation. How, when I arrived home from my visit to the specialist, Bart had said to me, 'I will look after you.'

I woke up in a hospital bed, my chest tightly wrapped in white cloths. An elderly nun in a white robe pushed the high bed to the window. 'Watch that sunset, dear, it is especially beautiful tonight.'

Miriam visited and gave me a letter. Here is an excerpt: 'I Still love you and I hope you will be Saved I am going to miss you at Easter Sunday. The Dogs will going to missed you and we hope you will be at home normal.'

I hugged my daughter so tight, and alone at night I wept with both sadness and laughter. My silent prayers were that I would see her and our sons grow up.

I returned home determined to find faith and healing in my garden. And eventually the day came when I found courage to look at my body in the mirror, to observe the physical damage, the raw scar, the imbalance. The long, slow recovery to strength was helped by a kind and sympathetic surgeon, Mr Michael Shackleton. And I acknowledged my real friends – those who, when they visited me, left their black, filmy shirts at home, clothing that showed their (to me) perfect breasts.

I often sat in our living room in the quiet hours after midnight, my fears for the children so deep as I worried what would happen if I could no longer care for them. I knew Foster and Ray would be all right, but what would happen to Miriam? How would her needs be met?

I stood in the garden amidst a riot of flowers – dahlias, day lilies and daisies. *Be strong, you'll survive this. Think positive.* Lydia's words over the phone: 'Pray to God, but keep rowing to the shore.' I didn't feel like praying, let alone rowing. I didn't have the nature of an Amazon or a Joan of

The apple tree

Arc. I wanted to hide. Hide my damaged body.

Will Bart still love me? This damaged body? Bart might leave me. He's popular with women.

The motto on my Dutch passport: *Je Maintiendrai – I Will Maintain.*

I said it out loud, again and again.

Je Maintiendrai.

At school I'd learnt about the young duke Willem of Nassau who in 1544 inherited the princedom of Orange from his cousin René of Chalons. The motto of the Chalons family was *Je Maintiendrai Chalons*. Prince Willem took not only the princedom but also its motto, which he changed to *Je Maintiendrai Nassau*. Later it became *Je Maintiendrai*, the Prince using the words in the wider sense of declaring and maintaining his honour and dignity for himself and his descendants.

As I recuperated I wandered around the garden, the place I thought of as my spiritual home. I picked dead flowers, sorted out which plants I would shift to a sunnier place in winter and ordered a delivery of compost.

I read survival stories – books about Amazon expeditions, mountaineers, cancer patients, thereby filling any barren part of my soul with new images. I found more in stories about goddesses from Greek mythology and began to understand the power of myth. I wondered whether I was a Hestia, goddess of the hearth – self-effacing and anonymous – or a Demeter with a strong maternal instinct.

Slowly I regained my strength. I knew that whatever happened, I would maintain my own dignity, the honour of being myself.

Je Maintiendrai.

Filling the house

And so the years moved on. Bart and I were busy with our jobs. We had an occasional clash of wills. His was strongest, fuelled by the time-honoured Dutch Father Knows Best tradition, but I was so used to giving way that it seldom came to an outburst. I needed support, so I enrolled in an assertiveness training course at the Cameron Centre. At last I learnt to voice any thought from my point of view.

We had boarders. Their contribution to the household helped with paying the mortgages. One year a young man from Motueka arrived on a motorbike. Peter was a particular joy to have with us and fitted well into our family. We took him skating; he played card games with the children; he helped Bart make concrete. He loved my cooking. We were sorry to see him go after two years' study at Otago.

But our family was our priority.

On Sundays we'd go to the beach. Brighton, Taieri Mouth, Karitane, St Clair or St Kilda. In summer the children and I waited in the surf for the right wave to throw us upon the beach. Then we'd go back again and again, waiting for another push of the ocean, the whippets shivering on the beach, watching us intensely. In winter we walked the dogs along the same beach and watch them chase the seagulls into the water.

I still loved the sea with its endless moods and movements. Long Pacific rollers slowly drawing themselves out

Filling the house

to nothingness, leaving behind the muddy brown of wet sand. I saw the extension from sea to sky, overlapping with its grey edges, and thought of all the places bordered by an ocean. Wide, spacious places with their own history and connections, strong as the rocks in our newly created wall. I wondered how those rocks would look in a hundred years. Who would live in our house then? What changes would have been made?

Often I'd sit in the yellow sand dunes – dreaming, enjoying the cleansing freedom of the sea. Down below on the beach the children would play with a blue kite, the dogs yapping and running with them. I'd hear their excited cries, stretch out my legs, lean back on my hands and look out over the ocean. Underneath the white foam of each wave was a shadow, dark and threatening, just before the wave hit the beach. I remember thinking: Oh, this beach, so wonderful, so clean and deserted.

We often spent our summer holidays in Central Otago. In Arrowtown with its river, Queenstown, Wānaka. We loved staying close to the lakes. Later we travelled to the Nelson area. Anywhere, as long as there was water. We'd sunbathe on our lilos, sometimes racing each other by paddling with our arms as fast as we could, other times dreaming and floating amongst that healing scenery.

We made friends in Dunedin who later moved to other cities. Invitations to visit arrived. Family members would continue to come to us from the other side of the world.

The house would be totally cleaned whenever family was due to stay. For weeks before an arrival I was totally neurotic, making sure everything was spic and span. 'What will people say?' was a frequent comment at those times when I thought the house wasn't up to the standard they'd expect, and the rambling garden was so different from Dutch gardens. How would they react?

Once they'd arrived and taken in our different lifestyle,

it was a delight to show our visitors around Dunedin and the South Island, caring for them in the best possible way we could. They soon found out how proud we were to live here. In turn they brought us up to date with news of the family, often small things nobody thought of writing about, yet part of the context of family life.

The first time she came here, Eef said, 'I can't put my finger on it but New Zealand has a special scent.' She said it again the second time she visited, and the third.

I don't think she meant the lingering smell of powerful household cleaning fluids used before her arrival!

AND YES, WE STILL LOVED LIVING IN OPOHO AND WERE grateful that the Opoho Church had sponsored us in 1960. For many years we were actively involved, Bart as a deacon and a Sunday school teacher, while I was an organist and a member of the Association of Presbyterian Women – first on the committee, later as secretary and vice-president. Our children went to Sunday school, and both Ray and Foster enjoyed being part of the active youth group, which was mainly made up of university students during the late seventies and early eighties when Dr Peter Gardner was our minister.

Opoho Church had a large contingent of students who used to come to the evening service before the youth group started. At any time there were also the – often older – theological students who attended Knox College in preparation for the Presbyterian ministry, many of whom had moved with their families to live in Opoho during their training. We regularly invited the youth group to come for supper after they'd completed their evening sessions. Once a month they and their families would come for tea – finding

Filling the house

places on chairs and on the floor – so they could have a change of scene from their student flats and enjoy being in a warm home. There was lots of laughter and it felt good to be surrounded by bright young people. On Saturdays the oven worked overtime, filling the house with its warm and enticing aromas of luscious cakes and heartening savouries – apple cakes, *kugelhupfs*, bacon and egg pies, mousetraps and whatever else I felt inspired to produce.

I often thought of the time when our children would leave home. We knew that eventually we would have to find a place for Miriam to help her development into adulthood. But what about the boys? They had done well at Otago Boys' High School, and in the mid-eighties went to university. Foster gained a surveying degree at Otago, while Ray went to Massey to study for a food technology degree, which he later changed to a chemistry degree. Where would they go once they'd completed their studies? What would their interests be to make their life richer?

At Foster's graduation in December 1987 I decided to become a student myself. I'd never had much confidence in myself and shrugged away suggestions of friends over the years to enrol at Otago and do some more study. *Oh, no, I'm too stupid. No, I can't do that – that is for other people.* But gradually the wish to know more about the horizons of other worlds was too tempting, and in 1988 I enrolled part-time for a paper in Greek and Roman literature. Reading and learning about *The Oresteia*, *Medea* and *Dido and Aeneas*, I kept thinking to myself, *Why do we think our lives are so important? It's all happened before.*

Together with Anne, a friend, I'd sit in the front row of the class, taking notes to the best of my ability. I observed the young people. They didn't worry when they were late for class – they would just swing their legs over the writing space in front of their seat and sit down, totally relaxed.

One day I'd known I was going to be late and had asked

Anne to save me a seat next to her in the front row. When I came in I could see the empty space waiting for me in the middle of the row, not at the end, which would have been easy to get to. I had no choice. So I decided to do like the younger students. I dashed for the seat, planted my bum on the desk in front of it, lifted my legs and threw them over to land in the place I needed to be. The trouble was I threw my legs with such force that my left shoe came off and flew right up to the top of the lecture theatre. It was returned, thank goodness, and I caught it – the class applauding the student who had caught the shoe mid-air and thrown it back, and me with the shoe in my hand, both of us grinning from ear to ear.

Then I got my first essay back. In Dutch there's a saying, *Een riem onder het hart steken*. A belt under your heart. That belt was a good mark and it made me feel I was on the right track.

Although I was working as well as going to lectures, I had a diminished household to look after with our sons flatting away from home. Gardening programmes appeared on television, enticing the nation to be more creative with their sections. Up till then Bart and I had mainly filled our garden with cuttings given to us by friends. Now we became more selective about the choice of plants that went into the soil. We'd always lived outside during the summer months, making the most of good-weather days, and Bart decided to build a beautiful fence to divide the leisure garden from the vegetable plot.

The fact that our daughter had Down syndrome was never a problem. Apart from the initial shock, we approached every situation with an open mind: *What can we do to help her on her way to a normal life? What can we do to improve anything that needs improving?* We knew we had to do everything ourselves. We did it, but I am glad that now

Filling the house

support is provided for a family with a DS baby and that there's support too for when there is a multiple birth in the family.

We experienced heartbreaking situations with unacceptable behaviour by others, but they were often caused by a lack of understanding. And that's why I found it important to talk about our daughter – perhaps a bit too much sometimes.

Bart would say, 'Why do you always have to talk about Miriam whenever we meet new people?'

'Oh, they asked if we had a family.'

Yes, we had a family, but part of this family was our disabled daughter. I was proud to talk about her achievements. I didn't want sympathy, or pity. I wanted the world to know how well she coped with her disability.

Miriam and I went shopping together and she chose her own clothes. She liked to dress brightly and I was amazed at her choice of combinations of colours. Television became an important part of her life – soaps, of course, but also documentaries, current affairs programmes, sports programmes. She knew the timetable of the television guide by heart. Not only the timetable but also details of the lives of actors she watched on TV. She knew exactly who was divorced, who was on drugs and who was in line for a major award.

Looking after Miriam had its own challenges but gradually she became more independent. On Saturday afternoons she'd take the bus into town to go to a film. I'd check with the theatre what time the film was finished and drove to town to meet her as the bus timetable was irregular on the weekend. Nowadays she would have used a cellphone.

Miriam attended a Living Skills course in Mosgiel. I thought the course would be good for learning what she needed to know when she eventually went flatting. However the art teacher took me aside: 'Did you know your daughter has a talent for painting?'

No. I didn't. I felt awful. Miriam liked colouring in, and I'd always raided bookshops for good colouring books for her, the more the better. The attendant would ask, 'What age group are you looking for?' And I'd say, 'Twenty-five? Thirty?' I discovered the Altair Design books with their intricate patterns, and Miriam made some colourful creations. But *painting?* Real paintings?

We enrolled her as an adult student in an art class at Queen's High School. She was a natural. The other girls in her class were amazed that she painted without having learnt special techniques, and the art teacher displayed her work in the school hall. When Miriam brought them home we were aware of their power. A painting of an angel floating above a madonna and child surrounded by green palms. A teddy bear waiting on his chair. Flowers dancing across a purple world. Always those strong images. Brilliant, vibrant colours. Dazzling with radiance.

We asked ourselves, where did it come from? What thoughts were in our daughter's mind to produce these amazing creations? We knew her as a quiet young woman who was limited in her ability to express her innermost thoughts. But her paintings were of the warmth of the sun and the brightness of the moon. Green grass overlapped the blue sky, holding the colours of all the flowers around the world. Brighter and brighter.

I sent some paintings to an international UNESCO competition. Miriam was proud when her work made it to the semi-finals in Paris. She said, 'Next time the final, Mum.'

But the highlight of Miriam's week was always Saturday night – Lotto night. Each Friday afternoon Miriam bought

Filling the house

herself a ticket and one for me. And each Friday afternoon she wrote an M on one ticket and an H on the other. She was in control of the tickets, checking them as the colourful balls rolled out of the giant container. Her ticket won lots of times. Little wins. She watched Lotto with a determination that mountain climbers must summon up when they confront another challenge. She established a ritual. Sitting in bed with a Lotto cap on her head, a wooden tray in front of her with the tickets, a pencil, paper and a rubber.

I remember my amazement when I discovered my daughter's determination and guile. It happened one Saturday night when Miriam came into the living room clutching the two Lotto tickets in her hands.

'I've won.'

Great excitement – it was a big win. Seventy dollars. But I noticed the pen scratchings around the M and H on both tickets.

'What happened to these letters? Did you change the initials?'

'No, I didn't.'

A few days later Adri visited. Miriam was as proud as a record-breaking athlete, telling her about the Lotto win. I put the kettle on, and while I was standing at the kitchen bench to pour hot water on the tea leaves I heard a little voice behind my back whispering softly, 'I did change the ticket.' I turned around, hugged her, and said, 'Oh, did you now?'

We loved having our daughter with us, she was quite independent, but every now and then we thought that it might be good for her to live away from home – to build on this independence on her own.

Miriam had established special relationships with Kitty and with Kirsteen. Kitty and her husband, Grant, had come to New Zealand from Chicago to be with their daughter

Elizabeth and family. Kitty's encouragement of not only my study but also of Miriam's art ensured that we saw a lot of each other. I was grateful for her infectious enthusiasm and loving care. I realised that this was something I'd missed out on in my youth and Miriam was lucky to have it.

Kirsteen often looked after Miriam when we went out, or when we went on a summer holiday. Miriam was always happy to have Kirsteen staying at our house. Kirsteen's thoughtfulness and artistic knowledge ensured that neither young woman was bored.

One day Miriam and I visited the classical section on the top floor of the Otago Museum. Standing in front of a plaster cast of a kore, I said, 'In the Greek and Roman ancient world gods and goddesses were heroic mythological characters with special gifts. They were considered to be living creations like us, with normal human attributes – the way they looked and behaved and how they reacted when they were sad or happy.'

With eyes as sharp as a blackbird's, Miriam looked at me. 'I'd like to be a Greek lady too.'

I'd met a lovely group of women through my study and every Thursday afternoon, after our Greek tragedy class, we gathered at the Otago Museum for coffee and to discuss that day's lecture. As mothers we felt deeply about Iphigenia being sacrificed, and shuddered when we read about Medea's internal conflict – where any wrong had to be revenged by justice even though it meant following an uncontrollable pattern of destructive behaviour. Whether it was through reading Euripides, or Aeschylus' *The Oresteia*, or plays by Sophocles, we talked about the Greek gods and goddesses as if they were our personal acquaintances.

'Why don't you join us on Thursday?' I said to Miriam. 'After you finish work you could take the bus to the Knox Church stop, and walk to the museum.'

The following Thursday morning after breakfast she

Filling the house

stood up and beamed. 'I'll see you at the Greek Ladies.'

From that day on she became part of the Greek Ladies group: Kitty, Kirsteen, Deborah, Jill and me, and sometimes Shanley. Even while Miriam was sipping hot chocolate and eating a piece of apple cake I was aware that her ears were wide open when we talked about the characters of the Greek myths and how they lived and worked.

Driving home one day along the one-way street, the leaves on the sports ground as golden as Agamemnon's mask, I told her in simple terms about the myth of Demeter and her daughter Kore. I said, 'In Greek mythology Demeter was worshipped as the goddess of the earth and her influence also stretched to the underworld. One day when Kore was out in the fields she stopped to pick a daffodil and Hades, the God of the underworld – who also loved Kore – grabbed her and took her down into the depths of the earth. From then on she was called Persephone. But Demeter was devastated that she had lost her daughter. She threatened that the earth would not produce any more fruit if her daughter had to stay in Hades and she could never see her again.'

Waiting for the traffic lights to go green at the Botanic Garden intersection, I turned to Miriam and said, 'I am so lucky to have you as a daughter and you can be sure I will always fight for you too.'

'Thank you, Mum.'

Little did I know that soon my daughter, like Persephone, would have to go into the depths of Hades. And I, as a mother, could not protect her, or follow her into that abyss of her own tragedy.

PART THREE

Retirement

A dull, grey autumn day in 2015. More rain is expected and the dryer is working overtime. It's intrusive to have it so close to the living room and to the small room where I sit behind my computer. Still, I don't have any other complaints living in this newly built retirement village.

We've been here nearly a year, surviving the shift from a five-bedroom house with an interesting garden to this two-bedroom apartment on the third floor of the Summerset Bishopscourt retirement village. It's warm, comfortable and ideally suited for our changing life situation. It feels safe.

Yet I miss my garden and the views of our home to those special hills that surround Dunedin – Flagstaff, Mount Cargill, Signal Hill. Each special in its own scenic environment.

In autumn and winter tūī and bellbirds used to flock to our balcony, circling around, waiting in trees until they could sip from bowls filled with sugar water.

When I look outside from this window I see seagulls hovering over the village, screeching for food they won't get. They settle on the balcony rail, bright eyes begging, but I can't feed them – everything is tidy here. They fly away over Highgate towards Aramoana. Towards the ocean, where they'll find their natural food supplies. Find the space to fly free.

The revolving dryer reminds me of my life, the moving and whirling of complicated situations, sometimes sudden, other times slow in reaching a climax. Tossed about by circumstances that could only be fully acknowledged by the passing of time and often hard work.

THE BALCONY DOOR IS WIDE OPEN. OUTSIDE A WARM nor'wester roars, shifting spring blossoms to unknown places. A young blackbird sits on the white railing, singing its heart out, singing about himself, how he wants to find a mate, how he needs to find a mate. It's that time of year where the urgency of procreation comes through in nature. Soon he and his mate will make a nest and try to be good parents. They don't know what will happen.

For them the time spent between morning dew and evening sun will have its free-flying flight path and landing spaces. They will endure calamities, storms and heavy rains that might destroy their freshly made nest. Perhaps a white heron will come and take the eggs away before they are hatched.

In a few weeks it will be quiet again. I will miss my little blackbird with its determined calling. He's been a surrogate for all the birds I left behind in Opoho. Even though I don't feed the blackbirds and sparrows any more they still come back and seek little patches of nourishment in and around the plants, impatiently throwing bits of soil out of pots containing daisies, geums and pelargoniums.

The last few months I've gone back into my past. Reaching into the depths of my psyche to bring together stories about events that have created such an impact on my life that even now I remember details with clarifying vibrancy. I did read somewhere that you don't have anything

Retirement

to write about your childhood if that childhood was a happy one. I always thought my childhood was normal. I never knew what to expect and took everything as it came. Already I've thrown away a lot of unnecessary baggage, physically and psychologically. But why are there knots of unresolved pain still waiting for release?

My mother was physically exhausted after I was born. She could never look after Lydia and me. There were always other women in the house who took responsibility for what the children needed, whether it was food or clothing or a visit to the doctor.

My mother needed to rest a lot. Only once did she take me out shopping: I was 12 and I needed to have my eyes checked at the hospital. I was told I needed glasses, and afterwards the two of us biked into town and Moeke bought me a blue skirt and a yellow towelling jersey. Even though she was mostly in the background she was still my security. My base camp.

When I became a mother I vowed always to have time for my children, give them all the love I had in my heart. As a young mother I loved and cared for Miriam and the boys with such an easy love, only made difficult because of inexperience and lack of communication skills. I think back to evenings when our sons were at high school. Sitting with them on the sofa, one teenager on each side, their arms clasped around me: 'You're the best mother.' Getting up in the middle of the night with my boys to watch international games of soccer and rugby. Nibbling chips and drinking hot chocolate.

The time came for them to get ready for their first Otago Boys' High School camp. New tramping boots needed to be run-in. Ray and Foster got dressed in their camping clothes, put on their boots, ran the bath and stood in it for a while. Afterwards they went on a long walk.

I'd often say to Bart, 'Why don't you take the boys for a

hike into the hills? They love the new tramping boots they've got for their school tramps.' But there was so much work around the house he couldn't see his way clear to taking them: a new lot of timber was waiting to be cut into the right size of four-by-twos, varnishing and painting needed to be done. New projects demanded attention.

There came a time though when even our sons' love for us was challenged and my path as a mother became as turbulent as the flight of a seagull on a stormy day.

I wanted to protect them, shield them, make life easy for them.

'You're spoiling them,' a friend told me. 'You're too soft.'

'What's wrong with that?'

I did my best. But that best wasn't always good enough.

Where did she go?

In March 1991 Lydia and Wim arrived back in Dunedin from their holiday in Melbourne, and we all flew to Tauranga for Foster and Frances' wedding. After the wedding we took our visitors for a holiday in the Bay of Islands while Ray and Miriam flew back to Dunedin, where she would be looked after by a friend. I don't think our family's religious differences were sorted out by then but we managed to have good family times.

Miriam was a bridesmaid, together with Frances' sister Hazel. They wore gorgeous deep pink dresses with delicate white edgings. Frances looked stunning in her white dress with a headband of pink roses and gypsophila, and so did the bridesmaids, presenting an impressive contrast – Miriam with her blonde curls and Hazel with her dark shiny hair. Miriam watched and copied every move Hazel made, making sure she did the right thing, undertaking her tasks with a vigour that nobody could have managed with more enthusiasm. She was alive, she was strong and she knew what she wanted.

I couldn't help wondering if her thoughts ever dwelled on whether or not one day there would be a big day like this of her own? On several occasions in the past she'd said, 'I want to be a teacher' or 'I want to be a nurse', but she never mentioned she wanted a boyfriend, or wanted to get married.

IN THE EARLY EIGHTIES WE'D HAD ANOTHER INFLUX OF overseas visitors, including my sister Jo and her husband Johan. A special joy was to welcome back Mijntje, accompanied by her husband, Harry. Mijntje had walked the Milford Track during her stay in New Zealand in the mid-sixties and now she wanted to show Harry our back blocks.

During their stay in 1980, Jo and Johan said to Miriam, 'One day you have to come and visit us in Australia.'

'Yes please!'

By October 1991 Miriam was looking forward to visiting Tante Jo and her family in Melbourne for the fourth time. With the support of Air New Zealand she had confidently managed the previous trips to Australia, and we hoped she would have another refreshing time and look back on many good memories to treasure during the coming year. My sister had said after her last visit, 'We love having Miriam here. She's so grateful for everything.'

Miriam packed her suitcase, carefully choosing what she wanted to take, as well as the small presents she'd bought for our large family on the other side of the Tasman.

As we had done during the last few years, we dropped her off at Christchurch airport, Miriam keen to undertake this adventure again. But as we waited for the plane to leave, I thought she looked worried.

Later that night I rang Melbourne to see how she was and she sounded elated. 'My cousins were at the airport. I like my cousins. I'm going to stay with Joke and Elly.'

A few days later I rang again. That night Jo's words came as an unexpected southerly blast: 'Miriam is very naughty, very strange. But then, it's been so hot here, 40 degrees, and I know she doesn't like the heat.'

'What do you mean naughty? What did she do?'

Where did she go?

'She's different.'

'How? Tell me.'

'I don't know.'

I then suggested I should change the booking so she would come home earlier, but Jo said, 'No, that's not necessary. She'll be fine. We'll take her to the zoo tomorrow.'

'Ring me if you have any more problems. Please!'

I couldn't relax, even though I was studying for exams. A few days later I rang again. Jo said, 'She's different, but she's all right. I'll keep a good eye on her.'

When Bart and I drove to the airport to collect her I said, 'It'll be lovely to have her home again. In her own calm way she's such a presence.'

'Yes, we do miss her.'

I'd been grateful for the quiet time of the past two weeks, especially since the first of my exams for that year started two days after Miriam's return, but at the back of my mind had been the constant worry that something wasn't quite right with her. Why had Jo said she'd been naughty? We didn't think the word *naughty* had ever applied to her. She was sharp, on the ball. She was cunning. She had guile. But naughty? Definitely not.

When we collected her from the airport the first thing she said was, 'I was afraid I was being kidnapped in Australia.'

Trying to keep my voice level, I asked, 'What made you think that?'

She turned her head away.

We talked to her, tried to tell her that she was safe with us and that she would sleep in her own bed that night. When we got home she said, 'I'll make a cup of tea.'

'Fine, darling. I've made you a welcome home cake. I know how much you like apple *kugelhupf*.'

As we came into the dining room she turned and walked backwards to the kitchen sink where she put water in the jug and switched it on. She then walked backwards again to the door of the hall and went downstairs to her bedroom. When I called to say that tea was ready she came upstairs, sat down, sipped her tea and ate a piece of cake, but then she sat very still and said, 'I don't want to talk.'

'That's fine, darling. We'll just sit quietly.'

Later that night I rang Australia to let the family know she had arrived safely home. I asked Jo, 'Did something happen while Miriam was with you? She seems so upset and worried she'll be kidnapped by a dingo.'

'No,' said my sister, 'we don't know what happened.'

IT'S HARD, EVEN NOW, TO RECALL THE TIME WHEN MIRIAM changed into a person I didn't know any more. I felt helpless as I fought to tell experts who hadn't met our daughter before that her behaviour wasn't normal, that there was another Miriam – a vibrant, interesting Miriam – inside the person she'd become.

That first weekend after her return from Australia her behaviour became very strange; she stayed in her bedroom and we realised that something was seriously wrong. She'd had a cheerful temperament, although we had learnt to understand and accept the occasional mood swing if there was a disruption in her routine or things didn't go the way she'd expected.

Now she couldn't answer my questions. Instead she'd say, 'I am Miriam Hellendoorn. I am from New Zealand. I am a Kiwi. I have two twin brothers. You are my real mother.' Miriam couldn't understand that 'two' wasn't needed in the context of twins. What she did know was that she had one real mother.

I was desperate, and trying always to reassure my daughter that she was safe. She repeated those words many times over

Where did she go?

the next few weeks, and whenever we went to town, she'd turn from left to right, right to left, and want to hold on to me. One day, while I stopped at the greengrocer in the North East Valley she locked herself in the car. When I got back into the car, she said, 'I don't want to be kidnapped by a dingo.'

I hugged her. 'You are safe with us, darling. There are no dingos in Dunedin.' I wondered what had made her so fearful that she might be kidnapped? What had she been told? Who had told her this? Had she seen a television programme about the Chamberlain child disappearance?

I made an appointment for her to see our new doctor. Our own very special GP, Dr Paul Moody, had retired and I counted myself lucky that Coleen Lewis had taken us on as her patients.

Miriam was sitting in the waiting room, and after we went into the doctor's surgery she screamed, 'I don't need a blood test!'

It was a struggle, but in the end she conceded to have the test, which revealed that she had hypothyroidism. She was put on medication but was distressed when it was time to take it. She yelled, 'Why are you doing this to me?'

Stroking her hair, I said, '*Schatje*, this medication will help make you feel better.'

'I don't take drugs, you know that! I'm not into drugs.'

And then she'd repeat her mantra again: 'I am Miriam Hellendoorn … you are my real mother. This is the truth.'

Something had gone really wrong. The medication she was given was slow to take effect. I kept asking myself questions, trying to pinpoint how we could have prevented this. Had something happened to her on the flight to Australia? Had somebody molested her during her trip and threatened that if she didn't comply, she would be kidnapped? Why, why, why? Why was our daughter so scared?

And so the whys, the hows and the whats kept on droning

in my head like an uncontrollable chainsaw. I carried within me guilt chips, raw squares of uncut Oamaru stone block, when I went to work and as I wrote my exams. *Why hadn't I noticed she was sick? Why had I let her go to Australia?*

I knew I might never have answers to my questions. She couldn't talk, apart from a few sentences. All we could do was to help her survive this Hades.

Miriam doesn't remember those long months. She couldn't go to work, she couldn't go to Queen's High School art classes, she didn't even want to get dressed. She stayed in bed all day listening to records on her stereo. She watched television. She kept the light on, the curtains closed. She said, 'I am safe with the light.'

How could we ever find out what really happened? I was beside myself with worry and fear. I read articles about mental illness in Down syndrome. I didn't find any answers. Miriam was full of internal pain, repeating her mantras. I knew she was functioning at different levels because occasionally she'd say, 'Oh, good, I'm back on Earth again!' But a short while later she'd say, 'I'm not on Earth!'

And then there was the greyest day ever, which in my memory can never ever appear in colour, not even in sepia. I had booked the day off work so I could take Miriam to the doctor. I came into her room, saying, 'We have an appointment with Coleen this morning. What would you like to wear?'

Miriam switched on the television and said, 'She's not a real doctor. The flying doctors are the real doctors.' Then, as she hid under the duvet, she howled, 'No! No! I'm not going.'

I rang the doctor to cancel the appointment, and after I'd explained what had happened she said she'd come over straight away. When Coleen arrived Miriam was in her bed, still hiding under the duvet, and the doctor had to try to talk to her through the bedding. After we left her room she

Where did she go?

said, 'I'll have to consult an expert on Down syndrome.'

I listened as she talked to the expert on the phone. I watched her face. Then she came to sit beside me on the sofa in the living room and took my hand, 'He thinks Miriam has pre-senile dementia.'

Miriam was in her bedroom downstairs. Beatles music blasting through the house. I sat on the sofa and I thought, *What do you do as a mother when you get told that your not-even-30-year-old daughter is senile?*

There were no more green hills to look at, there was no more sunshine to be enjoyed, there were no plans to be made for Christmas. My first question was, 'How long can I look after her?'

'As long as you can manage.'

'I don't want her to go into a home.'

'She can stay with you as long as you can manage.'

But her life was going to change. Ours as well. How could this have happened? There were other questions: what would we tell our sons: Foster in Brisbane, Ray in Christchurch? How would they cope? I would have to give up my job, my study. I felt selfish. I loved both of them. But I so dearly loved my unbelievably tough daughter.

The next morning the doctor phoned: 'I've talked to a psychiatrist at Wakari Hospital. She doesn't think that Miriam has pre-senile dementia.' Later we found out that undetected hypothyroidism can cause a psychotic state, and that thyroid disease is hard to diagnose in Down syndrome people because of an overlap in symptoms.

I knew then that one day, in her own time, Miriam would make the return journey from her Hades. The sun still shone, and the green hills on the other side of the valley would be enticing us all outside again. And our beautiful, amazing daughter would be all right. How we loved her. How we wanted to keep on caring for her.

Later, when I asked her what she'd like for Christmas,

she said, 'The best thing I'd like for Christmas is to be on Earth again!'

And I thought, my strong-willed, stubborn, solid daughter – where is she? Not only in Hades but also so far away from us in some mental stratosphere where we can't reach her, where everything she's known has become like something on another planet.

Each morning I wondered how we could help her in the way that was best for her. I mentioned to Kitty that perhaps I should look around for a kitten. We hadn't acquired any animals after our dogs and cat had died in the mid-eighties. Kitty's answer came quick and direct: 'Good idea. Don't do anything. We can help.'

And so on Waitangi Day Kitty's daughter, Elizabeth, brought Miriam a timid three-month-old kitten which we named Liesel. From that day on, Liesel, a grey tabby with beautiful marmalade markings in her coat, curled up close to Miriam when she was in her bed.

Our doctor set about organising an appointment for us with the psychiatrist who dealt with intellectually handicapped people. At that time he was still on sabbatical leave but would return in March. At our first appointment with him he prescribed a strong anti-psychotic drug. It had to be increased gradually, and when she took its highest dose the constant spasm made her mouth look as if it had an exaggerated pouting.

But after a few months we noticed a positive change: her mantras stopped, she smiled and talked again, and she decided that she'd like to go back to Queen's High School.

Miriam would never be able to reveal the inner struggle she had to go through during that year. Bart and I will never forget our loneliness. But how we treasured having our daughter back with us again … on Earth!

Where did they go?

Ray started work in Christchurch after graduating with a BSc in Chemistry. He'd met a young lass through the church he went to and they became engaged. The wedding was set for November. But earlier that year he'd lost his job through the restructuring of his workplace and found himself at a loose end. He wasn't able to find another position and became listless.

His wedding arrangements were cancelled.

One Sunday afternoon in October Ray rang. He sounded too quiet. I suggested he come home for a while. 'Dad wants to paint the house. You might like to help?'

'Yes. I'd like that.'

A few hours later he rang again. 'I don't think I'll come home.'

'Why not, son?'

'The people in the church think it's not such a good idea because you don't go to church.'

My heart sank. I didn't know what to say.

WE HAD STOPPED GOING TO CHURCH IN 1990 WHEN MIRIAM became ill. My own health wasn't good, and I just couldn't cope with caring for Miriam, working and studying. Well-meant but careless comments about Miriam's situation by parishioners also hadn't helped at that time. From then on our Sunday mornings became hallowed in their own way. Bart and I took our time to have breakfast, drink coffee together, listen to a Mozart Messe.

Trying to find peace inside. *Sanctus, Sanctus, Sanctus, Dominus Deus Sabaoth.*

I saw God in the dramatic sunrises and sunsets, in the ever-changing light on the hills we looked out to.

Hearing Ray's sad voice, I wanted to call those church people he mixed with and tell them what I thought of the advice they'd given to a fragile person. 'Darling,' I said, 'we might not go to church but your dad is the only person who still visits Mr S, who is in his nineties, and nobody else visits him. That is also one way of practising God's love.'

When Ray and Foster began university they'd chosen to join congregations with more active types of worship than the sort they had grown up with. They felt comfortable there. We accepted that. But what we could not accept was the way they had been indoctrinated to reject their parents' choice of how to spend a Sunday morning. We came to New Zealand to be free from religious oppression. *Would our sons ever understand what that oppression had done to us?*

The next day Ray arrived home. He was put on medication but slowly the depression got worse. It was unbearable to see him unhappy, without purpose, as he wandered through town. We loved our son but didn't know what to do.

In the meantime Foster and Frances had moved to Brisbane, where Foster had studied for a postgraduate diploma in surveying and after completion had started a new job there. Frances began her nursing career, but became ill and had to give up her job. They invited Ray to come over for Christmas and all seemed well. Then one morning, while on holiday at Tata Beach, we were woken by a neighbour with a message from Foster to say that later that day they

Where did they go?

were putting Ray on a plane to Christchurch.

We called our Hungarian friends Gus and Sylvia Doma in Christchurch, 'Can we stay one night? And if we can't be there in time, could you go to the airport, please?' We packed up and hurried northwards.

And so another time of utter sadness started. We again went through a heart-wrenching period watching our youngest son go through the hell of mental illness: his despair and loneliness, our despair and helplessness, as well as our inexperience in dealing with a grown-up son who in his anger had rejected us.

It took until June before Ray finally sought professional help, and with the support of a caring team, a slow and steady healing process started.

Ray attended a day-care programme for a while and later we had family meetings with Jo, a bubbly and caring occupational therapist. As part of his rehabilitation he also completed a bachelor degree in food science.

A few years later Ray had regular check-ups with a psychiatrist, who specialised in research on the occurrence of mental illness in twins. Our sons weighed seven and eight pounds respectively at birth and were born at full term. Imagine what it must've been like for those babies in a tight place stretched to its limit. Did they get enough oxygen?

Now years later, I see Ray as a man with the same quiet strength as his father. A man with a good sense of humour, understanding others who are going through the same experiences he's had. He became involved with ABLE, an organisation previously called Tapestry Clubhouse, where people with mental health issues can meet others and develop new skills.

More changes

Whilst working at the Otago Catchment Board, Bart had taken evening studies towards an NZCE and become a draughtsman, which led to work in the design office. In the meantime the board shifted from an old house in George Street to a new building in Stafford Street, and in 1989 it became the Otago Regional Council.

Because of the council's restructuring process in 1991, Bart's position in the design office came to an end. Instead he was offered a job in the records office with a drastic reduction in salary. He stayed there until he left in 2004 at the age of nearly 68. His health had been, and still was, excellent – even in September 1998 when he was told he needed a melanoma operation. This became a nine-hour ordeal. Bart was also told to get his affairs in order because he might not see Christmas. The staff gave him a portable CD player which he used every day, playing J S Bach's 'Wachet auf ruft uns die Stimme'. Lying on the sofa, eyes closed, his chosen healing process was on its way. His positive attitude and his dedication to life were admirable and it was a tremendous relief when after 10 years of regular checks he was discharged from the ENT department's recall list.

A defining speech

In December 1993 my work Christmas party at the university's Department of Surveying was to be combined with a triple-retirement function for Basil Jones – the then professor of surveying – and two senior lecturers, Allan Blaikie and Peter Hunt. Both Allan and Peter had also been acting heads of the department at various times in previous years.

A few weeks earlier I had been mortified when John Hannah, the new professor of surveying, told me I should give the farewell speech for Basil at this function. 'No, John,' I said. 'You can't do this to Basil. It's too embarrassing. A speech like that needs to be given by somebody more qualified.'

John's answer came back, 'You do it!'

That night I sat behind the old typewriter I'd bought from the department after we were given computers to work with. What could I write? What could I say about the man who had been such a wonderful boss – as had been all the other people I'd worked for at the university since 1971?

There was Jim Flynn in the political studies department who had given me such an unbelievably wonderful reference when I left to start work in surveying, even using the word 'intelligent' – he, the expert on IQ! I didn't take any notice of it at the time. I didn't think much of myself. I just did the work.

That damned inferiority complex. Always and always: I am no good.

The next day I went into John's room and threw the sheet of paper with my typed words on his desk. 'You'd better censor this. I don't think I can do it.'

I went back to my desk and got on with my administrative work.

Ten minutes later John stood next to me. I looked up at him. He said, 'I don't know what you're doing here. You should be at home writing all the time.'

I sighed, tears in my eyes. 'John, that's something I've always wanted to do but didn't think I could.'

I thought writers were gods and goddesses, clever people who could use words for all situations. I couldn't. I would be censored if I did. Even at home.

But the seed had been sown.

The next year I did four papers at university and graduated with a BA in December 1994.

John's words were engraved on my soul, in my heart.

Fly me to the sun

One of the papers I took in my last year of study was a communication skills paper organised by the Department of Management. I wanted to graduate in December 1994 with a BA majoring in classical studies, but this communication paper appealed to me. I especially enjoyed the tutorials where another woman and I, both in our late fifties, were slotted in with a group of male students. The tutor for our group was a woman called Paddy Richardson, a writer who had published stories on radio and in journals and was eventually to publish crime novels! She made our sessions interesting. She had a special way of getting us involved in the discussions relating to the topics that had earlier been dealt with in class. The young men would sit back and relax while Heather and I would be on high alert in case we missed anything important.

Towards the end of the academic year we had a lecture on cross-gender and cross-cultural communication. Never having had much confidence in communicating myself, I was enthralled by these lectures about how women had been treated by men, including how they had learnt to deal with abusive behaviour from their superiors.

After that particular class I had an appointment with a specialist in the Marinoto Clinic for a minor health problem. However, during this consultation I experienced a form of disparaging behaviour that changed for good my

ASTRIDE A FIERCE WIND

default attitude of wanting to please. In this case the 'ifs' are important. If I had not attended that lecture, I might have accepted the words of that expert as being true. I was lucky to have a supportive husband, good friends, a good job – but what if I hadn't? What if my days were spent at home, waiting for hubby to eat his dinner and then leave me on my own for the rest of the evening?

A year later the astute comment by professor of surveying, John Hannah, started me on a path that I'd thought I would never be good enough to tread. The following story was the beginning of a new way of communicating.

314

A woman I am

Imagine the scene. A warm sunny beach. A woman washing her hair in a tub. Singing how she's going to wash a man out of her hair, send him packing.

Well now. I wash my hair every day. Inside, under the shower, of course. But the whole idea of performing this routine has taken on a totally different perspective. You see, it has to do with how I see myself. How others see me.

As I walk along the main street, amidst a lunchtime crowd seeking the sun for the first warmth of the season, I think how good it is to be alive, to feel the sun on my face, on my head. Cars move past, horns toot, there are people everywhere. The large shop windows reflect my image. A middle-aged woman. Tall, broad-shouldered. Dark hair that waves with each step of my feet.

I have good reason to want to wash a man right out of my hair and send him on his way. I have no idea what sort of conditioning treatment I'll use, but it has to be the kind that radiates warmth and has a super-sensitive smell. The kind that will make me feel good.

I don't know yet where I want to send that man. To the deep ice valleys of Antarctica? To the frozen steppes of Russia? A tent in a desert with only a camel for company? Far, far away. Somewhere where he will suffer. Somewhere where he will learn. Isolated long enough so he'll learn how to give women the respect their intelligence and perception deserves.

I'm running ahead of myself but I'll tell you my story.

A few weeks ago I realised that this ageing body could benefit from some repair work and I made an appointment to visit a specialist. Again.

I arrive at the suite of the surgeon. Soft grey-wool carpet on which are arranged deep armchairs in tonings of navy blue. Oh, how I love this luxury. I feel so warm, so pampered. Modernist paintings on the palest of blue walls, framed with just that right amount of grey and chrome.

I'm led into the surgeon's room. After a series of perfunctory questions I'm told I'll need a small operation to clear my medical problem. It will mean just one day in hospital. I'm told that I'll be well looked after and that it will be a day of rest and relaxation. I feel awful. How can I disappoint him? How can I tell him that even one day is too much?

I ask him if he can give me another option to clear my problem. I don't want another operation.

He frowns. I smile and tell him that I have already had six operations, some more major than the others, and I'm reluctant to have another one.

As the doctor's voice drifts in perfectly modulated tones across his wide desk, I look at him. Dark, perfectly cut hair, beautifully tailored grey suit, good-looking in a polished kind of way. He tells me there is nothing else he can do to relieve my symptoms, and asks, 'What were the operations?'

I mention the hysterectomy, the mastectomy. I don't mention the months of recuperating, trying to accept what's happened, all intertwined with other internal blocks and tackles.

He leans back in his comfortably padded chair and with his fingertips touching looks at me, smiles and says in a calm, detached voice: 'I see, I see.'

A woman I am

What does he see? A thing of shreds and patches? Frankenstein?

Again he says, 'I see, I see.'

But this time there is more to come. A polite smile moves his mouth. 'So, if I am correct, with your hysterectomy and your mastectomy ... well, it really makes you only half a woman, doesn't it?'

He smiles as he looks at me, waiting for agreement. Does he want me to answer and say, yes, doctor, mister, you are right. I am only half a woman?

Oh, but then, this great wild anger slowly comes in my throat, from deep down in my innermost core of womanhood. A core that has been damaged many times but knows how to survive. Is it only my body that defines my womanhood? Is womanhood only significant if the body is without blemishes? I have carried, loved and brought up children. Soft limbs tired at the end of the day. Nurturing at night.

My supple song has been tuned many times.

Convention takes over; politeness is important. I was brought up well. But my reply is cold: 'I resent that remark very much. I may not be a lady, but I am a woman.'

But I want to hurt him. The smile of smugness is still there. I have visions of him surrounded by women in white silken robes. They dance around him, singing how they are women, wise and strong. Asking him how he would feel if he were called 'half a man'?

I have reached a stage in my life where there is no need to pretend any more. I have learnt a lot about life and living. But I feel helpless as I think of the damage this man causes with the power of his words. Does he see me as a statistic in that beautifully ordered, colour-coordinated world with mahogany furniture, desks dotted with expensive pens, bookcases lined with textbooks?

But I am not a statistic.

ASTRIDE A FIERCE WIND

I am not.

I'm ready to leave. The specialist puts out his hand and I shake it. My voice holds back words of anger – not because I am afraid of expressing them but because I would not know when to stop. Does he see a female body only as a conglomeration of cells, built and shaped to perfection? I think of thin, small-breasted women with inferiority feelings about their bra size. Searching for soft paddings. I think of tall, solidly built women conscious of their image, searching for diets that might supply the perfect form. Pounding the pavements in the hope that men will love them more. Will love their bodies more.

I'll keep the image in mind of a young woman washing her hair on the beach, singing and dancing, reaching her arms to the sky.

318

Flying off again

In 1995 both Bart and I were due a month of long-service leave. Combined with saved-up holidays, we thought it would be a good opportunity to visit our families overseas and see a bit more of the world before we got too old.

Foster and Frances were still living in Brisbane and we arranged to spend a night with them on our way to Europe. Since they were also planning a trip to Europe before returning to New Zealand, we looked forward to seeing more of them while we were on holiday.

Ray had settled well into a supportive flatting arrangement and had started part-time work. There was just Miriam to worry about …

About that time we had come to realise that Miriam would meet more people and have more outings if she moved into an IHC flatting situation. I felt as if I was betraying her when I made enquiries at the IHC for a placement.

There's an image stuck in my head of the day we took her to the flat in Wesley Street. She sat in her chair at the breakfast table, her face drawn, her tongue sticking out, her fork fiddling with the fried egg, bacon and tomato. I felt such guilt, such pain while I pretended to eat.

Inside my head the internal dialogue accelerated to top gear: How selfish of us, she is no trouble at home. *She needs to become more independent.* How can we let her embark on this, just because we want to have an overseas holiday? *It's time to let go; you deserve a break.* What will happen if her medication for the hypothyroidism runs out? *There will be proper supervision.* Will it be proper supervision? *Let go, let go.*

Driving home was a nightmare. I imagined her waking in the night. What if there was a power cut? Could she find the torch we had supplied?

When we got home the phone rang. 'Hello, Mum. It's Miriam. Are you home? How are you? How's Dad?'

'Yes, we're home. Dad and I are fine, darling. What about you?'

I settled myself on the sofa. I could visualise her in the little green-painted cottage. A new bed with her own bedspread. Her favourite dolls. A new television. Soon, new friends. And as I looked around our living room my eyes rested on the painting above the piano. This was one of her first paintings: a woman in the patrician style of the 17th century, sitting serenely in her chair. Her hands lie softly on the arm rests. A large white collar is draped around her neck and on her head she wears a bonnet. Her smile is wise, enigmatic.

And I thought of my daughter's smile. I thought of her strength.

She would be all right.

THOSE MONTHS TRAVELLING THROUGH EUROPE WERE inspiring and fulfilling. Between flying off to several destinations we stayed with our families, catching up on all the news. As always everyone was hospitable, making us feel welcome and introducing us to the cities we stayed in.

The lectures I'd had in Classics came alive while we travelled through Greece, Crete and Cyprus. In Cyprus

Flying off again

we stayed with Kyriaki and Elias, a young Greek couple we'd befriended while Elias studied in Dunedin. One day we travelled from Nicosia to Paphos. Shortly before we reached our destination, Elias stopped the car at the Rock of Aphrodite where, according to legend, the goddess of love and beauty rose from the waves. Creamy-coloured rocks, blue sea and grey pebbles around her, Kyriaki sat on a smaller rock, as beautiful as Aphrodite herself.

At Paphos we were fascinated to see rare Roman mosaics depicting mythological scenes, created by artists using pebbles and earthenware, and discovered in 1962 while the land was being ploughed. In Crete we travelled the north coast, with the highlight being a visit to Knossos. The wonderful museums with the well-known and not-so-well-known statues made me realise how lucky I had been not only to have learnt about the old civilisation but also to have had the opportunity to see everything in situ. From Athens we drove the winding road to Delphi and stood on that ancient hillside where the muses had spoken all those years ago – and still did. What is it about places like Delphi and Chartres, where people have worshipped at various times, that opens our souls and finds us reaching deeper and deeper into our psyche? It doesn't matter if we can't find whatever it is we are looking for, the healing work will still have been done.

We flew to Nice, rented a car and drove away into southern France, into a countryside of vineyards, lavender and olive trees. Rocky hills with picturesque villages, cathedrals, markets. We'd set off in the morning, not knowing where we'd sleep that night or what we would eat the next day. We loved that freedom, knowing that our children were well looked after and that for a change this time was our own.

Back in Holland we took part in Eef and Huug's fortieth wedding anniversary, meeting up with lots of cousins and their families. My sister Jo had also decided to take a trip to the northern hemisphere and it was lovely to be together again. Lydia and Wim had organised a family reunion at a camping ground in Switzerland where, after 35 years apart, the four sisters were together again. Surrounded by rocky mountains, listening to pelting rain hitting our caravans, Bart and I were deeply aware of the preciousness of the occasion, and the generosity and kindness of Lydia and Wim as hosts. We were there as a family and we laughed a lot together, but Bart and I knew that our lives were so different from my siblings. Having lived in New Zealand, we had learnt to live by different values.

We did some sightseeing in the Rhone Valley but most of the time we were just happy to spend time together, catching the sun, while the sisters caught up on family matters.

We ended that part of our travels in Cambridge, England, where we had a delightful stay with our friends, Ineke and John Field. While there, Bart and I took the train to London for an overnight stay, visiting the British Museum, the National Gallery and many other places. When we returned to Kings Cross station we passed a shop with its door open. The noise coming through that open door sounded familiar. We stopped, looked inside: the All Blacks were playing South Africa. We didn't mean to gatecrash and only wanted to find out the score. Within a minute we were shushed away.

WE STAYED WITH MIJNTJE AND HARRY IN GOUDA, A CITY close to The Hague and Rotterdam in the province of South Holland. It's known for its cheese and the seasonal cheese markets, and for its beautiful old buildings. Gouda has a charm of its own.

One morning Bart said he wanted to visit the Gouda

Flying off again

Windows at the St John's Church, the longest church in Holland.

'I remember going there on a school trip in 1955,' I said. 'Those windows are magnificent.'

The St John's Church was rebuilt after a fire raged through the town in the 15th century; a lot of work was done towards the end of the 16th century, when the nave was raised and the form of the church became a true crossbasilica.

Walking inside, listening with awe and wonder as an organist started to play a Bach fugue on the 18th-century baroque organ, I thought of all the people who had, through the ages, come to this place to seek refuge from religious persecution. First Roman Catholics, and later the Protestants who in 1573 removed all evidence of Catholicism after the church was assigned to them. People sat here, voicing their hopes, aspirations and perhaps resignations to their God. I wondered what was going on inside the minds of those occupying these old wooden pews now – tourists and regular church-goers listening to the deep sounds of the old organ. How deep into their souls did those sounds reach? It had been much simpler in the past. Blind faith. The difficulties of coping with complicated family relationships, racial or financial worries, and political instability in the world today might now be too strong for the healing sounds of an old organ to do their work.

'I feel overwhelmed by all these windows,' I said as we walked through the splashes of coloured light created by the stained glass. 'I keep thinking of the Church of the Good Shepherd in Tekapo.'

'Oh, Huub, how can you say such a thing? You can't mean that,' said Bart.

'Perhaps I do. I love that simplicity.'

I looked around at the wealth of sparkling colours in the stained-glass windows depicting religious, historical and political scenes. Windows that had been donated.

Philip II, King of Spain. Mary Tudor, Queen of England. I remembered learning that the inhabitants of Gouda removed the windows during World War II to protect them from the bombardments.

I moved on to the next window. *Freedom of Conscience*. The naked figure of a woman in a triumphal chariot, her left hand resting on the Bible and her right hand on her heart. Next to her stood an armed figure depicting Protection of the Faith, and beneath her chariot wheels lay a defeated Tyranny. Love, Justice, Harmony, Fidelity and Constancy.

We walked through the old city with its Gothic buildings still standing steadfast between new apartment complexes, wandered through quaint streets filled with people.

Later I said to Bart, 'Remember when we were in the St John's and I told you I didn't like the windows? That wasn't true. They are beautiful and amazing. But there was one window that brought so many of my buried feelings to the surface and seeing it again made me angry. It was called *The Woman Taken in Adultery*. I thought of my father and my mother.'

I recalled how, as a young girl, I'd looked at the pomp and richness of that window. I'd felt overwhelmed by an intensity of rage as my eyes focused on the woman in the centre of the panel being held by a soldier. The coldness in his eyes. Later I had looked at the figure of Jesus stooping at the woman's feet, 'He that is without sin among you, let him first cast a stone at her.'

'When I saw that window again,' I said. 'I realised why I had been so angry.'

I knew then that it was time to let my anger go. I remembered being scared of my father's parents. My grandmother locking me up. If I was scared, my father must have been scared too. How would he have been raised? He never said much. My parents were a product of their time – of the circumstances created by war, fear and poverty. If I wanted

Flying off again

to move on, forget the horrible times in the past, I knew I had to accept the power of unconditional love.

WE LOVED THE MARKETS HELD IN THE CENTRES OF THE OLD cities. The vendors shouting at the tops of their voices to attract prospective customers. In one, Mijntje, Bart and I bought large rollmops from a stall and found ourselves a seat where we ate the marinated fish. Carillons played in the background and all around us people were enjoying the fine weather, sitting outside restaurants, drinking coffee, beer or wine. 'This is heaven,' I said.

'Heaven, Huub?' Mijntje said, smiling. 'And how do you see hell?'

I sighed. 'War is hell.'

'Is it hard coming back here?'

'Sometimes. We've decided to visit the Arnhem-Oosterbeek War Cemetery. Remember the film *The Bridge Too Far* that was based on the Allied troops landing for Operation Market Garden?'

'We hardly ever go to see a film.'

'I remember Huub and I watching it when it first came out,' Bart said. 'The bridge at Arnhem became that bridge too far. Allied airborne forces tried to seize several bridges so they could move into northern Germany. But the operation failed in the end and the Arnhem-Oosterbeek cemetery lies on one of the former landing zones of some of the Allied forces.'

'Such a waste of life.'

'More than 1600 young men are buried there. It's been declared a British Commonwealth area. The Commonwealth War Graves Commission organises the maintenance of graves.'

We drove to Oosterbeek. Near the Old Church stood a monument. *Not One Shall Be Forgotten.*

My mind turned back to New Zealand. The Anzacs. How many graves of New Zealand and Australian soldiers would be at the Arnhem-Oosterbeek War Cemetery?

Large trees, rhododendrons, azaleas – and flowers everywhere at the graveside. A memorial stone: *Their Name Liveth for Evermore.* White crosses in straight lines. Endless white crosses. So many of them. Far too many. Four RNZAF casualties from New Zealand.

The Cross of Sacrifice at the far end. The sacrifice of war. The cross that faraway families of the deceased had to bear. Grieving from a distance.

Around us people turned to each other, hugging, crying. A young man came closer to me. 'I'll never forget this.'

I remembered the day my village was evacuated, walking next to my mother in the long queue, wanting to help push the pram that held Lydia. I closed my eyes, saw the foreign soldiers in their khaki uniforms standing outside the large villa, distributing tea and white bread. Lifting me up. 'How little you are. You are so beautiful. This is why we came. To help you.'

Because of their sacrifice, we had the opportunity to make a new life.

And I thought of how earlier that year we had attended the Dawn Service in Dunedin, Bart singing in the RSA choir. In the early morning darkness we had gathered quietly around the cenotaph, the air chilly with the first light frost of the season. It was hard to distinguish the faces of old and young people who'd gathered to lay wreaths at the base of the monument. Fresh, green, sharp-pointed leaves dotted with white roses and velvety carnations.

I'd looked at the people standing around me. So many had come to share with others the memories of those who

Flying off again

died in the war. For some those memories would be so painful that they still couldn't talk about it, didn't allow any silent anger and hurt to surface, afraid of not being able to control that pain.

I'd shivered as the booms of the single gun thundered across the Queen's Gardens, over the city and up the hills. Daylight gradually appeared. Bart and the RSA choir sang 'Gwahoddiad' – 'And He the witness gives to loyal hearts and free, that ev'ry promise is fulfilled if faith but brings the plea.'

I am coming home

And then there was always the homecoming. To our comfortable home, garden, lots of good neighbours and friends. Good colleagues.

We were so pleased to be back in Dunedin.

Home.

A home from where I could look at a certain hill, that special hill called Flagstaff.

A certain hill

I count myself fortunate to have lived opposite Flagstaff. Opening the curtains each morning meant the start of my emotional focus for the day. That beautiful view was the same but different depending on the season or weather.

When the children were young, we'd all walk to the top of Flagstaff and look down to the sprawling city of Dunedin – the harbour, the peninsula and the suburbs spread out over the surrounding hills. Later Foster and Ray took many long hikes there, including walking the Pineapple Track. The name goes back to nearly a century ago when people walking the track were accompanied by a local grocer, who supplied them with a few pieces of tinned pineapple after they'd hiked to the end of a steep section. Apparently lots of empty tins were left hanging on the trees.

In spring my eyes would travel beyond the blossom-covered apple trees outside our living-room window in Opoho to Pine Hill, one of the hill suburbs in Dunedin, then on to Flagstaff with its growth of mānuka, tōtara and other native trees as well as paddocks dotted with sheep. On still summer nights we could hear their bleating. Towards the summit any forest vegetation stops and dry tussock plants take over. The northern motorway winds its way between Pine Hill and the lower slopes of Flagstaff towards Waitati and ultimately to Christchurch.

Even in spring we could wake up to a sprinkling of snow

on top of Flagstaff, but once the weather had settled the hillsides were covered with bright yellow gorse, beautiful to look at but destructive with its rampant growth, gradually choking any other plants. Scottish settlers brought the first plants to New Zealand, hoping it would make them feel less homesick, but the climate here encouraged excessive growth and a lot of work was needed to clear this lovely weed.

Plants and homesickness. I knew that feeling so well. Indulging myself by buying tulips at the farmers' market in spring.

Getting up early on a clear summer morning, I'd sit on the balcony, camera ready. Often there was a haze, but through this haze the sunshine defined certain clusters of mānuka trees on the hill. Looking through the tall slender trunks made that part of the slope as mysterious as a Persian fairy tale, and I thought of the life going on there – possums, weasels, and wild cats that had thoughtlessly been abandoned.

I loved watching a long white cloud making its way from Mt Cargill to the west. Sometimes this cloud hung between the two hills and sometimes it edged close to the summit of Flagstaff. I remembered how in the early sixties top-dresser planes were active over those hills. Miriam would be outside in the pram (on advice from the Plunket nurse who said that fresh air was good for her) while I pegged the washing out, listening to the zooming of busy-bee planes in the distance. At that time of the morning it was a companionable sound, but it often made me think of the threatening drone of planes over Warnsveld during the war years. At least I didn't want to hide any more.

In July the first rays of the winter sun would hit the top of Flagstaff, usually before 8.30am – the beginning of lengthening days. In the late afternoon on or near the shortest day the dark pink shine would illuminate part of

A certain hill

the hill and we'd watch the sun disappear, often preceded by the most amazing sunsets. Then, before closing the drapes and turning the heater up, it was time to light a beeswax candle on the coffee table in the living room and start thinking about preparing dinner.

Weeks later the sun would hit the hill top from a higher point in the sky and we could see more clearly the gap between Pine Hill and Flagstaff. Each time I looked at those hills across the North East Valley an emotion demanded my attention. The beauty of the defining sun rays, the chilliness of the snow, the shouting yellow of the gorse. I couldn't ignore those views, and when occasionally I'd have a down day, I'd quietly lift my eyes to those hills and know I would be comforted.

The seasons have a way of running parallel to our emotions. Winter blues, spring and autumn storms, peaceful summer evenings. For me the hills were an inspiration to accept whatever the day would bring.

Even though I live closer to that 'certain hill' now in the retirement home, I don't have the wonderful view I had from our old house. But driving home I still see it in front of me, my eyes filled with memories.

The writing life

Sitting at home, driving through the countryside, or walking in the neighbourhood I always had words playing in my head, and at the end of 1995 I thought again of what John had said to me when he read my typewritten speech. I couldn't retire yet but what if I learnt how to write stories?

I knew writing stories would be different from writing letters, something I'd developed to a fine art. My family still complained about my newspaper-sized letters. Yet I'd been too scared to take a first year English paper as part of my degree. As always there was that constant fear of failure. Upbringing? Just an innate fear of being ridiculed? When I was a child I had regularly been ridiculed and suppressed by my older siblings. Perhaps they couldn't cope with somebody who dared to do things they hadn't thought of doing. I was the first person in the family who went to high school and learnt to speak other languages. Who wanted to learn to drive.

Toughen up, woman. Toughen up!

I rang Paddy Richardson, who had been a wonderful tutor and had been very positive about the assignments I had done for the communication paper. 'Paddy, what English paper could I take to help me with writing stories?'

The following words were spoken by Paddy in her speech at the launch of *The Madonna in the Suitcase*, a book I would

The writing life

come to write about Miriam. It was 6 May 2009.

*In 1994 when I was teaching a marketing paper in com-
munication skills I found myself particularly interested in
one of the so-called mature students – a gentle woman,
softly spoken with slightly accented speech and an obvious
sense of humour. You should have seen some of the male
phys-ed students tackling the 'getting to know yourself'
communication exercises. She was always dressed with style
and attention to detail – the earrings, the touches of colour
in her scarves and jewellery – who was this quietly elegant
woman?*

*One of the assignments required of students was to give
a seminar and Huberta's was especially memorable. She
spoke about her daughter Miriam who had, she told us,
Down syndrome. She spoke of her initial concerns and
then with pride and love of Miriam's life, of her talents, of
her place in the family, of her uniqueness. She spoke with
quiet confidence and assuredness and all of those young
students whose main topic of conversation seemed to be
what they got up to the night before sat up and listened
intently, in silence, and responded with such interest and
respect. This woman, I thought, had some stories to tell,
and once again I was made aware of those surprising and
unforgettable stories people carry with them.*

*Shortly afterwards I had a conversation with Huberta,
who spoke of wanting to write. She didn't know how or
where to begin. 'I'm a writer', I said. 'If you like I'll be
your tutor.' And so began a special year for both of us, the
beginning of a friendship which I value so very much and
the beginning of Huberta's development as a writer.*

*I knew, of course, having listened to Huberta's seminar,
that she had stories to tell, but the stories that seemed to
bubble so swiftly from her pen that year were astounding.*

For many she returned to Holland, and there were stories of growing up on the other side of the world, wartime memories told through the eyes of a child, stories of young immigrants new to New Zealand, a wealth of stories. For teachers of writing there is often a difficulty wherein while a student may have worthwhile stories to tell they may not in fact have the ability to tell them well. But this was not the case with Huberta. When you listen to or read her stories you hear her lyrical voice, her own special way with words, the rich imagery which tells of her love of the natural world – Dunedin's hills, trees, sea, her joy in gardens so evident. And so it wasn't surprising to me that Huberta soon began to have her stories taken by Radio New Zealand and journals.

HOW I ENJOYED THAT ONE HOUR PER WEEK WITH PADDY. Talking about books, about writing, about characters in books I thought I knew. I learnt so much, but I became also aware how much I had to learn. How difficult it was to write a short story, to put everything together. Never once was I made to feel a fool even though my writing produced a few chuckles. Paddy's attitude showed respect for my words and she was encouraging and uplifting. I was immensely grateful.

One of the first stories I wrote was about learning to play the organ. The feelings I had for the teacher, the fear I felt when he said I had to play in church one Sunday morning. That fear of failure was so strong that I got my mother to ring the teacher and cancel my playing. Paddy said, 'Send this story to *Sport*.'

It felt good to see my words in print. Later more stories followed.

The writing life

The next year Paddy asked me to join her writers' group – a group of women who met once a fortnight at Kath Beattie's house. It was called Kath's Group. That first night, with a wildly beating heart, I read out a story I'd written. I felt safe listening to suggestions for positive and possible changes. I felt I belonged.

Then began a period of happiness and fulfilment. New friendships. The richness of other people's stories, the laughter, the sharing. Writing our stories and articles came first. We shared joy when one of us had good news: a story on the radio or in a literary publication. The acceptance of a book by a publisher. Again so much to learn.

I found out that one of the group's members lived at the top of our street. Martha Morseth was a writer and a poet with a distinctive voice, and a wise woman. Like me she was an immigrant, born in the United States and moving permanently to New Zealand in 1972. We not only shared our love of writing but also our love for Dunedin. After we both retired, Martha and I spent precious times together, visiting galleries, seeing movies, drinking good coffee at the Botanic Garden's Crocodile Café. We talked about our writing and Martha encouraged me to write poems. I experienced such richness when she dedicated a poem to me.

Sadly, at the end of 2013, I moved to another suburb to the retirement home, and Martha and I don't meet up so much anymore, but we have both been grateful for the opportunity to experience true friendship.

ONE SATURDAY MORNING IN SEPTEMBER 1998, I ASKED Miriam, 'Would you like to make me a painting of a Madonna? I thought it might be nice to send it as a Christmas card to our family and friends. Everybody loved the other card you made. Of course I'll pay you!'

'Okay.'

In October Miriam was invited to be a delegate at an IHC conference in Tauranga, where she was going to be interviewed about her artwork. She'd had quite a bit of publicity by then: the IHC in Dunedin had bought a number of her paintings for their office and for some flats, and the clients enjoyed her work. The day before she left for Tauranga we dropped off a suitcase for her trip. I wanted to ask about the Madonna but thought better of it. She had enough on her mind.

She rang us soon after she returned, her voice full of excitement about the conference. 'I'm home! Can you pick up the suitcase?'

We arrived in the early evening. She beamed as she and Janine gave us a cup of tea, settled in their chairs and chatted a bit. Then Bart picked up the suitcase and put it into the boot. After we'd settled ourselves in the car I wound down the window, ready to wave goodbye. But I realised there was still something she wanted to tell us.

And then she said, an edge to her voice, 'The Madonna is in the suitcase.'

My mind jumping from Tauranga to a Madonna, I said, 'What? Oh, I see! You did it? That's wonderful! Thank you! I'll ring you.' When we got home we opened the suitcase – and there she was: Miriam's Madonna. Colours so bright, the mother stood within a frame of yellowed brush strokes on her left, red strokes on her right. The child's eyes had a mischievous spark. There was no meekness in this holy woman, but only a proud mother with her child safe in her arms from where it could look out into the world.

In January 2000 Dunedin's Moray Gallery showed an exhibition of Miriam's paintings. I was kept busy with the publicity that followed, answering requests for paintings

The writing life

and organising occasions for her work to be shown.

In 2003 I applied for and was given a mentorship by the New Zealand Society of Authors to write a novel. My mentor was going to be Lesley Marshall from Whangarei. Lesley had her own editing business, Editline, and from my first contact with her I felt safe to share my work. Writing in a second language will always bring problems but, like Paddy, Lesley's sensitive comments and deep understanding of the human condition greatly encouraged my efforts at creating a longer work of fiction. Every night after Miriam had settled down I'd go to my study and write, write, write. I sent chapters to Lesley who returned them with lots of helpful suggestions for improvement, at the same time letting me know that I was doing all right.

So I wrote a first draft, followed by a second draft, and there were many more drafts for somebody as inexperienced as I was. I found that caring for Miriam took more out of me than I had expected, leaving me less energy at night. I sent *The Orange Garden* away to publishers without success. One publisher in Christchurch offered to publish it if I could provide payment. I couldn't. I put it to one side.

One day I got the idea of writing a story about Miriam, her talents and her unusual way of creating art. And so I took the first steps of writing a long letter to her, using the second-person narrative and moving chronologically through her and our life. I remember the first time I read a chapter at the writers' group. Their reaction was humbling.

It became *The Madonna in the Suitcase*. I sent it to publishers and was at least grateful that their rejection letters were often heartbreakingly beautiful.

With loans from friends in the writers' group, and the support of other friends and organisations, the book was printed by Graeme McKinstry of McK Design and Print. It was launched at the Dunedin Library's Dunningham Suite. Nearly 150 people attended. Within two weeks I had repaid the loans. Radio New Zealand National asked me to adapt the story into five episodes which were first played on the morning programme, then later repeated in the afternoon and during the night programme. One night I was awake and heard an episode. What a thrill to hear Lloyd Scott's reaction. His sigh of appreciation.

That first year I spent packing up books and posting them all over the world. I was touched by the many emails, cards and letters I received from people who had read the book and whose hearts had been touched by the story. There is one letter I want to include here. It meant so much to receive this sensitively written literary critique of my book from a good friend on the day after the launch.

EXTRACT OF A LETTER FROM MAURICE ANDREW, RETIRED Professor of Old Testament Studies at Knox College.

MAY 2009

Dear Huubje

I have read The Madonna in the Suitcase *with great enjoyment and appreciation.*

The title itself suggests someone who has to be brought out, and you have done that superbly. The mosaic is an appropriate image that is carried through the book well: it gives expression to the colours that are also there both literally and metaphorically. The thing that strikes me most about Miriam's art is its composition and colour, and that is in the book as well.

You often give descriptions in pictures, and you clearly have a sharp memory for colours and the clothes that are

The writing life

themselves clothed in them. You see many links between life and art.

Such descriptions often make the reader feel with you both physically and emotionally. The pram was hard to push after your acquaintance failed to acknowledge Miriam. The meaning of the name, by the way, is not clear, but one suggestion is 'a wished-for child', and that would certainly be accurate in your case. But what a struggle you have had to bring other people to see that.

Your description of the loneliness of a mother of small children is moving. How many hurtful comments you have had to endure even from the 'experts', and what a trial to have to struggle to bring professionals to realise that Miriam had a struggle. You will have wondered sometimes how much more you were expected to put up with.

What a terrible time after the visit to Melbourne! But you kept going, and you take readers on this journey with you, even if they cannot join it completely.

Right from her birth you give a sharply focused picture of Miriam: the clothes she (and you) liked, the food, the people to whom she responded. It was important too that she knew her limitations, if that is a correct interpretation of her love of routine.

Your style too brings all this to clear expression: it is at least partly the address to Miriam that brings the reader to feel both physically and emotionally. Short sentences are often effective in expressing the growing confidence in both you and Miriam. The short comment at the end of a paragraph is a sharp summing up of what has preceded.

You often have an imaginative combination like the one between you, Hildegard and Holbein. So your style brings out your combination of human relations with learning and artistic appreciation. It would be praiseworthy in anyone, but in one for whom this was (once at least) a

ASTRIDE A FIERCE WIND

second language, it is doubly so. And you make clear that you haven't done it alone — Bart and the boys were an essential part of the whole.

340

A journey without an itinerary

At the end of 2000 Miriam was lucky to be selected into a polytechnic course to study for a certificate in employment skills. She loved that year.

The graduation date was early December, and she was beyond words. She was going to walk on that stage in the Town Hall, just as her brothers and I had done before her.

In November we had a short holiday in Golden Bay and arrived back home on the Saturday in time to pick up Miriam's graduation gown. But early on Sunday morning the phone rang. Her voice sounded muffled, as if her mouth were full of food. 'Mum!'

I knew something was wrong. 'We'll be right over, *schatje.*'

We raced to her flat. Janine opened the door. 'Miriam had a fall when she got up this morning.' I rushed into the flat. Miriam sat on the sofa. Stroking her cheeks, I said, 'What happened, darling?'

Her eyes were dull, empty. Her mouth was full of brown, mushy Weet-Bix and I used my fingers to gently remove it from her tongue, from the corners of her mouth.

'Darling, it'll be better if we take you to the hospital. Just to make sure.'

The ambulance arrived and two men entered the flat. I explained about the fall, about the lumps of breakfast in her mouth. One of the men said, 'Can you stand up, Miriam?'

ASTRIDE A FIERCE WIND

She stood but her movements were very slow. With her left hand she grabbed my hand, then sat down quickly. The ambulance men didn't seem to be too worried. Did they say we should put her back to bed? I can't remember, but I can hear my fighting lioness voice: 'This is not how our daughter is normally – she can't lift her right arm.'

I insisted they took her to hospital.

There were X-rays, blood tests. Finally in the middle of the afternoon an echocardiogram, which showed no cardiac abnormalities, and then a CT scan.

In the late afternoon the registrar came with the diagnosis: a stroke. Bart and I looked at each other while we held Miriam's hands. This wasn't real, this was a nasty dream. We stayed with her until she was settled in her bed in a ward. We drove home, we couldn't say a word. But the questions came soon enough.

What would that mean for her future life? For ours?

I was with her the next day when the neurologist came to her bedside. 'Miriam,' he said. 'I'd like you to make a fist for me with your right hand.'

She looked at him, her blue eyes dulled with exhaustion. But then she lifted her left hand and took it over to her right hand that was lying limp and still on the bedcover. With her good hand she picked up her right hand at the wrist and brought it to her chest where it flopped helplessly. I couldn't believe what happened next. As her eyes focused on the doctor she used her left hand to bend the fingers of her right hand into a fist.

There was no reaction in her face but I knew how her mind worked: if one solution wasn't possible she would change her path and try another one.

Even though she was sick, she knew and despaired that she had missed the polytechnic graduation ceremony. She kept repeating the word 'graduation' in a barely audible way.

The lecturer in charge of her course visited her. She said,

A journey without an itinerary

'Miriam, with the help of hospital staff I've organised for you to have a private graduation in a room on this floor.'

A few days after her classmates had graduated we dressed her in the blue graduation gown, which contrasted painfully with the long, stretchy white socks she had to wear below it. Bart pushed her in a special luxury wheelchair across the ward to a seminar room where, together with her classmates, friends and polytechnic staff members, we watched the head of the department at the polytechnic give her the well-deserved certificate.

The day after her graduation she went by ambulance to One Site One Service, the rehabilitation ward close to Wakari Hospital. Within a few days that room was transformed into a florist's shop.

And so we started on another journey, a journey without an itinerary.

Never ever did the staff allow us to think she would be a 'hopeless' case; they were there for her day and night. Later I realised I was on the defensive those first weeks. I fought for her, translated for her, wanting for them all to know her as she had been before the stroke: an intellectually disabled but also intelligent person.

Those first few weeks were hard. We wondered whether she would ever be able to feed herself, or even eat normal food again. Gradually the soft foods were replaced with solids, and after a few weeks it became clear there was progress.

After three months she was allowed to return to live with us in Opoho. With the team's help she had been trained to walk down the drive and climb the staircase though she was still conscious of each step she took.

And she kept improving.

I enticed her to go to the museum café. Before we had our coffee I'd say, 'First we have to have a little walk.' And so we initially walked a half-square of the museum grounds, and once I noticed she was getting stronger this became a full walk around the entire grounds.

One day I bought her a Word Find book at the bookstore and from then on it was a weekly challenge to get another book with lots of different word selections to be circled. She recognised so many words even though she couldn't pronounce them.

I put a pile of CDs in front of her. 'Which one would you like me to play?' Soon there were favourites: Celine Dion, Andrea Bocelli, Cliff Richard. I bought CDs of Hayley Westenra.

There was so much to learn, including a different kind of patience that had to include flexibility. During the day I tried to keep her occupied in interesting ways, working with clay, finger painting. She found it hard to use her right hand to hold a paintbrush, and cutting meat with a knife was a difficult task. I was aware she was missing out on people contact but I also sensed her frustration when she was with her IHC friends, knowing she couldn't take part in the general banter.

Our dreams for her were fulfilled when we heard about the Community Learning Centre in York Place, at that time run by Logan Park High School. She fitted well into the group from the first day we took her there, and ever since has attended the classes three days a week. Of course it meant dropping her off there in the morning and picking her up again in the afternoon. We spent a lot of time taking her to appointments and other engagements.

Word Find took over her life. At first she only did the puzzles during the day while sitting at the dining room table, but later she even worked on the books when she was watching television in bed. I wonder if the pages with their printed words were a substitute for the words she would've liked to use but no longer could?

A journey without an itinerary

Each day I observed her, her face full of concentration, her pen circling the new words she'd found in her booklet. Above her hung her Madonna painting, the colours as bright as her life has been.

We were grateful for the generous respite care provided to us by One Site One Service, giving us a chance to catch our breath, to enjoy a different horizon for short periods and Miriam loved the interaction with the nursing staff.

THREE YEARS AGO WE FILLED MIRIAM'S SUITCASE AGAIN, AND bought a bed and other furnishings for her room in a McGlynn Home in South Dunedin. It was a repetition of what we all had gone through in 1995 but this time her leaving was tinged with tremendous sadness. The sadness of finality – there was no return journey. A hard-to-find acceptance that it had to be done. I could no longer manage.

There was no relief from the grieving. At those times I felt as if I never would be a good Kiwi. I was ruled too much by my feelings and emotions.

Leaving home

I see my daughter lying asleep in her bed,
her life force reduced.
I remember her
as a woman who knew
determination:
going to town, taking a bus,
buying a Lotto ticket,
a cappuccino and a muffin
at the Muffin Bar.

One day she rang:
I've got fifteen books from the library,
I can keep them for three weeks.

Her hair spreads on her pink pillow,
her damaged hand lies still
on the lovingly made
wine-red handmade quilt.
Fingers gently spread,
the thumb apart,
the index finger slightly curved,
the same way she held her paintbrush.

Even in her sleep her presence
demands acknowledgement
of herself, her energy,
her understanding.

Tomorrow I'll have to let her go,
she'll sleep in a new bed
in a new place and her warm night-time smile
may be for someone else.

Life, eh!

Added to letting Miriam go were my fears for Bart, always so healthy, even after having gone through the massive melanoma operation in 1998. I now had to confront a future filled with loneliness and fear. With more changes.

I'd noticed a slow change in his behaviour. I tried to find excuses but eventually we were told he wasn't allowed to drive anymore and we were faced with a separation, not the separation of 'ties that bind' but one caused by the slow change in character and behaviour and the relentless unbinding of parts in his brain.

For me this heart-wrenching experience has been like walking through town with the aim of going to a favourite shop that has been in the same place for years. A shop where I know I can find the thing that I am looking for. A nice writing book, a little lamp for a desk. But when I arrive at that favourite place, I am met by a CLOSED sign on the door.

I peer inside but can only see the different degrees of darkness, with perhaps just a bit of light coming through a window somewhere. Even this minimal amount of light will not help me find what I am looking for.

Echoes from the cellar

Inside the cellar it is dark. Dark as the night that has just been, and dark as the feelings in the hearts of those who have sought shelter here. A candle on a high shelf makes a dim and unsteady circle of light on the ceiling. It's difficult to identify the shapes and faces of people, but they are shapes and faces of young and old people and of children.

Memories of childhood. What do we do with them as we grow up? Where do we store them? What causes them to emerge like growing roots, escaping when they become too large for the space a tree occupies?

I have written about my experience at the end of the war when our family had to hide in our cellar.

We waited on mattresses in the dark cellar, we and our neighbours. Houses and buildings around us lay in ruins.

When Bart and I emigrated to New Zealand in April 1960 we knew we had arrived in a land of milk and honey. Yet, though I was now living in a safe place I still had nightmares, remembering those last days of the war: the darkness, the hunger, the fear. Will the bombers come back? Will we be able to escape? What if the Bailey Bridge across the big river is destroyed as well? I remembered how shortly after the war, whenever a plane flew over at night, I'd run downstairs and stand in the doorway, waiting until the plane had disappeared. Did I think that by standing there I could run away in time if the plane should come down? Make my escape easier?

Then there were the dreams of being chased. Of not being able to move forward.

Living on the other side of the world, bringing up a young family, I often thought of the family who had lived next door to us in the village and who had shared the space in our cellar. A young family with three daughters, the youngest a baby of six months. Their house had been severely damaged by a straying V1 rocket a week before.

The mother had died 11 years after the war. What had happened to the girls? How had they dealt with life?

In 1997 I attended a writers' workshop in Dunedin led by Fiona Farrell. Our first exercise was to write about being in an enclosed space. That day it was as if an arrow zoomed from my subconscious into the reasoning part of my mind. I was again in that cellar, sitting on the steep, wooden staircase. When Jan, the young father, walked past me on the staircase I wanted to hold him back but I couldn't. I heard the cellar door open, saw a ray of light, heard the door being shut. I heard the front door open and close. I waited for those doors to open and close again.

Instead I heard the shrill whistling sound of a mortar grenade. Heard the silence.

I remember my father reading from the Bible: 'They that dwell in the secret place of the most High shall abide under the shadow of the Almighty.'

I saw that secret place as a cave in a towering mountain with walls so thick I couldn't hear the guns.

After he'd finished reading my father left the cellar. He returned, telling the young mother and her children, 'Jan is dead.'

Echoes from the cellar

SEVERAL YEARS AGO *DE STENTOR*, A DUTCH NEWSPAPER IN Gelderland – the province where I grew up – asked for stories from people who had moved abroad. Bart and I had just celebrated 50 years of living in New Zealand and my family suggested I send my impressions of our experiences since 1960. Arriving in Dunedin, making a new life, admitting that emigration often means living with one 'leg' that is occasionally weaker than the other. Always aware of living within that fragile balance. In August my comments were published in *De Stentor* and on their website.

Shortly after my article appeared I received an email from the eldest of the three girls who, with their parents, had sought refuge in our cellar. Joke wrote, 'You probably won't remember me.'

I wrote back, 'Joke, you and your sisters have never been out of my mind.' I told her what had happened at the writers' course, and that the cellar story had been read on the national programme of Radio New Zealand. She subsequently asked if she and her sisters could read the story. Before I sent it I was afraid that their feelings might be hurt. I explained that this story, although based on a real happening, had been embroidered with details from a writer's imagination.

Then came Joke's email. She was amazed that their experiences had been remembered on the other side of the world. She acknowledged that I had described the tense atmosphere in the cellar exactly as she and her sister Jannie remembered it – Jannie trying to hold her father back, grabbing the sleeve of his jacket, saying, *Don't go, Papa. Don't go.*

Joke wrote, 'I still remember your father returning, standing, waiting, at the top of the staircase. My mother's panicky voice, 'Where is Jan?'

Jan is dead.

Their mother had developed epilepsy after living with too much pain, too much sadness. Joke took the place of her mother by looking after Jannie and Hansje, the two younger daughters. After the mother's death the three girls were lovingly supported and cared for by their aunts, the ones Jan had gone to check on.

But they grew up with the unspoken rule: *Of the dead nothing but good.* They couldn't talk to their mother about what happened in the cellar, they couldn't talk to their aunts about it. Their memories were shelved and covered. But the pain festered.

Jannie wrote, 'Your story didn't cause us pain. It has brought us together. There was much recognition of our buried feelings.'

Jannie was five when it happened, yet she still remembers living with her mother's anger. *Why didn't he listen to me? Why did he leave me to cope with three small children?* She said, 'The episode in the cellar was never mentioned. There was no explanation, only helplessness. This prevented us not only from accepting what had happened but also from moving on.'

I have now talked with all three of the sisters. There is so much to catch up on, so many childhood memories to revive. Especially the good ones. I told Jannie that I was working on a novel called *The Orange Garden*, and that one of the chapters was about a Palm Sunday procession that each year was held in our village. Did she remember taking part? The next day she sent me an email with an attachment of photos taken of the first procession after the war. On that sunny morning in front of my computer in Dunedin I was there, back in Warnsveld, part of that procession, walking through the village, carrying Palm Sunday decorations, going past the windmill, past the still visible rubble in the surrounding area that had been hit by the V1.

I had remembered it exactly as it had been. The basis of so many stories.

A few weeks later Jannie sent me a DVD compilation of

Echoes from the cellar

old film footage from Warnsveld that she and her husband had put together on the occasion of their primary school class reunion. There again were all the other memories – not only the procession on the day before Palm Sunday, but also a Queen's Birthday procession. There was my best friend from my first day at school. The village streets, the 11th-century church, the old school … and me waiting in the queue to take a turn to play hopscotch! The film focused on familiar faces in the streets where I had once played, and as it zoomed through the wide tree-bordered lanes it offered even more glimpses into an earlier life.

What a gift. Sixty-five years condensed into a film of thirty minutes. I acknowledge the marvels of the life I have here, yet watching the film sent by Jannie, I felt deeply grateful to have had the opportunity to go back to a very simple childhood in a small village in Holland. Emigrating does not allow many windows to open to the past left behind. This was one of them.

It's especially been a gift to renew friendships that years ago were tainted with grief and sadness.

Several months after Joke's first reaction to the article in *De Stentor* I received an email from Henk Thate who had also read the article. Through him I found out even more about that dark time in our village during the last few weeks of the war. He sent books and photos, but the greatest gift was his offer of a painting by his father whose work is on permanent display in a gallery in Zutphen.

I chose a painting of St Martinus Kerk. This church was in the view I looked out to from our house. This was the church Bart and I were married in and, where as a child, I played happily, surrounded by old bones.

Home

A new year has started. A fresh summer's day. Our holiday in Golden Bay was good. That beautiful Tata Beach, the West Coast mountains on the other side of the bay. The warm weather.

But now I am home in our retirement-village apartment in Wakari, a suburb of Dunedin. Bart is away for the day and I sit on the balcony with a coffee, watching the gulls sweeping above me. Down below the lawnmower roars while cars try to find a park. People amble along, taking time to stop for a chat with other villagers.

It is home. Our new home.

I feel restless and decide to go to Taiaroa Head. I need space, need to see the ocean.

I get into the car, drive through town, along Portsmouth Drive. Just before Anderson's Bay inlet I turn right. I'll take the top road. There've been so many changes since we arrived in Dunedin more than 55 years ago. Each year there are more camper vans along this narrow, winding road, more tourists stopping to take in the views – the wide seascape beyond the gently rolling hills.

I think of Holland, its neatness, the sense it has of the ages of civilisation of Europe. The ancient buildings. The old bones in the churchyard in my village – the bones of my family.

Here there is rugged farmland. Smallholdings or lifestyle

Home

blocks. The rough outbuildings are just patches in the paddocks. Always this space, the wide open spaces of Aotearoa. Blue and green, ocean and land. In the distance are seabirds, and closer in the waders around the tidal inlets – spoonbills, plovers and herons. Seals and yellow-eyed penguins.

I drive on to Taiaroa Head. Ahead of me is the albatross colony. At the café I sip my flat white outside and watch giant birds flying over the colony, testing the wind, letting themselves drift away on its power. When the albatross arrive they want a safe breeding place. But there are predators. Ferrets and stoats. Cats as well. Seemingly soft and appealing, but predators in the wrong places – for their victims!

How can a child be protected from predators?

Let it go. Let it go. Find healing in unconditional love.

I am here, so far away from the bones of my ancestors. Here with my family. New growth which has sprung from ancient trees.

Loss and love. Sorrow and joy. It is how life is.

The weather has changed; a storm from the southwest, coming straight from Antarctica, is headed for the mainland. I stand for a while, watching the sea, hearing the boisterous waves. Feeling the energy of the wind. I think of all the places bordered by ocean, all those spaces with their own history and connections, as solid and enduring as the rock I stand on today.

I walk further to the outcrop, the wind howling around me. Wild waves crash on the rocks below.

> *De Zee, de Zee klotst voort in eindeloze deining,*
> *De Zee waarin mijn Ziel zichzelf weerspiegeld ziet.*

A poem from high school. One that made me aware of the

connection between sea and soul. The sea, the sea heaves forth in endless swell. The sea in which my soul sees herself reflected.

This ocean. Not only a connection to the soul but to others, other people, other sorts. Their sound is gone out into all lands and their words unto the ends of the world.

With wind and light around me, I see myself as a young girl dashing into the sea. So keen to taste the salt, so curious about the magic of different worlds at the other side of that blue expanse. Here I can see in all directions – the dark clouds in the southwest, white clouds still over Flagstaff and Mount Cargill.

And here is another memory. Bart and I standing at the railing of the ship that would bring us to New Zealand. Those fears for the future. Fears buoyed by young love, by optimism.

That sea brought us to a new life. Customs, habits, new ways of fitting in. Oceans connecting worlds. Strangers who became friends.

Māori canoes. Sailing ships. Ocean liners. Passengers arriving to find this jewel in the ocean. This fine, green land. Our journey from Christchurch to Dunedin. That train which wound along the harbour, groaning and whistling, readying itself for arriving at the station, dropping us into a whole new world.

The wind has eased, white cloud formations replacing the grey masses. All these years. Love and loss and longing for safety. Longing for a home where I would feel safe. My life divided up like voices in a choir, each demanding its own score, but blending into the progression of sound. Sometimes pleasing to the ear, sometimes a hard-to-understand cacophony. It's like the life of an immigrant. Happiness and loneliness at the same time.

But now I'd better make my way home. I walk to the

Home

car, carrying with me the young girl sitting in a cellar. The young married woman. The mother. The sadness of not being a grandmother.

Going home to a different life. Not alone, but lonely at times, happy at times.

Driving down the steep hill from the albatross colony, I feel the summer sun on my face. Last night I listened to Elisabeth Schwarzkopf singing *Four Last Songs* by Richard Strauss and my tears fell freely.

> *Wir sind durch Not und Freude*
> *Gegangen Hand in Hand;*
> *Vom wandern ruhen wir*
> *Nun überm stillen Land.*
>
> Through joy and sorrow we have
> walked hand in hand;
> we are resting from our wandering
> now above the quiet countryside.

I think of the girl who found silver and gold beneath a plain-looking mound.

The girl who took her treasure home.

I recognise now my mother's gift, that wealth of silver and gold stored within me that I have learnt to treasure. A wealth created from richnesses found within darkness and brought out of the shadows into the light of the southern hemisphere. The place I travelled to, astride a fierce wind.

I open the front door – 'I'm home!' – and walk through the apartment, opening wide the windows and the door to the balcony. Bart is back from his daycare programme. We sit quietly, sipping our coffee.

I have acknowledged my past.

I am happy that I've grown old here.

Acknowledgements

An earlier fictionalised version of the chapter 'A woman I am' was published in *Fiction Plus*, April 2001, under the title 'Conditioning Treatment'. The poem 'Coffee bones' on p.176 was selected by Sue Wootton for the *Otago Daily Time*'s 'Monday's Poem' on 21 April 2014. An earlier version of the chapter 'Echoes from the cellar' was published in *The Press*, and 'The cellar' was adapted for *Standing Room Only*, RNZ National, on 13 November 2016.

I would like to thank the New Zealand Society of Authors for awarding me a mentorship, and Lesley Marshall for her superb mentor companionship.

Special thanks must go to the members of Otago Writers Network, my treasured writing group: Paddy Richardson for empowering encouragement; Martha Morseth for wise and loving support; Carolyn McCurdie for her enthusiasm after reading the final draft and for suggesting both title and publisher; Penelope Todd for unwavering assistance; and for the safety net of inspiration – Beatrice Hale, Claire Beynon, Elizabeth Brooke-Carr, Eva Wong Ng, Jackie Ballantyne, Jane Woodham, Jenny Powell, Kath Beattie, Maxine Alterio and Shirley Deuchrass.

Grateful thanks also to Majella Cullinane for her question after she'd read the script of my unpublished novel *The Orange Garden*. 'Why,' she asked, 'is this a novel and not a memoir?' Her question gave me confidence to no longer hide behind a fictitious character. I had after all written this book to save myself.

Special thanks go to Sue and Robin Harvey for their ongoing love and support, and Reece Arnott for ensuring smooth computer use. For Dutch war photos and advice I am grateful to Henk Thate, Henk Mulder, Jan Rossel, and the late Jannie Martinus. And I am grateful to Wolfgang Gerber of McK Design & Print for working wonders with old family photos.

Thanks and love to Bart and my family for being there.

Bart and I would also like to acknowledge the friendship of so many wonderful people we've met since 1960. Friends that made us feel part of their families, sharing our lives and giving us memories that will last.

Finally, heartfelt thanks go to Mary McCallum and Paul Stewart of Mākaro Press, especially for Mary's brilliant editing and strong support during the editing process, and Paul's stunning design of the book.

This is my personal story, sometimes misty and at other times enriched with imagination, but at all times imbued with the emotional truth of my life on both sides of the world. For more information about Dutch immigrants and their life in New Zealand, please refer to *Tasman's Legacy: The New Zealand – Dutch Connection* by Hank Schouten.